GLOBAL ENVIRONMENTAL CHANGE AND INTERNATIONAL LAW

Prospects for Progress in the Legal Order

Lynne M. Jurgielewicz

University Press of America, Inc.

Lanham • New York • London

4720 Boston Way
Lanham, Maryland 20706

3 Henrietta Street
London, WC2E 8LU England

Printed in the United States of America
British Cataloging in Publication Information Available

Library of Congress Cataloging-in-Publication Data

Jurgielewicz, Lynne M.
Global environmental change and international law : prospects for progress in the legal order / Lynne M. Jurgielewicz.
p. cm.
Includes bibliographical references and index.
1. Environmental law, International. 2. Global warming--Law and legislation. 3. Ozone layer depletion--Law and legislation. I. Title.
K3585.4.J87 1996 341.7'62--dc20 96-1087 CIP

ISBN 0-7618-0284-3 (cloth: alk. ppr.)
ISBN 0-7618-0285-1 (pbk: alk. ppr.)

∞™ The paper used in this publication meets the minimum requirements of American National Standard for information Sciences—Permanence of Paper for Printed Library Materials, ANSI Z39.48—1984

TO MY PARENTS

For keeping the faith

Christmas 1996
To Joey,
One of my biggest
supporters!
Love,
Aunt Lynne

It reminded me of what most of us, really, know: that pessimism and despair are childish, that the only realistic stance toward life is optimism. Because we always survive. Through the most terrible and horrendous moments of human history, through all the purges, long marches, wars, gulags and floods, we survive and go on and increase and make our rude progress. A family begins, a baby is born, a young man gets out of law school and puts up a shingle, a lady in a ball dress is applauded and curtsies back in tribute.

Peggy Noonan
Life, Liberty, and the Pursuit of Happiness

CONTENTS

ABBREVIATIONS

CFC	Chlorofluorocarbons
CH_4	Methane
CO	Carbon monoxide
CO_2	Carbon dioxide
Copenhagen Revisions	Copenhagen Amendment and Adjustments to the Montreal Protocol to the Vienna Convention on Substances that Deplete the Ozone Layer
FCCC	Framework Convention on Climate Change
HCFC	Hydrochlorofluorocarbons
ICJ	International Court of Justice
ICJ Reports	International Court of Justice Reports
IUCC	Information Unit on Climate Change
IPCC	Intergovernmental Panel on Climate Change

London Revisions London Amendment and Adjustments to the Montreal Protocol to the Vienna Convention on Substances that Deplete the Ozone Layer

Montreal Protocol Montreal Protocol to the Vienna Convention on Substances that Deplete the Ozone Layer

N_2O Nitrous oxide

NO_x Nitrogen oxide

O_3 Ozone

OECD Organisation for Economic Cooperation and Development

PCIJ Permanent Court of International Justice Reports

SO_2 Sulphur dioxide

UNCED United Nations Conference on Environment and Development

UNGA United Nations General Assembly

UNEP United Nations Environment Programme

Vienna Ozone Convention Vienna Convention for the Protection of the Ozone Layer

VOC Volatile organic compounds

PREFACE

As a graduate student at the London School of Economics and Political Science, my interest in international affairs was heightened. Not a terribly difficult accomplishment, considering the hallowed halls of that famous institution resonate with all the languages of the globe. Nevertheless, I became seduced by the hows and whys of international relations. (Actually, that is a small lie. My father's insistence that one should read The New York Times on a daily basis first whetted my appetite for international affairs.)

Having been trained in the law, it was quite natural that my studies at the LSE focused on the stepchild of international relations — international law. In addition, my scientific background lent itself readily to environmental issues. I therefore found myself studying international environment affairs. Thus, this book traces its ancestry to my doctoral research and indeed, served as my Ph.D. thesis.

At the time of my thesis submission, I naively believed that I would never again undergo the type of perceived agony that accompanied turning my research into an acceptable Ph.D. thesis. My assumption, however, has turned out to be quite wrong and it has been even more daunting to turn my thesis into a book. It was not the work involved per se, however, but rather that the work was done under the condition animi fracta, or more literally, au coeur brisé. Miraculously, however, this book has found its way to the publisher and into the reader's hands, reminding me of the words from a Chris Isaak song, *I Believe*. Something about the fact that angels do listen and God does hear our prayers. Amen, alleluia, and all that.

ACKNOWLEDGMENTS

One of the protagonists in the film *The Black Robe* proclaimed that he wished that he were a Jesuit, then he would have an answer for everything. Having attended a Jesuit university as an undergraduate, I can vouch for the authenticity of that remark. Not having an answer for everything, however, has meant that I have had to rely on the help of others in order to complete my Ph.D. thesis and to have it published as the book you see before you. The amount of time devoted to the scripting of this acknowledgement section is woefully inadequate in comparison to the time spent on the rest of the book, considering that those accounted for in this section are the reason the rest of this work exists. Nevertheless, in this brief space I will attempt to shed some light on those persons without whose help I would never have succeeded.

My thesis supervisors, Dr. Glen Plant of the LSE Law Department, and Mr. Mark Hoffman of the LSE International Relations Department, provided me with valuable guidance and constructive criticism every step of the way. The interdisciplinary aspect of my thesis did not make their jobs any easier, yet both were willing to travel this uncertain road between two disciplines. In addition to my supervisors, I was helped along in my research by many persons knowledgeable in the area of my work. These include, among others, Professor Rosalyn Higgins of the LSE, Myles Allen of Oxford University, Dan Reifsnyder of the US State Department, Tim Swanson of Cambridge University, Philip Whyte of the Bank of England, and the UN Information Unit on Climate Change, Geneva, of which I benefitted from as much as

I contributed to, through my consultancy work with them. I would also like to thank Dr. Margaret Doxey, who was a source of inspiration. Thanks as well to the immediate past Convener of the LSE Law Department, Professor Carol Harlow, and Professor Tom Brogan, Chair of the Political Science Department at Albright College, whose general support was much appreciated.

My friends, both in London and in the United States, provided me with plenty of distractions, without which my thesis and book might have been completed a lot sooner. Nevertheless, they were there when I needed them and hardly ever questioned my tendency to disappear for weeks at a time. In particular, I have to thank Jane Hawes for providing me with daily pearls of wisdom via electronic mail, especially David Letterman's "Top Ten Good Things About The Greenhouse Effect," Gary Solis for his always-excellent-advice, Demetra Pappas for sharing some long intercontinental telephone calls regarding au coeur brisé, the Hirschbaeck's for their general enlightenment, and Joost Houtman for letting me know that "if I want it to be there, it's there." Thanks also to Todd Mavis and Dan Turner, and in particular to Joan Lowden, who has pointed out once or twice that "everything is negotiable." A special thank you is necessary for Gabrielle Marceau, for having survived "the London years" with me.

Finally, and most importantly, there is my family whose love, support and prayers saw me through to the end. My parents, who provided me with this wonderful opportunity to study in London, also gave me the confidence to finish this project. My sisters: Stefne, Anne and Janet; my brother Joe; my sister-in-law Rita; and my brothers-in-law Bill and Tom, could always be counted on for their support, be it letters, phone calls, "Bundles for Britain" or passing along articles for research. (Or risking life-and-limb driving in a snowstorm to deliver a forgotten thesis draft to the airport before a certain flight took off for London.)

While this book can only be a very small contribution to the vast amount of knowledge already accumulated in this world, it is nonetheless a contribution from what US historians have labelled the "13th generation," so-called partly for the gauntlet its members see in its "bad" reputation and partly since it is the 13th generation to know the American flag. Although perceived as a "lost generation," as historians William Strauss and Neil Howe note in their work *Generations*, this generation may not have seen Nirvana, but they can achieve something. Something, perhaps, to pass along to the next generation. I cannot finish here, then, without mentioning those members of the next generation closest to my heart, my six nephews and my niece: Thomas Jr., Joseph III, James, my godson Andrew, Michael, Brian, and Stephanie Elizabeth.

Portions of Chapter 2 and Chapter 3 originally appeared in Bartlett, et al., ***INTERNATIONAL ORGANIZATIONS AND ENVIRONMENTAL POLICY*** (Greenwood Press, Westport, CT, 1995). Reprinted with permission; all rights reserved.

Excerpt from Peggy Noonan, ***LIFE LIBERTY, AND THE PURSUIT OF HAPPINESS***, copyright © 1994 by Peggy Noonan (Random House Publishers, NY, 1994), reprinted with permission; all rights reserved.

CHAPTER 1

An Introduction

INTRODUCTION

The purpose of this book is to examine the ability of the international legal order to deal effectively with issue-areas in need of international regulation, specifically through the concept of international regimes ("regimes").[1] Numerous definitions of regimes have evolved and these will be explored in detail in Chapter 3. For the present, it is enough to cite the oft-quoted definition of Stephen Krasner whereby regimes are "principles, norms, rules and decision-making procedures around which actor expectations converge in a given issue-area."[2]

While the concept of regimes has been explored for some time within the discipline of international relations, it has only recently begun to find favor among legal scholars.[3] Thus, this book contributes to the understanding of international law through the application and analysis of regimes within the discipline of international law. This is done not by way of repetition of the work done in the international relations field, but from the perspective of the discipline of law. As Oran Young has stated:

> ...It seems likely that the most important thing the legal community and the social science community have to offer each other in broadening and deepening our understanding of international regimes is their distinctive modes of reasoning.[4]

Both regimes to be examined in this book involve aspects of global environmental change: climate change resulting from global warming, as well as depletion of the ozone layer.[5] These have been chosen because both climate change and ozone layer depletion are global environmental issues that demand inter-national legal action — unilateral action will not be able to provide solutions. Therefore, both "require a high degree of international cooperation with due respect for national sovereignty of states."[6] They are also similar environmental problems in terms of their "critical issues."[7] These factors justify a comparative evaluation regarding the respective international regimes formed in the areas of climate change and ozone layer depletion. Based on the conclusions drawn from these regimes, an argument will also be made for the importance of the role of international regimes within the discipline of international law in general. An international lawyer might be tempted to "complain that regime theorists are simply restating the obvious — that international legal rules, norms and decision-making procedures facilitate cooperation."[8] Yet "international lawyers have been all too willing to accept this premise as an article of faith rather than as a theoretically deducible and empirically verifiable phenomenon."[9] Research into how the international legal order promotes cooperation among states should be conducted; this will strengthen the argument for the importance of the legal order. One way of doing this is to study regimes:

> International regimes are more and more salient features of international...law. Since they visualize complexity as well as flexibility they facilitate insight especially into a step-by-step approach...[to international law-making].[10]

Global environmental change is an interdisciplinary matter, encompassing broadly the critical areas of science, economics and development[11] which this book will take into account. The study of regimes is also necessarily interdisciplinary.[12] Thus, while this book is primarily concerned with the *legal* characteristics of regimes, it must also look at other aspects of the model regimes examined here, notably their scientific, economic and development aspects. As Oscar Schachter points out, law has a distinctive character:

> Law is not wholly autonomous; ...it has causes and consequences; ...it involves power and values; ...it is an aspect of a larger social and political process... [but] law is not the same as politics, sociology or philosophy.[13]

Thus, the international lawyer will look for a legal framework within which to place regimes in the international legal order. While regimes are influenced by extra-legal considerations and may include factors influencing state behavior that have not yet acquired the status of law, to be counted as "law" regimes must satisfy the criteria of international law-making.[14] This is necessary in order to maintain a distinction between legal and non-legal rules and principles; for example, between a legal order requiring behavior and a public order conditioning behavior. The generally accepted sources of international law include treaties, customary law and general principles of law.[15] These criteria are well-known and all major schools of international law accept them. The policy-oriented school,[16] however, is particularly receptive to examining law as a process of decision-making, including extra-legal policy considerations. For this reason, the policy-oriented approach is emphasized in this work as the school most conducive to the development of thought necessary to understand and respond to the particularly serious environmental challenges in question, as well as allowing for the incorporation of regimes within its framework.[17]

SCIENTIFIC BACKGROUND ON GLOBAL ENVIRONMENTAL CHANGE

Nothing surprised Indiana Jones -
after all, he was a scientist.[18]

Climate Change Resulting from Enhanced Global Warming[19]

Global warming is a natural occurrence on our planet. It results from the entrapment of heat radiated from the Earth. The sun emits energy in the form of short wavelengths of radiation, some of which is absorbed by the Earth. The Earth in turn reflects its own radiation, but in longer wavelengths because its temperature is lower than the sun's. The "greenhouse" gases and particles present in the Earth's atmosphere are opaque to these longer wavelengths of infrared energy, while at the same time transparent to the shorter wavelengths emitted by the sun. This prevents the heat from escaping beyond the Earth's atmosphere and creates a *natural* "greenhouse effect," one of the "most well-established theories in atmospheric science".[20]

The primary naturally occurring greenhouse gas is water vapor. Other naturally occurring greenhouse gases include carbon dioxide (CO_2), methane (CH_4), nitrous oxide (N_2O) and ozone (O_3). Without the presence of these *naturally* occurring greenhouse gases in the atmosphere, the temperature of the Earth would be approximately 33 degrees celsius (^{0}C) cooler, preventing the existence of life on the planet.[21] However, the presence of *manmade* sources of CO_2,[22] CH_4,[23] N_2O,[24] tropospheric O_3,[25] as well as chlorofluorocarbons (CFCs) and hydrochlorofluorocarbons (HCFCs),[26] create an *enhanced* greenhouse effect which may increase global temperatures and lead to climate change. This enhanced greenhouse effect is exacerbated by the loss of storage or absorption sinks for these gases through modern human activity.[27] The possible effects of climate change are well documented, and include rising sea levels and a shift in climatic zones, affecting ecosystems, agriculture, water resources and human settlement.[28]

The scientific explanation for this warming effect was first put forward in 1896 when a Swedish chemist, Svante Arrhenius, calculated that a doubling of CO_2 in the atmosphere of the Earth would raise the global temperature by 4-6^{0}C.[29] The majority of scientific opinion supports the theory of global warming, including the Intergovernmental Panel on Climate Change (IPCC), set up under the auspices of the UN Environmental Programme (UNEP) and the World Meteorological Organization (WMO) to assess the impacts of climate change.[30] The IPCC 1992 Supplementary Report affirmed its earlier 1990 Report placing the climate's sensitivity to doubled CO_2 in the range of 1.5 to 4.5^{0}C, with a best estimate of 2.5^{0}C.[31]

The extent to which a rising temperature of the Earth's surface can be attributed to the build up of the greenhouse gases remains, however, a point of controversy. While there has been a rise in the average surface temperature of the Earth over the past century,[32] a causal link with the buildup of greenhouse gases and the temperature rise has not been proved beyond doubt.[33] Thus, distinguishing natural warming from warming attributed to an enhanced greenhouse effect is a problem climatologists must cope with. In effect, these scientists are searching for a greenhouse "fingerprint" to link a rise in temperature to the buildup of the greenhouse gases.[34] The leading climatic changes that might indicate a greenhouse fingerprint are particular global temperature patterns, uniform sea surface temperatures, an increase of water vapor in the atmosphere, and changes in the relative intensity of the seasons.[35] Scientists believe that these indicators can be distinguished from natural changes[36] in the climatic system and thus are characteristic of global warming.

Computer simulations utilizing general circulation models (GCMs) are currently considered the best available technology for predicting the range of possible temperature change.[37] The climatic conditions usually simulated by GCMs are a doubling of pre-industrial CO_2 atmospheric concentrations which have revealed a range of global average temperature increases of 1.9 to 5.2^{0}C (3.4 to 9.4 degrees fahrenheit).[38] The inability to refine this estimate further is the result of the GCMs' limitations.[39] For instance, current GCMs inadequately depict crucial factors such as cloud cover. In addition, only a limited number of GCM simulations are available at present and this results in the inability to adequately determine a more specific value within the temperature range or even to eliminate temperature changes of less than 1 degree or more than 5^{0}C.[40]

In addition to the above uncertainties encountered in the modelling of the impacts of man-made greenhouse gases, a number of additional unknowns need to be taken into account in modelling, including the indirect effect on global warming of other pollutants, as well as the relative effectiveness of the various greenhouse gases in trapping heat, feedback mechanisms, and sinks.

Firstly, there are other pollutants that have an indirect effect on global warming, in particular sulphur emissions. The cooling effect of sulphur is not, however, included in the general circulation models for predicting climate change.[41] Sulphur is emitted in gas form mainly as sulphur dioxide (SO_2), but changes to fine aerosol particles when reaching the atmosphere.[42] These aerosols may affect the absorption of radiation by the atmosphere, as well as affecting the density and brightness of clouds, increasing their cooling effect. Both of these consequences may result in significant regional cooling and an abatement of sulphur emissions might increase global temperatures.[43] Indeed, the period of cooling interrupting the warming trend of the past century, beginning around the 1940s and most prominent in the northern hemisphere, may be due to the simultaneous and significant rise in sulphur emissions from industry.[44]

Aerosols comprised of sulphuric acids and water from volcanic eruptions could also lead to a cooling which could counter a global warming temporarily.[45] Climatologists state that eruptions such as Mount Pinatubo in 1991 will exert a marked cooling effect on the planet, delaying by several years the time when a global warming due to increased greenhouse gas emissions might become obvious.[46] That same eruption also probably smothered the potential warming effect stemming from the return of "El Nino" in 1992.[47] Therefore, rising sulphur emissions from industry and volcanic eruptions might have an ephemeral cooling effect and temporarily mask any global warming.

Other pollutants that can affect global warming indirectly include nitrogen oxide (NO_x), volatile organic compounds (VOCs), and carbon monoxide (CO). Their relevance to global warming stems from the fact that they are precursors of tropospheric ozone, one of the greenhouse gases.[48] However, there is difficulty in predicting trends and distribution of nitrogen oxides since their atmospheric lifetimes are relatively short compared to other greenhouse gases, and there are inadequate monitoring procedures.[49] Trends of the other pollutants are also difficult to predict.[50]

A second variable within modelling is that the degree of "global warming potential" or effectiveness in trapping heat of each greenhouse gas is different, as is the amount of time each gas will remain in the atmosphere.[51] Thus, while CO_2 is considered the main greenhouse gas at present by virtue of sheer volume emitted, other gases are more effective in trapping heat and last longer in the atmosphere and so may take on relatively greater significance in the future.[52] Thirdly, it has been suggested, employing the theory that warming stimulates the release of carbon dioxide, that global warming will build on itself in a classic feedback mechanism.[53] This theory suggests that global warming would release naturally stored CO_2 and naturally stored methane.[54] The effects of clouds which both trap and reflect radiation depending on the circumstances may also contribute to this feedback mechanism.[55]

A fourth variable in the modelling equation is the presence of "sinks" such as oceans or forests which aid in the removal from the atmosphere of the greenhouse gases through natural assimilation,[56] another factor not well understood at this time.[57]

All these variables contribute to the uncertainty in modelling regarding the definitive cause and extent of surface temperature rise.[58] For instance, the IPCC had predicted in its 1990 report that average global temperatures would rise by 0.3^0C per decade, but has since revised that figure in its Supplementary Report of 1992. It is now "expected to be less," since the GCMs did not include all possible factors.[59] In addition, the 1992 IPCC Report noted that confidence in the regional changes simulated by computer models remained low.[60]

However, as techniques improve, models are becoming more reliable as scientific tools.[61] For example, GCMs have recently been able to incorporate deep sea ocean circulation factors, allowing the thermal absorption capacity of deep oceans to be taken into account. Preliminary results of the inclusion of these factors suggest that global temperatures may not be rising as quickly as previously thought.[62] In addition, scientists are now working with terrestrial biogeochemical models (TBMs) which incorporate underlying biophysical and biochemical processes. These models can be useful in aiding the understanding of the global carbon cycle and estimating the change increased anthropogenic CO_2 will have on the cycle.[63]

An independent check on the computer predictions has apparently affirmed the conclusions reached by GCMs.[64] In this study, climatic data from two different era, 20,000 years ago in the depths of the last Ice-Age when the average global temperature was 3-5^0C cooler than today, and the mid-Cretaceous period of approximately 100 million years ago when the temperature was 6-12^0C warmer, was analyzed to determine how the climate changed in response to certain forces ("forcing"), including greenhouse gases. From this information, a calculation was made of the change in both temperature and "forcing" between those periods and today. An estimation of climate sensitivity, as depicted by temperature change resulting from CO_2, could then be made. The study concluded that during the Ice-Age, the sensitivity of the climate to a doubling of CO_2 would have resulted in raising the average global temperature by approximately 2^0C, while a similar scenario during the mid-Cretaceous period would have raised the average temperature by approximately 2.5^0C. Combining the two results, the study predicted that a doubling of CO_2 will lead to a warming of 2.3^0C, plus or minus 0.9 degrees.[65]

According to scientists, this study is more reliable than the results of GCMs, since it analyses both a colder and a warmer climate than that prevailing today, not just the modern climate observations of GCMs. More importantly, the analysis includes the effect of key unknowns of GCMs such as the effects of clouds, which climate modelers do not yet know enough about.[66] The study includes these effects since the actual temperatures of the time periods utilized would include the net result of such unknowns as clouds.

The importance of global warming depends on the extent of resulting climate change. Although some states might be labelled as climate change "winners" and some as "losers", particularly in terms of agriculture,[67] it has been stressed that surveying the situation "on the nation-state level may not be appropriate," since "if significant climate change occurs, it's going to be a lot of individuals in the world who are disadvantaged. At one level, it doesn't matter so much which country they're in."[68] Nevertheless, a recent study revealed that crop yields would actually increase in some states following a global warming.[69]

Scientists debate the sources of global warming and the rate of climate change.[70] Recently published scientific papers have argued that the effects of global warming to date have been relatively benign.[71] These papers argue that the warming has increased nighttime temperature lows rather than daytime highs, and that, in the northern hemisphere, the warming is occurring primarily in winter and spring with summer temperatures no warmer than were present in the 1860s and 1870s. In addition, the increased cloud cover causing the nighttime warming and daytime cooling is probably caused by the warming itself and so is likely to moderate a warming effect by keeping daytime temperatures lower.[72] Finally, some scientists question whether a doubling of CO_2 will occur at all, partly because of the limited availability of fossil fuels.[73]

The outcome of this debate, which is beyond mere scientific discourse, will influence the implications of science for legal policy.[74]

Ozone Layer Depletion

Ozone layer depletion is another contributor to global environmental change. The ozone layer, located in the stratosphere approximately 13 to 35 miles above the earth's surface, prevents the entry of harmful ultraviolet (UV) light radiated from the sun into the Earth's atmosphere and causing injury to the world's vast assortment of species, including man.[75]

Concern over possible deleterious effects on the stratosphere were raised during the 1960's with regard to the supersonic transport project (SST).[76] Additional concerns over ozone layer depletion were raised in respect to nuclear testing and the agricultural use of fertilizers. But it was not until 1974 that ozone layer depletion received international attention. In that year, a scientific study revealed that CFCs could deplete the stratospheric ozone layer.[77] CFCs are manmade chemicals used in refrigeration, air conditioners, aerosols, solvents and plastic foams.[78] Ultraviolet light acts to break down CFC compounds, releasing chlorine monoxide, which in turn destroy ozone.[79] Scientists estimate that for every 1% depletion of the ozone layer, between 1 and 2% more of harmful ultraviolet radiation reaches the Earth's surface, depending on seasonal temperatures.[80]

An ozone "hole" (in actuality, greatly diminished ozone levels) was discovered above the Antarctic Circle by a British team in October 1984, and confirmed the following year by NASA satellite photographs.[81] In 1987, proof that ozone layer depletion was definitely linked to chlorine monoxide was provided by a NASA-sponsored expedition to the Antarctic. This was followed six months later by the report of the Ozone Trends Panel, composed of more than 100 scientists from 10 different countries, confirming that chlorine monoxide was the basis of ozone layer depletion.[82]

Observations by the US National Oceanic and Atmospheric

Administration (NOAA) in 1992 revealed that ozone layer depletion over Antarctica was beginning earlier and occurring faster, by as much as 15%, than the previous year of 1991.[83] Although scientists are unsure whether the acceleration was due to man-made or natural causes, such as the Mount Pinatubo and Mount Hudson volcanic eruptions in 1991,[84] the rate of depletion was a matter for concern. Recently, ozone above Antarctica reached a record low, with all of the ozone between 8 to 11 miles above Antarctica having been destroyed.[85]

In addition, the threat of an Arctic ozone hole remains high due to the presence of chlorine monoxide and other chemicals, and was prevented in 1992 only by a warm winter, according to scientists.[86] A report of the World Meteorological Organization stated that ozone levels in northern Europe, Canada and Russia the previous year were 12% below average, "an occurrence never before observed in more than 35 years of continuous ozone observations."[87] Early 1993 monitoring figures showed an even greater decrease. NASA satellites detected that ozone levels over the northern hemisphere were at their lowest level in 14 years and that ozone levels in the first three months of 1993 were 10 to 20% below their normal range in the middle latitudes of the northern hemisphere.[88] Scientists cautioned, however, that the decline may have been a transitory effect from the eruption of the Mount Pinatubo volcano in 1991.[89] In 1995, the Arctic ozone layer shrank by a record amount, increasing concerns of a future Arctic ozone hole.[90]

In a 1987 study, the US Environmental Protection Agency (EPA), stated that if no action was undertaken to prevent ozone depletion, there would be a likely dramatic increase in skin cancer and cataracts, and the human immune system would be adversely affected.[91] The report also linked UV radiation with possible damage to phytoplankton, which form the base of the oceanic food chain.[92] More recently, researchers have compiled greater evidence that UV rays may interfere with human immune systems, including irregular immune responses to skin cancer, contact allergies and infectious diseases.[93]

In April 1991, US EPA Administrator William Reilly revealed NASA data which indicated that, since 1978, the ozone layer over the United States has depleted at twice the rate previously believed.[94] The EPA estimates that based on the new information, approximately 12 million Americans will develop skin cancer, with over 200,000 resulting fatalities. While this was a US-based study, the results can be extrapolated to other geographic areas with similar ozone layer depletion levels within the northern hemisphere. The EPA study does not, however, take into account lifestyle habits of sunbathing, which, if on the increase, could account for the extra cases of skin cancer. Nevertheless, in revealing the 4.5 to 5 percent decrease in the ozone layer, the EPA chief stated that: "It is unexpected, it is disturbing and it possesses implications we have not yet had time to fully explore," adding that the new data called for a "reappraisal of both US and international policy on the control of the ozone-destroying chemicals."[95]

This reappraisal in the form of international action to curb ozone layer depletion[96] has apparently begun to reap rewards, notwithstanding the record lows of ozone depletion reported above in this book. Scientists now claim that the build-up of the industrial chemicals most responsible for depleting the ozone layer has slowed considerably, and if the trend continues, the increase in the chemicals should halt before the end of this decade. The worst of the ozone destruction should come around the turn of the century, after the maximum load of chemicals wafts up to the stratosphere. As the chemicals are gradually destroyed by natural processes, the ozone layer should begin a recovery lasting 50 to 100 years.[97]

CONCLUSION

While much research has already been completed in the areas of climate change and ozone layer depletion, there is still some scientific uncertainty as to their potential effects.[98] This factor plays a critical role regarding international cooperation within the legal order by making cooperation more difficult. Without substantiated scientific data, support for international action is diminished.[99] Nevertheless, legally binding agreements are sometimes reached as scientific uncertainty diminishes or even sometimes where it remains largely undiminished, but where public opinion or a perception of danger help drive international action. The ozone layer depletion and climate change regimes provide evidence of this.[100] Growing scientific knowledge should contribute to the strengthening of regulations, as within the ozone layer depletion regime.[101] Uncertainty regarding other issues critical to the regime must also be overcome as well,[102] for the law-making process to continue.

Regimes help reveal this law-making process through their step-by-step approach to strengthening the international legal order, since regimes:

> ...begin with commitments 'merely' to norms and principles, and either lack regulatory rules or possess only very weak ones. This is exactly as it should be. If states waited... until there was enough concern and scientific understanding to adopt strong rules, they would wait much too long...[as they] are needed early on to help create the conditions that make strong rules possible...[103]

The following chapter will examine the schools of thought in international law, followed by an examination of the law relevant to climate change and ozone layer depletion prior to the formation of the regimes concerning those issues. Chapter 3 is concerned with the concept of regimes and why they are an essential part of the international legal order. Then, Chapter 4 will examine the critical issues and catalysts specific to the climate change and ozone layer regimes and how regimes can address the uncertainty associated with critical issues. Chapters 5 and 6 are analyses of the climate change and ozone layer depletion regimes. Finally, conclusions will be drawn in Chapter 7 as to the viability of regimes within the framework of the international legal order in general.

NOTES

1. This book is concerned with international regimes and not domestic regimes. This does not mean that domestic factors are not important within international regimes. Rather, the purpose is to examine international regimes involving more than one state rather than a domestic regime within one state.

2. "Structural Causes and Regime Consequences: Regimes as Intervening Variables," in *International Regimes*, ed. Stephen D. Krasner (Ithaca: Cornell University Press, 1983), p. 1.

3. One of the leading international relations scholars in the area of regimes states: "There is little evidence, however, that lawyers and legal scholars have made a conscious effort to examine, much less to debate, the conceptual and theoretical issues raised by their reliance on the idea of regimes or legal regimes in international society." Oran Young, "Understanding International Regimes: Contributions from Law and the Social Sciences," paper presented at the annual meeting of the American Society of International Law, Washington, DC, 1-3 April 1992, p. 32.

4. Ibid., p. 38.

5. Although ozone layer depletion may contribute to climate change by altering the atmospheric climate system, for the purposes of this book it will not be included in the term "climate change" in order to avoid confusion.

6. Intergovernmental Panel on Climate Change (IPCC), *Policymakers Summary of the Formulation of Response Strategies*, Report of Working Group III, (NY: WMO and UNEP, 1990), p. v. While the IPCC was referring to climate change resulting from global warming, the statement applies to ozone layer depletion as well.

7. See, *infra*, Chapter 4.

8. Anne-Marie Slaughter Burley, "International Law and International Relations Theory: A Dual Agenda," *American Journal of International Law* Vol. 87, No. 2 (April 1993), p. 221.

9. Ibid.

10. Winfried Lang, "The International Waste Regime," *Environmental Protection and International Law*, ed. Winfried Lang, Hanspeter Neuhold and Karl Zemanek (London: Graham & Trotman, 1991), p. 148.

11. As will be shown below, science, economics and development are critical issues in the ozone layer depletion and climate change regimes. See, *infra*, Chapter 4. The uncertainty involved is partially attributable to "politicization." The Oxford Dictionary defines this as the act of "giving political character to." Politics, then, is taken into account through politicization of these issues rather than as a separate critical issue. See, *infra*, Chapter 4.

12. See, *infra*, Chapter 3, Introduction to International Regimes.

13. *International Law in Theory and Practice* (Dordrecht: Martinus Nijhoff Publishers, 1991), p. 4.

14. See, *infra*, Chapter 3, Formation of Regimes.

15. See, *infra*, Chapter 2, Sources of International Law.

16. See, *infra*, Chapter 2, Policy-Oriented School.

17. See, *infra*, Chapter 2, Policy-Oriented School. In that regard, international law and regime theory can be brought closer together, thus overcoming perceived methodological difficulties. See, Young, "Understanding International Regimes: Contributions from Law and the Social Sciences," *supra*, n. 3. While Young does indeed recognize the "distinctive modes of reasoning" between the legal community and social science community, the view of this author is that the two can be reconciled, particularly within the policy-oriented approach to international law. Indeed, Young himself suggested in a panel discussion of his paper that there are ways around the "two-cultures problem," but that it requires breaking down deep-seated mindsets that keep these cultures separate, and identifying the best intellectual opportunities for collaboration. He suggests sources of obligation or determinants of compliance as examples of such opportunities. Oran Young, "Remarks," *American Society of International Law: Proceedings of the 86th Meeting*, Washington, DC (1992), p. 174.

18. *Indiana Jones and the Temple of Doom*, Paramount Pictures, 1989. While global environmental change involves economic and development considerations as well as scientific factors, it is at its core a scientific problem with economic and development ramifications. Therefore, it is necessary to explain the scientific basis of the problem in order to properly evaluate economic and development concerns, as well as to better understand the scientific uncertainty involved. These critical issues will be addressed in Chapter 4, *infra*.

19. For a general survey of the many social and economic aspects of climate change see *Scientific American: Managing Planet Earth* (Special Issue) Vol. 261, No. 3 (September 1989). Climate change and global warming are not interchangeable terms. Global warming is a "symptom" of climate change, which is the "disease." See, UN Information Unit on Climate Change (IUCC), Fact Sheet 9, "Why 'Climate Change' and 'Global Warming' Are Not the Same Thing," *Climate Change Dossier* (Geneva: IUCC, 1992).

20. Stephen H. Schneider, "The Greenhouse Effect: Science and Policy", *Science* Vol. 243 (10 February 1989), p. 771.

21. IPCC, *Policymakers Summary of the Scientific Assessment of Climate Change*, Report of Working Group I (NY: WMO and UNEP, 1990), p. 4.

22. CO_2 buildup results from the burning of fossil fuels and the net loss of CO_2 absorption from diminished forest "sinks" because of deforestation. Other sinks include the atmosphere, the ocean, the soil, and biomass (plants and animals). See, for instance, J.T. Houghton, B.A. Callander and S.K. Varney, *Climate Change 1992: The Supplementary Report to the IPCC Scientific Assessment* (Cambridge: Cambridge

University Press, 1992), pp. 31–34. See, also, National Academy of Science, *Policy Implications of Greenhouse Warming*, Report of Synthesis Panel of the Committee of the National Academy of Sciences, the National Academy of Engineering, and the Institute of Medicine (Washington, D.C.: National Academy Press, 1991), pp. 3–9 and IUCC, Fact Sheets 1 & 2, "An Introduction to Man-Made Climate Change" and "The Role of Greenhouse Gases," *Climate Change Dossier* (Geneva: IUCC, 1992).

23. CH_4 emissions stem from fossil fuel burning, enteric fermentation, rice cultivation, landfills and deforestation. The main sink is a chemical reaction with a hydroxyl radical to form water vapor. Houghton, et al, *Climate Change 1992*, *supra*, n. 22, pp. 35–37. Recent studies, however, have indicated that the amount of CH_4 in the atmosphere may be levelling off, and will stop increasing around 2006. "Methane in Atmosphere Is Levelling Off," *International Herald Tribune*, 30 July 1992, p. 8.

24. N_2O buildup has been thought to result mainly from biomass burning and fossil fuel combustion. The main sinks are stratospheric photo-oxidation and photo-dissociation, and perhaps consumption in soils, but that has not yet been evaluated. Houghton et al, *Climate Change 1992*, *supra*, n. 22, pp. 37–38. However, new studies have downgraded N_2O production from fossil fuel combustion and biomass burning, suggesting that the major source of N_2O has yet to be identified or that a known source has been underestimated. W.R. Cofer et al, "New Estimates of Nitrous Oxide Emissions From Biomass Burning," *Nature* Vol. 349 (21 February 1991), pp. 689-691.

25. Tropospheric O_3 results from the interaction of ultraviolet light and traffic and industry emissions. Sinks for tropospheric ozone precursors include soil uptake and stratospheric oxidation. Houghton et al, *Climate Change 1992*, *supra*, n. 22, p. 40.

26. The leading source of CFCs and HCFCs is industry use in refrigerants, solvents, aerosol propellants and foams. The main contributors are CFC-11, CFC-12 and HCFC-22. Because of their ozone layer depleting effect, CFCs and HCFCs are regulated by a separate international agreement and protocol. See, *infra*, Chapter 1, Ozone Layer Depletion. The only significant sink for these sources is photolysis (slow destruction by sunlight) in the stratosphere and a chemical reaction with a hydroxyl in the troposphere. Houghton et al, *Climate Change 1992*, *supra*, n. 22, p. 38.

27. See, *supra*, n. 22–26, for a description of the sinks for the greenhouse gases.

28. See, for example, IPCC, *Policymakers Summary of the Potential Impacts of Climate Change*, Report of Working Group II (NY: WMO and UNEP, 1990); Department of the Environment, *The Potential Effects of Climate Change in the United Kingdom* (London: HMSO, 1991); and National Academy of Sciences, *Policy Implications of Greenhouse Warming*, *supra*, n. 22.

29. Svante Arrhenius, "On the Influence of Carbonic Acid in the Air Upon The Temperature of the Ground," *Philosophical Magazine* Vol. 41 (April 1896), pp. 237–276. The idea that the atmosphere acted like a greenhouse, letting in heat but not allowing heat to escape, was first argued by the French mathematical physicist, Jean Baptiste Fourier. See, "Les Temperatures du Globe Terrestre et des Espaces Planetaires," *Memoires de l'Academie Royale des Sciences de l'Institut de France* Vol. 7 (1824), pp. 569–604. Shortly after, John Tyndall observed that radiation from certain atmospheric gases was responsible for the trapping of heat. See, "On Radiation Through The Earth's Atmosphere," *Philosophical Magazine* Vol. 4 (March 1863), pp. 200–07.

30. See, IPCC, Report of WGI, *supra*, n. 21, and Houghton et al, *Climate Change 1992*, (IPCC Supplement) *supra*, n. 22.

31. Houghton, Climate Change 1992, *supra*, n. 22, pp. 17, 101. See also, William K. Stevens, "Estimates of Warming Gain More Precision And Warn of Disaster," *The New York Times*, 15 December 1992, p. C9. Unless emission rates change, scientists estimate this doubling from preindustrial concentrations to occur by the middle of the next century. National Academy of Sciences, *Policy Implications of Greenhouse Warming*, *supra*, n. 22, p.25. A revised date of 2100 has been reported, however. "Scientists Confront Renewed Backlash on Global Warming," *The New York Times*, 14 September 1993, Section C.

32. IPCC, Report of WGI, *supra*, n. 21, p. 2. See, also, Peter Aldhous, "1990 Warmest Year on Record", *Nature* Vol. 349 (17 January 1991), p. 186.

33. See, "Reading the Patterns," *Economist* 1 April 1995, p. 65. See, also, Philip D. Jones and Tom M.L. Wigley, "Global Warming Trends," *Scientific American* Vol. 263, No. 2 (August 1990), p. 91, where the authors state "it is impossible as yet to interpret accurately the undeniable global-scale warming that has occurred during this century." See, also, Houghton, et al, *Climate Change 1992*, *supra*, n. 22, p. 5 where the authors affirm the finding of the first IPCC assessment that the observed temperature increase could possibly be a natural occurrence and not due to a human-induced greenhouse warming. See, also, Chapter 4, *infra*, for a discussion of the issue of scientific uncertainty.

34. See, Houghton, et al, *Climate Change 1992*, *supra*, n. 22, pp. 162–165.

35. Ibid.

36. Ibid.

37. See, IUCC, Fact Sheet 14, "How Climate Models Work," *Climate Change Dossier* (Geneva: IUCC, 1992).

38. National Academy of Sciences, *Policy Implications of Greenhouse Warming*, *supra*, n. 22, pp. 17–18.

39. This contributes to the scientific uncertainty within the climate change regime. See, *infra*, Chapter 4.

40. National Academy of Sciences, *Policy Implications of Greenhouse Warming*, *supra*, n. 22, pp. 18–19.

41. US Department of State, Bureau of Oceans and International Environmental and Scientific Affairs, *Environmental Documentation: United Nations Framework Convention on Climate Change*, Washington, DC, September 1992, p. 3.

42. Stephen H. Schneider, "The Changing Climate," *Scientific American* (Special Issue on Managing Planet Earth) Vol. 261, No. 3 (September 1989), p. 76.

43. Ibid.

44. Ibid.

45. See, US EPA, *The Potential Effects of Global Climate Change On The United States: Report To Congress*, ed. Joel P. Smith and Dennis Tirpak, EPA-230-05-89-050 (Washington, DC: EPA 1989), p. 15.

46. See, Houghton et al, *Climate Change 1992*, *supra*, n. 22, p. 164. See also, James Hansen, Andrew Lacis, Reto Ruedy, Makiko Sata and Helene Wilson, "How Sensitive is the World's Climate?" *Research and Exploration* Vol. 9, No. 2 (Spring 1993), pp. 155–157.

47. El Nino is the huge pool of extra warm seawater that appears in the eastern part of the Pacific Ocean periodically and changing jet stream patterns temporarily so as to make some areas of the Earth wetter, drier, or warmer than usual.

48. See, *supra*, n. 25, and Houghton et al, *Climate Change 1992*, *supra*, n. 22, p. 40. Other precursors of tropospheric ozone include non-methane hydrocarbons. International regulation of NO_x, SO_2, and VOCs fall under the Geneva Convention on Long Range Transboundary Air Pollution Convention and Protocols, *International Legal Materials* Vol. 18, No. 9 (1979), pp. 1442-1455; [NO_x], Vol. 28, No. 1 (1989) pp. 212–230; and [SO_2], Vol. 27, No. 3 (1988) pp. 707–711. A VOCs Protocol was signed on 19 November 1991, Vol. 31, No. 3 (1992), pp. 568–611.

49. Houghton et al, *Climate Change 1992*, *supra*, n. 22, p. 40.

50. Ibid., pp. 40, 90–92.

51. See IUCC, Fact Sheet 7, "Measuring the 'Global Warming Potential' of Greenhouse Gases," *Climate Change Dossier* (Geneva: IUCC, 1992).

52. See, Houghton et al, *Climate Change 1992*, *supra*, n. 22, pp. 51–67, and IUCC, Fact Sheet 7, *supra*, n. 51. For example, approximate lifetimes are 50-200 years for CO_2, 10 years for methane, 132 years for N_2O and from 55-500 years for the various CFCs. Over a 20 year period, one molecule of methane traps approximately 35 times more heat than one molecule of CO_2 and so has a Global Warming Potential (GWP) of 35, relative to CO_2. The GWP for N_2O is 260, and for CFCs, the GWP ranges from 4500 to 11,000 depending on the particular CFC. Over a 100 year time period, the GWP for methane decreases to 11, for N_2O it remains about the same, and for CFCs, the GWP depends on the CFC in question.

53. See, D. Rind, E.W. Chiou, W. Chu, J. Larsen, S. Attman, J. Lerner, M.P. McCormick and L. McMaster, "Positive Water Vapor Feedback in Climate Models Confirmed By Satellite Data," *Nature* Vol. 349 (7 February 1991), pp. 500–502, where studies suggest a strong case for the existence of water vapor feedback mechanisms.

54. Ibid.

55. National Academy of Sciences, *Policy Implications of Greenhouse Warming*, *supra*, n. 22, p. 92.

56. Houghton et al, *Climate Change 1992*, *supra*, n. 22, pp. 29–42. See, also, *supra*, n. 22–26 for the known sinks of the greenhouse gases.

57. For example, research indicates that approximately 40% of the carbon dioxide released into the atmosphere from human activity remains there for decades, while about 15% appears to be assimilated into the ocean. The whereabouts of the remaining 45% is unknown, thus creating uncertainty as to the rate of increase of atmospheric carbon dioxide. National Academy of Sciences, *Policy Implications of Greenhouse Warming*, *supra*, n. 22, p. 10.

58. See, IPCC, Report of WG I, *supra*, n. 21, p. 20, National Academy of Sciences, *Policy Implications of Greenhouse Warming*, *supra*, n. 22, pp. 17–19, and IUCC Fact Sheets 1, "An Introduction to Manmade Climate Change," 5, "Is the Earth Warming Up Yet?", & 8, "How Predictable Is the Climate?"(UNEP: Geneva, 1992). Also, ozone layer depletion, see *infra*, Chapter 1, results in cooling at certain levels of the atmosphere in northern latitudes, which may mask the greenhouse signal. See, Houghton et al, *Climate Change 1992*, *supra*, n. 22, pp. 6 & 14. There is also the "El Nino" phenomenon, whereby natural factors warm equatorial seas resulting in global weather changes, *supra*, n. 47.

59. Houghton et al, *Climate Change 1992*, *supra*, n. 22, p. 17.

60. Ibid., p. 101. A revised report of the IPCC is scheduled to be issued in late 1995.

61. See IUCC, Fact Sheet 15, "Are Climate Models Reliable?" *Climate Change Dossier* (Geneva: IUCC, 1992).

62. Graham Chapman, "Editorial," *The South-North Centre for Environmental Policy Newsletter* No. 9 (May 1993), p. 4, citing Sir John Mason, "The Greenhouse Effect and Global Climatic Change," annual James Forrest Lecture to the Institute of Civil Engineers, London, 16 April 1993.

63. See, I. Colin Prentice, "Process and Production," *Nature* Vol. 363 (20 May 1993), pp. 209–210.

64. Eric J. Barron, "Lessons From Past Climates," *Nature* Vol. 360 (10 December 1992), p. 533 and Martin I. Hoffert and Curt Covey, "Deriving Global Climate Sensitivity From Paleoclimate Reconstructions," *Nature* Vol. 360 (10 December 1992), pp. 573–576.

65. Barron, "Lessons," *supra*, n. 64, thus narrowing the inner and outer limits of the GCM predictions, *supra*, n. 40.

66. See, *supra,* n. 40.

67. See, IUCC, Fact Sheet 110, "Climate Change Scenarios: The Issue of Winners and Losers," *Climate Change Dossier*, (Geneva: IUCC, 1992). See also, National Academy of Sciences, *Policy Implications of Greenhouse Warming, supra*, n. 22, which states that "countries like the United States, which encompass many climate zones and have active and aggressive agricultural research and development, would probably be able to adapt their farming to climatic changes deriving from greenhouse warming. Poorer countries with less wealth or fewer climate zones may have more difficulty avoiding problems or taking advantage of better conditions," p. 37.

68. Statement of Professor Dan Magraw, General Counsel for International Activities, US EPA, quoted in *The New York Times*, "In a Warming World, Who Comes Out Ahead?", 5 Feb. 1991, p. C8.

69. Conducted jointly by the Oxford University Environmental Change Unit and the US Goddard Institute for Space Studies. See, Joe Rogaly, "Cost of Norfolk Claret," *Financial Times* (London), 8 December 1992, p. 14.

70. See, William W. Kellogg, "Response to Skeptics of Global Warming,"*Bulletin American Meteorological Society*, Vol. 72, No. 4 (April 1991), pp. 509–510.

71. See, "Global Warming," *USA Today*, 4 April 1995, p. 3A, discussing the results of a study performed by Sallie Baliunas, a Harvard astrophysicist, for the George C. Marshall Institute which concluded that global temperatures are rising 0.1 degree Celsius a decade or three times less than computer projections. See, also, *Research and Development*

Vol. 9, No. 2 (Spring 1993), particularly Richard Lindzen, "Absence of Scientific Basis," pp. 191–200, Robert C. Balling, Jr., "The Global Temperature Data," pp. 201–207, and Patrick J. Michaels, "Benign Greenhouse," pp. 222–233.

72. Cloud cover makes nights warmer by absorbing ground heat and radiating it back to the Earth. Days are cooler since clouds block sunlight. See, Michaels, "Benign Greenhouse," *supra*, n. 71.

73. S. Fred Singer, letter to the editor, *The New York Times*, 28 September 1993. Mr. Singer is Director of the Science and Environmental Policy Project, Arlington, Virginia.

74. See, *infra*, Chapter 4.

75. See, for instance, UNEP, *Action On Ozone* (Nairobi: UNEP, 1989).

76. Lynton Keith Caldwell, *International Environmental Policy: Emergence and Dimensions*, 2d ed. (Durham: Duke University Press, 1990), p. 262.

77. F.S. Rowland and Mario Molina, "Stratospheric Sink for Chlorofluoromethanes: Chlorine-Atom Catalyzed Destruction of Ozone", *Nature* Vol. 249 (28 June 1974), pp. 810–812. Since then, other ozone depleting chemicals have been identified, including halons, HCFCs, *supra*, n. 26, carbon tetrachloride, methyl chloroform, methyl bromide and hydrobromofluorocarbons (HBFCs). Halons are used in firefighting equipment, carbon tetrachloride and methyl chloroform are primarily used as solvents, and methyl bromide is primarily used as a pesticide. World Meteorological Organization, *Scientific Assessment of Stratospheric Ozone*, Global Ozone Research and Monitoring Project (Geneva: WMO, 1989) and Friends of the Earth, *Methyl Bromide-Ozone Destroyer* (London: FOE, 1992).

78. See, US EPA, *How Industry is Reducing Dependence on Ozone-Depleting Chemicals*, Office of Air and Radiation (Washington, DC: EPA, 1988). See, also, *supra*, n. 26.

79. After the UV light breaks down the CFCs, releasing chlorine atoms (Cl), the chlorine atoms attack ozone (O_3):

$$Cl + O_3 = ClO + O_2$$
$$ClO + O = Cl + O_2$$

In the first reaction, the chlorine monoxide (ClO) is an unstable and highly reactive compound with an odd number of electrons. ClO will then react with a free oxygen atom in the atmosphere in order to obtain an even number of electrons. The oxygen in ClO is then attracted to the free oxygen atom to form an oxygen molecule (O_2), leaving Cl free to start the cycle all over again. See, Sharon Roan, *Ozone Crisis* (NY: John Wiley & Sons, 1989), pp. 8–9.

80. See, "Ozone Depletion Linked to Rise in Harmful Radiation," Independent (London), 23 April 1993, p. 2 and Martin Chipperfield, "Satellite Maps Ozone Destroyer," *Nature* Vol. 362 (15 April 1993), p. 592.

81. See, Richard Elliot Benedick, *Ozone Diplomacy* (Cambridge: Harvard University Press, 1991), pp. 18–20, and Roan, *Ozone Crisis, supra*, n. 79, pp. 125–141.

82. The Panel was organized by Robert Watson of NASA. See, Benedick, *Ozone Diplomacy, supra*, n. 81, pp. 108–111, and Roan, *Ozone Crisis, supra*, n. 79, pp. 219–220. Along with chlorine, bromine also has been found to destroy ozone.

83. See, D.J. Hofman, S.J. Oltmans, J.M. Harris, S. Solomon, T. Deshler, "Observation and Possible Causes of New Ozone Depletion in Antarctica in 1991," *Nature* Vol. 359 (24 September 1992), pp. 283–287. See also, "Ozone Depletion Over South Pole Accelerates," *The New York Times*, 27 September 1992, section 1, p. 29. The drop in ozone usually occurs just prior to the break-up of the polar vortex, a mass of very cold stagnant air, at the end of the southern winter.

84. Ibid.

85. Gabrielle Walker, "Weather Contributes to Record Ozone Loss," *Nature* Vol. 365, 21 October 1993, p. 683.

86. Warren E. Leary, "Scientists Say Warm Winter Prevented Arctic Ozone Hole," *The New York Times*, 1 May 1992, p. A12.

87. "UN Agency Cites Lowest Recorded Levels for Ozone," *The Boston Globe*, 14 November 1992, p. 5.

88. See, "Ozone Layer Over Britain Shrinks," *Independent*, 23 April 1993. p. 1 and "Northern Hemisphere Ozone at 14-Year Low," *The New York Times*, 23 April 1993, p. A26.

89. Ibid.

90. "Arctic Ozone Layer Shrinks," *The New York Times*, 4 April 1995, p. C5.

91. US EPA, *CFCs and Stratospheric Ozone* (Washington, DC: Office of Public Affairs, 1987).

92. Ibid.

93. "Rays of Sun May Affect Body's Immune System," *Reading Eagle* (Pennsylvania) 25 December 1992, p. B10.

94. "EPA Weighs Fees, Other Options to Expedite Phaseout of Ozone-Eating Chemicals," *Inside EPA*, 12 April 1991, p. 3.

95. "Ozone Loss Over US Is Found To Be Twice as Bad as Predicted," *The New York Times*, 5 April 1991, p. A1. Previous estimates of skin cancer were only 500,000 with 9,300 deaths. At the same time, it is important to keep in mind that safe substitutes may not be readily

available for banned CFCs. HCFCs are currently being substituted for many CFCs, but HCFCs also have ozone depleting properties. See, *infra*, Chapter 5, Economic Uncertainty, for a discussion of the status of replacements for ozone depleting substances.

96 See, *infra,* Chapter 5, International Action Regarding Ozone Layer Depletion.

97. JW Elkins, "Decrease in the Growth Rates of Atmospheric Chlorofluorocarbons 11 and 12," *Nature* Vol. 364, 26 August 1993.

98. This is less true of ozone layer depletion, where documented studies have estimated the degree of harm to humans. *Supra*, Chapter 1, Ozone Layer Depletion.

99. The importance of scientific certainty will be discussed in Chapter 4.

100. Other international agreements allow for scientific research to be taken account of as necessary, such as the UN Convention on the Law of the Sea, Art. 61, and the International Convention for the Regulation of Whaling, Art. V, (amendments shall be based on scientific findings, but other factors can also be taken into account).

101. See, *infra*, Chapter 5.

102. See, *infra*, Chapter 4.

103. Peter M. Haas, Robert O. Keohane and Marc A. Levy, "Improving the Effectiveness of International Environmental Institutions," in *Institutions for the Earth*, ed. Peter M. Haas, Robert O. Keohane and Marc A. Levy (Cambridge, Mass: MIT Press, 1993), p. 413.

CHAPTER 2

The International Legal Order and Global Environmental Change

The 'acceleration of history' and the individualization of justice have brought about a situation inimical to the development of... international law in its classical sense.[1]

An examination of the general international law broadly concerning climate change and ozone layer depletion is outlined below to show the lack of applicable law for these issue-areas prior to the formation of the climate change and ozone layer depletion regimes.[2]

It is first necessary to outline the main approaches to international law, in order to properly place the concept of regimes within the international legal order and distinguish it from other forms of controlling behavior (such as morality) since "the legally binding nature of norms of international law distinguish them from other social norms which function in the inter-State system (...political norms, norms of international morality...)."[3]

The basic tenets of each of the main schools of thought will be discussed below. As Oscar Schachter has pointed out, "one could say, with only slight exaggeration, that at the present time the universe of international lawyers divides roughly into the instrumentalists (policy-oriented) and the positivists."[4] Nevertheless, the naturalist school of thought will also be addressed. The emphasis, however, is on the policy-oriented school. It is this approach that is most conducive to the development of thought necessary to understand and respond to the particularly serious environmental challenges in question, and that can best incorporate regimes within its jurisprudential framework.[5]

SCHOOLS OF THOUGHT

"All organized groups and structures require a system of normative conduct — that is to say, conduct which is regarded by each actor, and by the group as a whole, as being obligatory, and for which violation carries a price."[6] Brierly similarly stated that "there can be no society without a system of law to regulate the relations of its members with one another."[7] Thus, while the conduct of states may be conditioned by factors in addition to law, a normative system of international law "makes possible that degree of order if society is to maximize the common good — and indeed, even to avoid chaos in the web of bilateral and multilateral relationships that society embraces."[8] There are, however, various theories employed to explain the concept of international law.

Naturalists

For the naturalists, international law is based on absolute values.[9] Thus, there is an appeal to a superior source of obligation.[10] Although different values have been put forward as this superior source of obligation, they can be roughly placed in two classes: those based on some religious source, and those based on a secular source, such as a characteristic of human nature or of the physical environment.[11] Whatever the chosen source, however, critics contend that this school of thought remains "mystic or ideological, because the basic tenets of ...[the] theory ultimately prove scientifically unverifiable by others."[12] Vattel, while basing his works on natural law, distinguishes between laws of morality or conscience and laws of action, thus minimizing natural law in the process, but which nevertheless continued to exert influence over unlimited state sovereignty.[13] In the 20th century, the naturalists' emphasis turned to the purposes and direction of the international legal system. Thus, Koskenniemi suggests that natural law obligations, once associated with divine law, became associated with what is necessary for subsistence and self-preservation.[14] A distinction, then, is made between the:

> traditionalist, absolutist point of view holding that Natural Law is a higher kind of law from which no derogation is permitted. Positive law has to conform to this superior law and, if it does not, it must be considered invalid. In the more modern, relativist view... Natural Law is a standard to which rules of positive law should conform without necessarily being invalidated, if this proves not to be the case.[15]

While the naturalists may not at present occupy center stage in international legal theory, some of today's international legal ideas and principles, such as that of human rights in international law, including intergenerational rights,[16] find their roots in natural law and the relevance of ethics and justice.[17] In addition, the concept of international *jus cogens* was developed under the strong influence of the naturalists, who claimed that states were obliged to respect certain fundamental principles of the international community.[18] Notwithstanding these contributions, policy-oriented proponents, discussed below, claim that naturalists make little contribution to a comprehensive inquiry about empirical processes affecting decision-making. As a result, the establishment of goals by the use of exercises in faith, rather than common interest, can only provoke the assertion of different and possibly opposing goals by those professing a different faith.[19] Positivists also find fault with the natural law, particularly its "mysticism" and unverifiability.

Positivists

The positivist school of international law views the legal order as a body of authoritative rules which determine the behavior of individual states. Thus, values and ideals are not a matter of legal concern for the purely positivist school. According to Austin, the "founding father" of legal positivism, law consists of commands from a political superior to a political inferior:[20]

> Every positive law, or every law simply and strictly so-called, is set by a sovereign individual or sovereign body of individuals,

to a person or persons in a state of subjection to its authority.[21]

Austin's theory, however, "entails entirely negative consequences with respect to international law," since it leads him to deny international law the character of law.[22] Kelsen constructs a complex theory of positive law, which posits a "grundnorm" from which all subordinate norms derive their validity. In his "Pure Theory of Law," Kelsen argues that the grundnorm of international law was international custom as a law-creating fact: in other words, that states ought to behave as they have customarily behaved.[23] From this norm identifying custom as the source of law, Kelsen is able to trace the validity of all other legal rules, including treaties which draw their validity from the principle of *pacta sunt servanda*, itself a rule of customary international law.[24] In addition, Kelsen's view of a legal order requires the capacity of states to apply sanctions.[25] These sanctions do not necessarily have to be applied, but "ought" to be, by which is meant that the application of a sanction to a breach of a normative standard is legal, in other words, ultimately sanctioned by the "grundnorm."

Although Kelsen takes into account the role of both international organizations and individuals within the legal order,[26] he views states as the creators of normative standards. This conviction, along with his view of international law as a coercive, sanctioning order accentuates the idea of a formal international legal order, with little regard for the social processes and choices undertaken. Kelsen's "pure" view of the primary role of states in international law, as well as the formal separation of legal and political processes is representative of the traditional, positivist school of international law in which customary norms and treaties create obligations.

Hart views law from a more sociological viewpoint, although maintaining a positivistic outlook. For Hart, law is a system of rules, both primary (behavior standards) and secondary (means of identifying, developing and changing primary rules).[27] A rule of recognition provides a test for determining whether a rule is legal; if the rule has been created or enacted in the way stipulated by the rule of recognition, then the rule is binding.[28] Thus, for Hart there are two ways for a rule to acquire legal status: the rule has been created or enacted in conformity with a secondary rule of recognition and 2) in primitive societies, a rule can become binding if it is accepted as a standard of conduct.[29]

Hart considers international law to consist only of primary rules, since that legal order lacks a legislature and compulsory enforcement procedures. Thus, for Hart, the international legal order was not a system of rules, since a rule of recognition or basic norm has yet to evolve with which to trace the validity of other rules. Instead, Hart believes rules of international law are binding because they are accepted and function as such.[30]

Hart's view of law has been labelled "new positivism"[31] in that it occupies a middle position between traditional positivism as in Kelsen's pure view of law, and the policy-oriented approach described below. But the views of what have come to be called neopositivists are still not free from criticism. Critics contend that a rule-oriented approach fails to take account of decision or choice in the legal process and gives insufficient attention to the policies for which rules are devised: "divorced from policy and context, rules are skeletons without body and soul."[32]

Policy-Oriented School

The principal competing theory to positivism views international law as a policy-oriented process of decision-making which conforms to shared expectations derived from common values. Thus, the policy school arose as a challenge to the positivists and their view of international law as a system of rules. In addition, while sharing the view of the legal realists that law involves policy-choices,[33] the policy-oriented approach attempts to demonstrate that the role of international law in conflict resolution is not limited to low-conflict situations, something the realists could not accept. Thus, the school moved beyond the Realists into the jurisprudence of problem solving. The challenge the approach presents to international legal scholars is:

> (1) to develop a jurisprudence, a comprehensive theory and appropriate methods of inquiry, which will assist the peoples of the world to distinguish public orders based on human dignity and public orders based either on a law which denies human dignity or a denial of law itself for the simple supremacy of naked force; and (2) to invent and recommend the authority structures (principles and procedures) necessary to a world public order that harmonizes with the growing aspirations of the

> overwhelming numbers of the peoples of the globe and is in accord with the proclaimed values of human dignity enunciated by the moral leaders of mankind.[34]

This policy-oriented or "New Haven Approach"[35] to international law is best understood in terms of a map outlining "a continuing process designed to become part of the intelligence and appraisal functions of the world community."[36] This map includes systems of public order included within the larger context of a world social process in which persons pursue values or preferred events through institutions, organized and unorganized, utilizing available resources. These values include power, enlightenment, wealth, skill, well-being, affection, respect and rectitude.[37]

Within the global social process, the policy-oriented school is concerned with the shaping and the sharing of power. The social situation concerned with this process is labelled an "arena": "The identifying characteristic of an arena is a structure of expectations shared among the members of a community; that is, choices affecting the community are made which, if opposed, will in all probability be enforced against opposition."[38]

Thus, a process of decision-making in which choices are made occurs. Within the arena there are various participants including governments, international organizations, nongovernmental organizations, pressure and interest groups, as well as individuals acting alone or through organizations.[39]

The perspectives of these participants may diverge and be highly individualized. Participants continuously attempt to achieve their own goals through their "bases of power" or resources, made effective by various strategies used to affect outcomes. These strategies utilize indulgences or deprivations, resulting in isolation or coalitions of the participants.[40]

For this school of thought, international law is thus not just a body of rules but a continuous process of decisions made by authoritative decision-makers, guided by community perspectives and choosing among policy alternatives:

> ...an appropriate conception of law will include not merely certain allegedly autonomous, technical rules, inherited from the past, but also a whole contemporaneous process of decision — a process in which decisions are taken through orderly procedures by authorized decision-makers, not by naked force or

> calculation of momentary expediencies but by the reasoned relation of alternatives in choice to fundamental community expectations about how values should be shaped and shared.[41]

Thus, the policy-oriented school takes the perspective of the decision-maker. While the positivist is concerned with the identification of sources of law, the policy-oriented school is concerned with social choices encountered in decision-making: "the prescription and application of policy in ways that maintain community order and, simultaneously, achieve the best possible approximation of the community's social goals."[42] The decision-making process is further broken down into the following components:[43]

> (1) Intelligence: Gathering, processing, and disseminating information essential to decision making; (2) Promoting: Advocacy of general policies and urging proposals; (3) Prescribing: Projecting authoritative community policies about the shaping and sharing of values; (4) Invoking: Provisional characterization of a certain action as consistent or inconsistent with a prescription or law that has been established; (5) Applying: Final characterization and execution of prescription in concrete situations; (6) Appraising: Evaluating performance in decision process in terms of community goals; (7) Terminating: Ending a prescription or arrangement and the social arrangements based on them.

Decision-making includes the making of the law as well as its application though courts and other institutions. It extends across the scope of social organization and the hierarchy of power. Thus:

> For purposes of policy-oriented inquiry, the most appropriate [i.e., usable conception of international law] requires emphasis not upon rules alone, but upon rules *and* operations, and further, not upon authority alone or control alone, but upon authority *and* control (original emphasis).[44]

Authority and Control

International law, then, is the entire process of authoritative decision-making, involving both authority and control. Thus:

> New Haven reserves the word 'law' for processes of decision that are both consistent with the expectations of rightness held by members of the community (authoritative decisions) and effective (controlling decisions). While the particular mix of authority and control may vary widely, a conception of law as authoritative and controlling decision avoids exercises in irrelevance, whether because of absence of authority or absence of control.[45]

Authority refers to expectations regarding the decision-maker, while control is defined in terms of effectiveness, thus introducing an element of power and incorporating political and social processes into law. "...A conception of law as authoritative and controlling decision avoids exercises in irrelevance, whether because of absence of authority or absence of control,"[46] and prevents legal scholarship from drifting off into the "fantasy lands of naked power or semantic law."[47] The degree of effectiveness depends on the social and decision processes between transnational and national communities.

Thus, in the policy-oriented school of international law, the process of creating legal obligations depends on shared expectations of legitimacy (authority) and effectiveness (control). Oscar Schachter has succinctly outlined the policy-oriented view of legal obligations.[48] The critical test for obligation is the response of the target audience to the express or implied assertion of authority, or, a test of legitimacy and effectiveness.[49] Accordingly, five processes are necessary for the establishment of obligatory norms:

> (1) the formulation and designation of a requirement as to behavior in contingent circumstances; (2) an indication that designation has been made by persons recognized as having the competence (authority or legitimate role) to perform that function and in accordance with procedures accepted as proper for that purpose; (3) an indication of the capacity and willingness of those concerned to make the designated requirement effective in fact; (4) the transmittal of the requirement to those to whom it is addressed (the target audience); and (5) the creation in the target audience of responses-both psychological and operational-which indicate that the designated requirement is regarded as authoritative (in the sense specified in (3) above) and as likely to be complied with in the future in some substantial degree.[50]

The perception as to the legitimacy of the norm is a psychological as well as a political event. The psychological factor is not new to international law; it has been addressed with respect to the traditional concept of customary law and *opinio juris*.[51] But Schachter differs from the usual approaches to characterizing the psychological factor (consent of states, state conduct, and the like)[52] and instead focuses on the *expectations* of the target audience. For him, (as for the policy-oriented school) "the question with regard to any given possible norm or practice is whether the target audience *will* regard it as authoritative and effective, not simply whether it has done so in the past" (emphasis in original).[53] Thus, for legal prescription to result under the policy-oriented school, there must be present initially (and continuously for the prescription to endure) a "policy content," an "authority signal" and a "control intention."[54] Explicit content does not necessarily equal prescription, since there may be absence of prescriptive intent. In less formal settings, content must often be inferred. The application of content may differ in future situations, depending on the context.

The authority signal may also be explicit or implicit, as well as changeable. It must be something that distinguishes demands backed up only by credible threats from law. It is the audience that gives the prescriber or law-maker authority.

Power entails the element of control, that those who are prescribing intend and can make the prescription controlling. The power "elite" will vary from circumstance to circumstance, depending on the relevant parties. Sometimes only a few states will be critical. The objectives of the parties, the importance they attach to the norm in question and the investment they are willing to make to sustain the prescription are all important. Control does not require unanimity or even wide consensus: norms are effective because some elites have enough interest to make them effective.

The "overriding aim [of the policy-oriented school] is to clarify and aid in the implementation of a universal order of human dignity."[55] Within the decision-making process, the policy-oriented school outlines five intellectual tasks towards achieving that objective to be performed by those involved in decision-making, including: clarification of goals, analysis of past trends to examine the degree to which the goal has been achieved in past decisions, analysis of the factors that influenced past decisions, projection of future trends with regard to different decision options, and the invention and evaluation of policy alternatives in order to achieve the preferred goal.[56]

Criticisms

Notwithstanding the attraction of the policy-oriented school to those concerned with integrating power and authority, the school has been the subject of much criticism:

> Common criticisms are that the system's meta-language is hard to understand; that its approach is open-ended and susceptible to subjective manipulation; that it generates more uncertainty about law than it provides general and stable guidance for conduct; that the entire approach is too complex, cumbersome, and demanding to apply; and that it is merely a wordy way of stating the obvious.[57]

Specifically, a "key issue in the controversy between the policy-oriented and rule-oriented schools (positivists) [is] the question whether specific rules and principles of international law may legitimately be overridden by policies or major purposes of the States concerned."[58]

In reply to the above criticism, it is necessary to outline the essence or necessity of the New Haven School, which can be summed up with regard to its role in three critical areas of law-making: determining legal obligation when there are competing legal principles at play, when legal rules have fallen into disuse and when new legal rules have come into existence.[59] In each of these three areas, policy must be taken into account to determine the existence and context of legal obligation. This does not mean that the traditional sources of international law are discarded. Rather, policy is taken into account during the decision-making process in order to determine the presence (or not) of a legal norm "by the use of analogy, by reference to context, and by analysis of the alternative consequences."[60] Thus,

> ...International law is most usefully conceived, not as a pre-existing body of rules, but as a comprehensive process of authoritative decision in which rules are continuously made and re-made; the function of the rules of international law is to com-

> municate the perspectives (demands, identifications, and expectations) of the peoples of the world about this comprehensive process of decision; and that the rational application of these rules in particular instances requires their interpretation, like that of any other com-munication, in terms of who is using them, with respect to whom, for what purposes (major and minor), and in what context.[61]

More importantly, the intellectual tasks of the lawyer and scholar outlined above cannot be carried out irrespective of policy considerations. This is particularly true with regard to situations such as (1) the "quasi-legislative" activities of the "General Assembly and other UN bodies purporting to lay down, expressly or by implication, requirements of state conduct or to terminate or modify existing requirements;" (2) "the recognition of so-called 'rules of the game,' based on implicit understandings or unilateral actions;" (3) "the social revolutions which have overturned traditional orders and have challenged the assumptions on which prior conceptions of authority were based;" (4) "the growing interdependence of states-especially in economic and technological activities-has vastly increased patterns of cooperation and reciprocal behavior which have not been institutionalized in the traditional modes of lawmaking;" (5) "the increased 'permeability' of national States has resulted in a diminishing barrier between matters of international concern and those of domestic jurisdiction, (due mostly to the force of the UN Charter bringing domestic activities before collective organs for appraisal on the base of international criteria);" and (6) "the expansion of science and technology with international impact both beneficial and harmful has given rise to informal means of setting standards and exercising supervision without entering into tight and tidy legal instruments."[62]

What was true in 1968 is even more true today, particularly in light of such occurrences as the breaking up of the Soviet bloc and Yugoslavia, and the humanitarian intervention in Somalia. Some of these trends can also be seen in the area of climate change and ozone layer depletion: notably, the global impact of environmental problems as well as the expansion of science;[63] economic and technological interdependence;[64] and the involvement of the United Nations.[65]

Thus, reliance on rules alone, or the trend of past decisions, especially when that trend is not clear, is of little assistance when attempting to deal with a changing political world. The emphasis and concern with policy alternatives for the future, then, is necessary, since a "jurisprudence which purports to be 'scientific' only is [not] adequate."[66] While

> international law has its own inbuilt methods for change (treaty revision, progressive development through the International Law Commission, codification, custom)... these methods... are slow. Hence, to rely merely on accumulated past decisions (rules), where their context has changed and their content is unclear, is to encourage contempt among international relations scholars.[67]

Brief mention should be made here of legal functionalism.[68] While not a framework of inquiry such as the policy-oriented school, it is a "jurisprudential orientation that generates a certain style of inquiry and concentrates on certain sorts of legal developments."[69] Functionalism's aim is to examine those activities not considered politically significant, concentrating on the "role of law at the margins of international conflict."[70] Thus, the functionalists claim that, where the vital interests of states are concerned, states will not be concerned with rules of international law. Where non-vital interests are at stake, however, such as telecommunications, postal services, etc., states are willing to support international law and organizations serving it.

However, regardless of the degree of political interest, because "the legal process is part of the process of decision which in turn is part of the social process as a whole,"[71] law and politics cannot be separated, no matter how critical the issue. Thus, the "halfway house" approach of functionalism is damaging in that, while it claims to deal with policy, it does not provide a systematic structure for doing so.[72] The policy-oriented approach does provide that structure.[73]

This book argues that the best choice is the policy-oriented approach to international law-making. This process of decision-making does not avoid, like other schools, the essential relationship between law and policy, but deals with it openly and systematically, instead of achieving unconsciously desired policy objectives which are then given the label of "correct legal rule."[74] Because, moreover, the policy-oriented approach can accomplish this, which neither the naturalists nor the positivists attempt to do, it is conducive to the inclusion and study of international regimes within the international legal order. This does not mean, as already stated, that the approach ignores rules; rules play a vital part in the process of lawmaking. In this school's view, focusing on the traditional view of the sources of law is not wrong, but is an incomplete approach to law. Accordingly, these sources will now be examined.

THE SOURCES OF INTERNATIONAL LAW

Article 38 of the Statute of the International Court of Justice (ICJ) lists what are generally considered to be the traditional sources of international law: international conventions, international custom and the general principles of law recognized by civilized nations. Included as subsidiary sources are judicial decisions and the writings of highly qualified publicists.[75] Each of these will be discussed in turn.

International Conventions or Treaties

International conventions or treaties are agreements governed by international law, binding only upon the parties to the particular agreement unless the treaty represents or comes to represent customary law.[76] Thus, it is an "obligation of international law voluntarily undertaken — or, if it be preferred, the instrument whereby such an obligation is undertaken."[77]

The 1969 Vienna Convention on Treaties sets out conventional rules for treaties concluded after 1980, when the Convention came into force.[78] The three basic approaches to treaty interpretation; literal (centering on the actual text of the agreement and emphasizing the analysis of the words used), the effective (intentions of the parties), and the teleological (object and purpose of the treaty), are all taken account of in the Convention.[79] To confirm interpretation of the treaty in accordance with the ordinary meaning of the words in their context and in the light of the treaty's object and purpose, recourse may be had to supplementary means of interpretation, including the preparatory work of the treaty and the circumstances of its conclusion.[80] This recourse is also allowed where the interpretation leaves the meaning ambiguous or obscure or leads to a manifestly absurd unreasonable result.[81] The Convention also allows for reservations so long as the reservation is not incompatible with the object and purposes of the treaty, or unless the treaty prohibits reservations or permits only specific kinds of reservations.[82] While reservations encourage greater number of parties, writers point out that reservations tend to undermine the effectiveness of treaties, "by enabling states to protect their economic and other interests."[83] This has affected, for example, the Convention on Trade in Endangered Species, where objecting Parties are not bound to trade restrictions concerning species listed in treaty appendices.[84] On the other hand, the impermissibility of reservations in the Law of the Sea Convention has prevented a sufficient number of ratifications needed for the treaty to enter into force. As stated above, however, the issue of reservations is closely linked to uncertainty regarding economic and other issues which prevent substantive agreements, and so might be overcome as uncertainty is overcome.[85]

The concept of *jus cogens* is also recognized in the Vienna Convention, whereby states cannot opt out of the observance of certain basic norms of international law. Thus, there are "rules of customary law which cannot be set aside by treaty or acquiescence but only by the formation of a subsequent customary rule of contrary effect."[86] The Convention describes a peremptory norm as that which is "accepted and recognized by the international community of States as a whole..."[87] The concept is controversial, however. Brownlie points out that "more authority exists for the category of *jus cogens* than exists for its particular content."[88]

Nevertheless, it can be argued that the acceptance of certain norms as fundamental "would represent an advancement and refinement in the international legal system, and the system for this step forward does not depend on itself, but rather upon its principal participants, states."[89] Norms of *jus cogens*, then, would not retain their peremptory status if the world community as a whole did not regard them as such. Thus, "the status of norms that we hold dear is to be protected by our efforts to invoke and apply them, in turn ensuring that they do not totally lose the support of the great majority of States."[90] As such, advancement *is* possible and the observance of how these and other legal norms develop can only help in the development of such norms.[91]

Once treaties have entered into force, they are binding on the parties under the customary principle of *pacta sunt servanda*. Non-parties can become bound to treaty provisions should they become part of customary law, so long as the provision is "of a fundamentally norm-creating character such as could be regarded as forming the basis of a general rule of law."[92] Third parties can also become bound by treaties providing benefits or obligations for them as long as the third parties agree, which must be in writing to incur an obligation.[93]

While treaties may be successful in achieving binding rules, they also have drawbacks. Treaties may take a long time to negotiate, as well as to enter into force. This can be due both to delays regarding individual state ratification and political unwillingness to enter into the treaty.[94] Examples of uncertainty inherent in preventing development of international law will be examined, *infra*, in Chapter 4, and discussed in regard to ozone layer depletion and climate change in Chapters 5 and 6.

Long delays may not always occur, however, as "multilateral treaties can provide an efficient means of urgent global or regional law-making when necessary."[95] Treaties can overcome delay by providing a "framework" of general obligations and avoiding contentious areas of substantive obligations until such time when agreement is more forthcoming. Both the Vienna Convention on Substances that Deplete the Ozone Layer and the Framework Convention on Climate Change follow this approach.[96] Further protocols can be added as agreement is reached regarding scientific and technical issues. This can be seen in the development of the ozone layer depletion regime, *infra*, Chapter 5. In addition, treaties sometimes provide for protocols or annexes to be amended separately from the basic treaty, thus allowing for easier revision.

The references made above to delays and possible solutions are important, since they indicate that there are factors critical or catalytic to treaty formation and development within the legal order. The determination and observance of these factors would seem to be an important consideration for international legal scholars.[97] This is true not only for those involved in the negotiations at hand, but also for legal scholars seeking to learn lessons from past treaty negotiations for application to future negotiations. Regimes can aid in the study of such legal development.[98]

Customary Law

Regarding customary law, the International Court of Justice (ICJ) stated in *The Case of Nicaragua v. United States* that:

> ...The Court has to emphasize that, as was observed in the *North Sea Continental Shelf* cases, for a new customary rule to be formed, not only must the acts concerned 'amount to a settled practice', but they must be accompanied by the *opinio juris sive necessitatis*.[99]

Thus, "customary international law results from a general and consistent practice of states followed by them from a sense of legal obligation."[100] Various alternative theories for the necessity of both opinio juris and practice for the formation of customary law have been put forth. These include a focus on the objective element or practice alone,[101] and a focus on the subjective element or opinio juris alone.[102] Yet the ICJ and the Permanent Court of International Justice (PCIJ) have always stressed the need that both elements be present for the formation of customary law.[103]

In principle, customary international law binds all states whether or not they have given formal consent, unless, as is widely accepted, a state persistently objects to the rule while it is being formed.[104] Thus, "new norms require both practice and opinio juris before they can be said to represent customary international law. And so it is with the gradual death of existing norms and their replacement by others."[105] The requirements and determination of practice and opinio juris, however, have given rise to considerable controversy within international law.

While it is generally agreed that state practice includes conscious acts or abstentions that have direct or physical consequences, as well as entry into binding agreements, there is some divergence in national digests of state practice and disagreement among scholars as to what other acts, such as claims and statements, are and should be treated as examples of state practice.

Brownlie includes the following within state practice:

> diplomatic correspondence, policy statements, press releases, the opinions of official legal advisers, official manuals on legal questions, eg manuals of military law, executive decisions and practices, orders to naval forces etc., comments by governments on drafts produced by the International Law Commission, state legislation, international and national judicial decision, recitals in treaties and other international instruments, a pattern of treaties in the same form, the practice of international organs and resolutions relating to legal questions in the United Nations General Assembly.[106]

Akehurst includes physical acts, claims, declarations in abstracto such as General Assembly resolutions, national laws, national judgments and omissions.[107] Thus, under his view General Assembly Resolutions can qualify as state practice if they claim to be declaratory of existing law, with the value of such resolutions depending on factors such as voting numbers and reasons for votes.[108]

The Restatement includes in state practice "diplomatic acts and instructions as well as public measures and other governmental acts and official statements of policy, whether they are unilateral or undertaken in cooperation with other states." Inaction may also constitute state practice.[109]

D'Amato, however, restricts state practice to those acts having physical consequences, such as nuclear weapon testing, which provide concrete evidence of state practice. Thus, for D'Amato, statements and claims, including General Assembly Resolutions do not qualify as state practice since they are poor indicators of what states will actually do.[110]

Although there is disagreement regarding the content of state practice, the general view appears to be that "state practice covers any act or statements by a state from which views about customary law may be inferred,"[111] including omissions to act and silence. While individuals may play a role in pressuring state behavior, usually through non-governmental organizations,[112] it is state behavior that remains the decisive factor. The ICJ has taken notice of unilateral declarations in the *Nuclear Test* case,[113] and the *North Sea Continental Shelf* case.[114] Omissions were considered in the *Lotus* case.[115] In addition, the Court has accepted

General Assembly Resolutions and resolutions of other international organizations as state practice.[116]

The extent of practice necessary to qualify as customary law is not clear. The ICJ has mentioned "general acceptance"[117] and "extensive"[118] state practice.[119] Regarding duration and consistency, "most jurists accept as a general rule that duration has an inverse relationship to consistency: the shorter the duration of a practice, the more consistent it must have been."[120] The ICJ in the *North Sea Continental Shelf* cases stated the necessity of "virtually uniform" state practice.[121] In the *Anglo-Norwegian Fisheries* case, "substantial uniformity" was required, thus allowing for some inconsistency[122] while in the *Asylum* case the ICJ found state practice too inconsistent to establish customary law.[123] Thus, Brownlie states that uniformity and consistency of practice is "very much a matter of appreciation and a tribunal will have considerable freedom of determination in many cases."[124]

In the *Nicaragua* case, the ICJ agreed that opinio juris needed to be confirmed by state practice. But the Court added that state practice did not have to be universally consistent, so long as inconsistent conduct is treated as an exception to the rule, and not an indication of a new rule:

> The conduct of States, should, in general, be consistent with such rules, and that instances of State conduct inconsistent with a given rule should generally have been treated as breaches of that rule, not a indications of the recognition of a new rule. If a State acts in a way prima facie incompatible with a recognized rule, but defends its conduct by appealing to exceptions or justifications contained within the rule itself, then whether or not the State's conduct is in fact justifiable on that basis, the significance of that attitude is to confirm rather than weaken the rule.[125]

Opinio juris, because it is a psychological as opposed to a material element, is difficult to identify; problems of proof arise. In the *Lotus* case, the PCIJ found that customary law had not been established, as there was no evidence that states had refrained from criminal prosecution because they had been conscious of a duty to do so.[126] In the *North Sea Continental Shelf* cases, the ICJ found no evidence that states had felt legally obligated to act in a certain way.[127] Thus, the Court seemed to require "unequivocal evidence of a consciousness of legal obligation."[128] How this is to be revealed is not clear: "occasionally the Court seems to have identified opinio juris in state practice itself. The *Lotus* and *North Sea Continental Shelf* cases imply, however, that evidence of opinio juris is to be found mainly in explicit statements made by states about the reasons for their actions or abstentions."[129]

Attempts have been made to deal with the difficulties of establishing opinio juris. D'Amato states that opinio juris is satisfied if "an objective claim of international legality is articulated in advance of, or concurrently with, the act [or abstention] which will constitute the quantitative elements of custom." In so doing, a state will give notice of legal implications.[130] Akehurst also accepts statements by states as more important than actual belief by the state in the truth of the statement.[131]

In *Nicaragua*, the ICJ stated that opinio juris could be deduced "with all due caution" from the attitudes of the parties concerned and other states toward certain General assembly resolutions, particularly the Declaration on Friendly Relations.[132] The Court stated that state consent to such resolutions was "an acceptance of the validity of the rule or set of rules declared by the resolutions themselves."[133] Thus, a customary rule included in a treaty does not discontinue its status as a customary rule with its ensuing obligations.

Notwithstanding the *Nicaragua* case, the legal value of General Assembly resolutions continues to be debated. Higgins describes the various views as part of a spectrum, ranging from those skeptical about the relevance of the resolutions to the middle of the spectrum, where resolutions may be evidence of developing trends of customary law, to the radical end, where there are those who give "considerably greater legal significance" to resolutions.[134]

The Court in the *Nicaragua* case has come under criticism for its view of the formation of customary law:

> It [the ICJ] envisages certain actions (such as participation in treaties or voting for resolutions in international fora) as constituting both state practice and opinio juris and thus giving rise readily to an "instant" customary law... Thus a significant international obligation can be created by non-objection to a consensus resolution.[135]

D'Amato agrees, claiming the "Court...completely misunderstands customary law" with regard to state practice and opinio juris: "First, a customary rule arises out of state practice; it is not necessarily to be found in UN resolutions and other majoritarian political documents. Second, opinio juris had nothing to do with 'acceptance' of rules in such documents. Rather, opinio juris is a psychological element associated with the formation of a customary rule as a characterization of state practice."[136]

In addition to theoretical debates concerning custom, there are practical concerns as well. Unfortunately for pressing issues of international importance, customary law usually takes time to develop, although it is possible for customary law to develop quickly or even on a regional or bilateral basis.[137] However, it is difficult for any semblance of universal state practice to develop at all, let alone quickly, when there are an ever increasing number of states joining international society, particularly where issue-areas are global in nature, such as climate change and ozone layer depletion.[138] Thus,"...customary law provides limited means of social engineering, and there is a particular need for the development of new institutions, standards, and localized regimes to deal with the protection of the environment."[139] Brownlie, however, is quick to point out that customary rules should not be undervalued as they provide the basis for the development of the law.[140] Indeed, since the time Brownlie made that statement in the context of the environment, international environmental law has developed greatly.[141] Many new concepts such as the precautionary principle, common concern and intergenerational equity,[142] introduced in various documents and resolutions, may become part of customary law eventually.

Customary law has been described as part of a "process of continuous interaction, of continuous demand and response" among the decision-makers of different states which "create expectations that effective power will be restrained and exercised in certain uniformities of pattern."[143] By describing custom in this way, an evaluation is made of the several interdependent features of the process of customary prescription which might aid in determining the degree to which participants share expectations about their future behavior. Under this policy-oriented view, international custom refers to the flow of communication and acts of collaboration among persons across national state boundaries which create expectations among them regarding the requirements of future decision in the shaping and sharing of all values or preferred events.[144] As this book is adopting the policy-oriented approach to international law, then this view of customary law will also be adopted.

General Principles of Law

General principles of law are difficult to define precisely. Although the drafters apparently had two aims in mind: 1) they wished to expand the sources of international law by introducing natural law principles into international relations and 2) to avoid the possibility of the Court declaring itself incompetent through lack of applicable rules (non liquet),[145] as Brownlie has noted: "In the committee of jurists which prepared the Statute there was no very definite consensus on the precise significance of the phrase."[146]

Consequently, there is disparity regarding the extent to which general principles are considered sources of law.[147] Jennings points out that "it seems possible to hold either that the general principles are a distillation from some essential notions found in municipal laws generally... or that it means nothing more or less than the principles of natural law."[148] While Jennings cautions against the dangers of general principles, he concludes that on balance the provision is a "salutary addition to Article 38 if used with caution," as it allows apparent gaps in the law to be turned into opportunities for progressive development.[149]

The Restatement (Revised) of the Foreign Relations Law of the United States categorizes general principles as only a supplementary source of international law.[150] One academic notes that "even Verdross, one of the most authoritative and staunch advocates of the importance of Art. 38, conceded in 1968 that the role of the 'principles' had greatly dwindled as a result of their gradual absorption into treaty and customary law."[151]

Alexandre Kiss, however, points out that the underlying concept of general principles, identifying common principles, remains valid.[152] The importance of the principles lies with their ability to fill in gaps within international law. There is a problem, however, with the lack of general principles that are applicable in specific areas, or, being applicable, they are vague and unhelpful.[153]

Nevertheless, general principles remain a valid source of international law, and are useful in non liquet situations. As international law develops, then more general principles may become accepted as international law.

Subsidiary Sources

Judicial decisions and the writings of publicists are included in the ICJ Statute as subsidiary sources of international law. While they do not qualify as formal sources under the Statute, they both can contribute to the development of international law.

Although ICJ decisions are not binding precedent in theory, they can provide compelling evidence of the law.[154] Several decisions have been notable for their contributions to the development of international law, including the *Nottebohm* case[155] (genuine link between individual and claimant state), the *Reparation for Injuries* case (legal personality of the UN),[156] the *Genocide* case (treaty reservations),[157] the *Anglo-Norwegian Fisheries* case (persistent objection to formation and unilateral claims).[158] Cases dealing with the environment are discussed *infra*.

Art. 38 does not limit judicial decisions to the ICJ. Thus, other international courts and tribunals, as well as the decisions of municipal courts can be considered under this category, such as the European Court of Justice and the US Supreme Court.[159] Domestic courts, then, can have an effect on the development of law, as can be seen in regime development.[160]

Although judicial decisions are a subsidiary source of international law, there is still high value placed on these decision. This is because judicial decisions "often produce a degree of certainty where previously confusion and obscurity existed" as well as invoke familiar principles with "assurance and certainty."[161] In rapidly evolving areas of law, however, there may not be any applicable judicial decisions to provide evidence of the law for the situation at hand.

Writings of prominent publicists are highly looked upon in the international law community, particularly by those less familiar with international law, such as arbitral tribunal and domestic courts.[162] They may be subjective, however, reflecting national and other prejudices and may not adequately reflect shared state interests.[163] One writer states that "since academic sources do have a role, albeit a minor one, in the creation of rules of international law, it is crucial to the validity of one's conclusions not to confuse the snowballing acceptance of a rule by academics with snowballing acceptance by states."[164] Yet this "should not lead us to dismiss the value of writers, but rather to assess correctly the writer within his particular environment."[165]

It is not possible to prove which publicists are "the most highly qualified,"and so opinions as to authority of writings can differ greatly.[166] Nevertheless, the International Law Commission, Harvard Research drafts and other similar bodies are considered highly authoritative.[167] UN reports and drafts, as well as EC recommendations could also have some significance.[168]

Soft Law

"'Soft' law is a paradoxical term for defining an ambiguous phenomenon;" "...a new process of normative creation which jurists feel uncomfortable analyzing does exist...;"[169] "soft law means different things to different people;"[170] "...its precise meaning is still debated;"[171] "there is no uniform opinion... regarding the exact definition..."[172]

Statements such as these underline the imprecision of the term "soft law" and underscore the difficulty in examining the phenomenon. Nevertheless, an attempt will be made to dissect this concept, which differs from international regimes, described in the next chapter. Regimes are institutional arrangements within the legal order. As such, they provide a framework of analysis regarding cooperation between states in which soft law may be taken into account in the analysis.

In keeping with the statements made above regarding soft law, definitions of soft law vary. They:

> range from treaties, but which include only soft obligations ('legal soft law'), to non-binding or voluntary resolutions and codes of conduct formulated and accepted by international and regional organizations ('non-legal soft law'), to statements prepared by individuals in a non-governmental capacity, but which purport to lay down international principles.[173]

Thus, definitions vary from a narrow to a wide view of soft law. For the purposes of this book, the definition of soft law will include binding as well as non-binding obligations. Both types are underdeveloped from the perspective of substantive international law; the first type, while binding, is "soft" on substantive obligations, and the second type is non-binding. The underlying reasons for underdevelopment, as well as the prospects for future development, can be examined in the framework of regimes and their critical issues.[174] Essentially:

> 'Soft law' is by its nature the articulation of a 'norm' in written form, which can include both legal and non-legal instruments; the necessary abstract norms in issue which have been agreed by states or in international organizations are thus *recorded* in it, and this is its essential characteristic (original emphasis).[175]

While non-legal soft law is, of course, not binding under international law, the repetition of principles through non-binding instruments can indicate a new opinio juris emerging among states.[176] Combined with state practice, opinio juris signals the emergence of customary law.[177] There is some debate, however, as to whether soft law instruments alone establish state practice.[178] This contributes to the dissatisfaction with customary law in general:

> Perhaps it is time to face squarely the fact that the orthodox tests of custom — practice and opinio juris — are often not only inadequate but even irrelevant to the identification of much new law today. And the reason is not far to seek: much of this new law is not custom at all, and does not even resemble custom. It is recent, it is innovatory, it involves topical policy decision, and it is often the focus of contention. Anything less like custom in the ordinary meaning of that term it would be difficult to imagine.[179]

Claims as to the legal force of non-binding soft law are an inevitable result of the international law-making process. These claims are made by arguing either that soft law has "hardened" or that the sources of international law have changed.[180] The problem for the international legal order is that inclusion of non-binding soft law within the category of sources would force a structural change in traditional international law. However, such soft law should not be regarded as having no legal significance simply because it does not fit into the categories of sources.[181]

In an attempt to resolve this dilemma, one scholar advocates a distinct legal category for non-legal soft or "declaratory" law in order to allow the recognition of such norms that are in the process of articulation and effectuation.[182] Under this category, a law is declarative when a minority considers it binding or a majority considers it non-binding. Declarative law, then, would lack one of the elements of customary law; either the material element or the psychological element. Such a view, however, would require the sources of law to be changed, something that could not easily be achieved without a major re-thinking of legal theory. Indeed, such a view ignores the premise that, since soft law by its label differentiates itself from "hard" law, there must be some advantage to it being so labelled.

The advantage lies in the subjectivity inherent in soft law: discretion with regard to obligation due either to vagueness or the exigibility of the obligation because of an escape clause.[183] On the other hand, non-legal soft law may allow states to accept precise, but non-binding, obligations,[184] which may eventually harden.

Nonetheless, it is argued that the concept of soft law contributes to a blurring of normativity regarding law and non-law.[185] Rather than being considered a "normative sickness," however, soft law is more of a sign of the times and a product of necessity[186] and "is not per se a legal pathology."[187] Indeed, soft law serves important purposes within the legal order.

Soft law can indicate trends in international law-making, as well as define standards of acceptable behavior.[188] As Pierre Dupuy has pointed out, soft law may result in the setting of standards of "due diligence"[189] in international cooperation as well as serving as a point of reference for national legislation, and is "both a sign and product of the permanent state of multilateral cooperation..."[190]

Soft law can help create expectations as to state behavior,[191] either that it will be respected or that it is binding. Precision or the legal form of soft law "induce" this expectation, although it is argued that expectations differ depending on whether the norm is legal or non-legal.[192] When states do not wish to commit themselves to rigid obligations, but rather wish to allow themselves flexibility with regard to compliance, they are apt to choose non-legal obligations. Flexibility is particularly important in an increasingly diversified world of newly created states with discrepancies in economy, which make agreement regarding obligations harder to reach.[193] This often happens under the stress of international negotiations.[194]

Soft law can also play a role in overcoming disputes. Taking due account of this role, Birnie considers the label "soft settlement" more accurate than "soft law."[195] Soft law allows states to negotiate and interpret ambiguous terms "without exciting complaint,"[196] an important consideration in a decentralized international legal order. In this regard, institution building in the form of regimes aids in the dispute-settlement procedure, in which soft law can be utilized.[197]

Soft law thus appears to play a large role in implementing international law and cooperation. It has been pointed out that:

> Soft law instruments allow for the incorporation of conflicting standards and goals and provide States with the room to manoeuvre in the making of claims and counterclaims. While this process inevitably causes normative confusion and uncertainty in terms of the traditional sources of international law, it is probably the inevitable consequence of unresolved pressures for change in international law.[198]

The concept of soft law underscores "that it is excessively simplistic to divide written norms into those that are binding and those that are not."[199] Treaties may require little in the way of obligation, while "instruments of lesser dignity," ie technically not binding, may prove more influential regarding state's behavior.[200] Legal scholars have correctly advocated for some time the benefits of "soft law" as a basis for development of "hard law." Thus, soft law should and does play a role in the international legal order, including regime building.[201]

POLICY-ORIENTED LAWMAKING

The above discussion has highlighted some of the difficulties associated with formal sources of international law, particularly delays in treaty-making and creating customary law. But the recognition that customary international law and treaties can be brought about when the conditions warrant it, as well as the promise of soft law, suggest optimism for the development of the international legal order in the form of regimes, as will be described in the following chapters. The policy-oriented school of international law is well suited for the examination of regimes, as the school advocates the study of expectations about appropriate behavior in determining lawmaking. Similarly, regime theory explores why states cooperate.[202]

The critical test for determining the establishment of obligatory norms is the response of the target audience to the assertion, whether express or implied, of authoritativeness. If the rules of the game developed by states are perceived by themselves and by other parts of the community (ie organizations) as "state practice" carried out by appropriate decision-makers for that purpose and by appropriate procedures, then that practice would be considered authoritative (legitimate). This does not imply that the practice of two or three states imposes obligations on others; it means that such practice is viewed as authoritative by those others. If that practice is also perceived as likely to be complied with, it would then be appropriately characterized as "practice accepted as law," or *opinio juris*.[203] The test in brief is authority (legitimacy) and control (effectiveness). To fully understand the policy-oriented communications model of lawmaking or prescription (both custom and treaty) is to speak of it as an ongoing process where the observer can identify: 1) the participants, 2) the subjectivities, 3) the situations, 4) the resources, 5) the strategies, and 6) the outcome of the process.

Firstly, there are the participants (both the "prescribers" and the "target audience"), including international and national officials, elites of multinational enterprises, many interest and pressure group, and individual leaders within these groups. The extent to which the prescribers represent the principal participants among the target audience is also important: "The fact that divergent political and ideological viewpoints have been harmonized is widely treated as persuasive evidence that the draft has an enhanced authority."[204]

While states possess the maximum authority in the world arena, the activities of other participants may also be relevant,[205] in particular the United Nations. International governmental organizations are both distinctive participants and provide necessary structures of authority for other participants:[206]

> While the obsession with the paramount nature of sovereignty still reigns supreme in power politics, the law of Specialized Agencies, in so far as it follows in the wake of scientific and technical progress, has tended to intensify methods of functional co-operation and promote a measure of world integration.[207]

Other non-state actors also participate in the prescribing of international rules, including nongovernmental organizations and transnational corporations.[208] In addition, all group participants are associations through which individuals cooperate in order to fulfil their demands; "in the final analysis, these group forms are highly malleable instruments created and maintained by people to clarify and secure their common interest."[209]

Secondly, there are the subjectivities (identifications, demands, expectations) or perceptions of the participants about the content of their communications and its relation to existing law. This could vary from those identifying with a global system to those identifying with a more exclusive unit; demands could vary from those seeking world order to those seeking solely self-interest, expectations could vary from the most realistic to the most fantastic.

Thus, the participants may have differing subjectivities. The concern here is primarily with the shared expectations regarding future behavior. Since subjectivities are not open to direct examination, they can only be distinguished from a contextual analysis of past behavior;

Thirdly, there are the situations in which subjectivities are mediated and expectations about authority and control are played out, ranging from the most formal and specialized (international organizations and conferences) to the most informal and unorganized. Thus, in determining proper authority, the inquirer can look to the relation between the prescriber participant and the situation in which he has acted, ie acting in an official capacity such as diplomatic correspondence, as a UN representative, etc., as well as the temporal and geographical extent of interaction.

Fourthly, there are the resources and other bases of effective power and authority which all would-be prescribers use to give weight to words and deeds; ie knowledge and skill. The degree to which the prescriber participants are able and willing to use means to make their policy effective and controlling, as well as the procedures they utilize in doing so are taken into account.

Fifthly, there are the strategies or modes of communication used in generating the flow of words and behavior, ranging from those relatively explicit (both verbal and written) to those which are relatively implicit (eg judicial opinion) or other patterns of behavior revealed over any period of time; Finally, the outcome of the process, exhibited as a pattern of communication and response, may or may not be a prescription, in the sense of expectations shared by politically relevant groups (the target audience) that certain policies are authoritative and controlling.[210]

Thus, the above process is important in ascertaining whose expectations are relevant, how these expectations can be ascertained in such a diverse international community, and what will result if only divergent expectations can be found. The relevant expectations depend on the subject and situation; the extent to which the issue is of concern to the actors. There are methods to ascertain shared expectations within the world community, such as diplomatic correspondence, international agreements, judicial decision, scholarly studies, public statements of leaders and national legislation. As to the prospect of divergent expectations, the decision-maker can look to duration frequency, geographic extent, consistency and continuity. But even if divergences cannot be resolved through such techniques, Schachter emphasizes "that the extent and obduracy of such difficulties are subjects for investigation, not for surrender. They involve questions of fact; they change in time and in relation to changing environmental factors and to new perceptions of needs, interests, and values."[211]

Rule-oriented approaches to law-making cannot easily take account of new perceptions or expectations; it is in that respect that:

> the further one moves away from positivism and rules, the less important becomes the distinction between *lex lata* and *lex ferenda*...If law as rules requires the application of outdated and inappropriate norms, then law as process encourages interpretation and choice that is more compatible with values we seek to promote and objectives we seek to achieve. But it is only to a rule-based lawyer that this is to be classified as 'law as it

> should be' standing in contrast to 'law as it is'. To the law as process, this is in large measure a false dichotomy...[212]

The policy-oriented approach can best analyze the entire process of international lawmaking, and will be applied in the analysis of the ozone layer depletion and climate change regimes. Before doing so, there is a need to show why these regimes were needed.

INTERNATIONAL LAW APPLICABLE TO GLOBAL ENVIRONMENTAL CHANGE

The following sections will examine the international law applicable to climate change and ozone layer depletion, prior to the formation of the respective regimes. This is done to help explain the shaping of expectations (as the policy-oriented school uses that term) for more substantive regulations for both climate change and ozone layer depletion. An examination of the relevant "new concepts" that have been introduced within international law will also be made, which although controversial within international law, can still help to shape expectations regarding future lawmaking.

Prevention of Environmental Harm

The appropriate starting point for the examination of the duty to prevent environmental harm is what Kiss and Shelton refer to as the fundamental principle of international law concerning transfrontier pollution.[213] This principle is stated in Principle 21 of the 1972 Stockholm Declaration on the Human Environment:

> States have, in accordance with the Charter of the United Nations and the principles of international law, the sovereign right to exploit their own resources pursuant to their own environmental policies and the responsibility to ensure that activities within their jurisdiction or control do not cause damage to the environment of other States or of areas beyond the limits of national jurisdiction.[214]

Principle 21[215] has its historical roots in the Roman maxim *sic utere tuo ut alienum non laedas*.[216] This maxim was later expanded in the well known *Trail Smelter Arbitration*, which gave credence to the prevention of harm principle.

The *Trail Smelter Arbitration*[217] was concerned with the issue of fumes from a Canadian smelter that were adversely affecting property across the border in the US state of Washington. The tribunal affirmed that:

> Under the principles of international law,... no state has the right to use or permit the use of its territory in such a manner as to cause injury by fumes in or to the territory of another or the properties or persons therein, when the case is of serious consequence and injury is established by clear and convincing evidence.[218]

While *Trail Smelter* aided the development of international environmental law, it "is actually a rather modest contribution to the jurisprudence"[219] because of its limited application. The damage contemplated included only tangible injury which could be given a monetary figure; the incident had to be of "serious consequence"; and the injury had to be "established by clear and convincing evidence."[220] In addition, the tribunal dealt only with property damage and placed "no value on wider environmental interests such as wildlife, aesthetic considerations, or the unity of ecosystems."[221]

Under *Trail Smelter*, "the victim has to wait for the harm to be done before he can take action."[222] However, it has been pointed out that if *Trail Smelter* had prescribed otherwise, not only would the Trail Smelter have been closed, "but it would have also have brought Detroit, Buffalo and Niagara Falls to an untimely end."[223] In addition, the case is unusual since Canada admitted its responsibility, the two states having agreed to the use of a tribunal to determine the question of damages and future operation of the smelter.[224] Notwithstanding its limited scope of application, *Trail Smelter* did provide a precedent for international environmental law through the use of an international tribunal to deal with harm from transboundary pollution.[225] So while the shortcomings of *Trail Smelter* can be criticized, the decision did contribute to the development of international environmental law. And, as scientific knowledge advances "as to the nature of 'damage' that pollution wreaks" and as technology advances to permit greater industrial production with a lesser amount of pollution, the decision of *Trail Smelter* becomes stronger.[226] Still, such knowledge cannot resolve the problem of unwillingness to pay for higher standards of environmental protection; without the acceptance of such a responsibility by industrialized states, the developing world will similarly disregard such a duty.[227]

Expanding further on the concept of *sic utere tuo* and the prevention of harm principle, in the *Corfu Channel* case, the ICJ held Albania responsible for damage caused to British ships in its territorial waters, because Albania failed to warn the ships of the presence of mines.[228] Specifically, the Court iterated that it is "every State's obligation not to allow *knowingly* its territory to be used for acts contrary to the rights of other States",[229] thus establishing a "...*prima facie* liability for the harmful effects of conditions created even by trespassers of which the territorial sovereign has knowledge or means of knowledge."[230] However, while the "rights of other States" could be identified in this context as the right of innocent passage, the specific rights are not as clear where the harm may be to common resources.[231]

Further supporting the prevention of harm principles is the *Lac Lanoux Arbitration*,[232] which resulted from a Spanish claim that France was illegally diverting waters from reaching Spain, without the consent of the Spanish government. The tribunal held that if France had impaired the waters through pollution, Spain would have had a valid claim.[233]

In the *Nuclear Tests* cases, Australia and New Zealand brought an action against France in an effort to stop French nuclear testing in the South Pacific.[234] Interim Orders restraining the tests were made, but the case was later declared moot when France agreed to stop its atmospheric testing, although the ICJ did state that the unilateral declaration of a state created a binding legal obligation to conform its behavior to that stated in the declaration.[235] At least one scholar believes that the Court "would have succeeded in identifying a legal principle on which to base a decision," such as the reliance on equitable principles in the *North Sea Continental Shelf* cases.[236]

As stated earlier, these cases have led to the development of the "fundamental principle" concerning transfrontier pollution, formulated in Principle 21 of the Stockholm Declaration on the

Human Environment,[237] adopted at the 1972 United Nations Conference on the Human Environment.

Attended by delegates from 113 states,[238] the Conference adopted a fundamental Declaration of Principles (the "Stockholm Declaration") concerning the human environment, a resolution on institutional and financial arrangements, and an Action Plan of 109 recommendations for environmental assessment.[239]

Principle 21 of the Declaration, described earlier,[240] expands on the restrictive bounds of *Trail Smelter* by expanding the responsibility of states to prevent environmental damage for "activities within their jurisdiction or control", not just activities within their territory. Also, the Principle extends the scope of protection to "areas beyond the limits of national jurisdiction", thus including common areas. In addition, damage is not qualified by the term "serious,"[241] and includes damage caused by persons under the state's control, wherever they may act.[242]

However, the Principle also underscores the sovereign right of states "to exploit their own resources pursuant to their own environmental policies." Even though the Principle does not give states unlimited freedom regarding its environment, it has been suggested that more distinct guidelines referring to the "common good" should have been articulated.[243] A stronger principle, however, might have precluded any agreement at all.

The Principle has also been supported by declarations adopted by the UN General Assembly, including the Charter of Economic Rights and Duties of States, in which Article 30 reiterates the responsibility of states laid down in Principle 21.[244] In addition, the 1979 Geneva Convention on Long Range Transboundary Air Pollution (LRTAP)[245], the 1982 UN Convention on the Law of the Sea,[246] the Vienna Convention for the Protection of the Ozone Layer (Vienna Ozone Convention),[247] the Framework Convention on Climate Change (FCCC)[248] and other agreements also reiterate or otherwise give support to Principle 21.[249]

Principle 2 of the Rio Declaration on Environment and Development,[250] however, rephrased Principle 21 to read: "States have... the sovereign right to exploit their own resources pursuant to their own environmental and developmental policies." Thus, the addition of "developmental policies" would mean that states' responsibility in the exploitation of their resources is no longer subject solely to its environmental polices, but to its economic development policies as well.[251] The Declaration appears, then, to equate environmental with developmental policies and rights.

While some may bemoan this inclusion of "developmental policies" in the Declaration as a "skillfully masked step backwards,"[252] its inclusion was insisted upon by the G-77 group of developing states. This was due to the "perception [of the G-77] that developed country rhetoric was shifting dangerously in the direction of globalizing certain selected environmental resources..."[253] Such a statement underscores the importance of development issues in environmental policies and signals that it should not be taken lightly in lawmaking. Indeed, the issue of development is critical to both the ozone layer depletion and climate change regimes.[254] Thus, even as non-binding soft law,[255] the Declaration helps shape the expectations of states with regard to future regulations and the concept of "sustainable development."

First introduced in the 1987 Brundtland Commission Report *Our Common Future*, the term "sustainable development" has been frequently used to describe an ideal model of development that takes into account the environmental needs of both present and future generations.[256] How this is to be achieved, however, is not quite clear. The Declaration attempts to do so in Principle 8, where it states that "to achieve sustainable development and a higher quality of life for all people, States should reduce and eliminate unsustainable patterns of production and consumption and promote appropriate demographic policies."

Thus, the Principle "achieves one of the most delicate balancing acts of the entire Rio Declaration," by addressing itself to both developed and developing countries.[257] The Declaration, then, contributes to the shaping of future expectations regarding sustainable development through its soft law basis. There are other examples of the legally "soft" Declaration concerned with the duty to cooperate, *infra*, which also help shape expectations.

It can be concluded that a general duty of prevention of harm to the environment exists. Birnie and Boyle point out that recent conventions, discussed above, "point to international acceptance... that states are now required to protect global common areas," in addition to preventing transboundary harm.[258] This duty, however, almost always exists as a "qualified duty of prevention,"[259] according to existing case law and treaties. In addition, it is unclear as to what standard of liability a state will be held responsible: due diligence or strict (or absolute) liability.

Liability for Environmental Harm: Due Diligence or Strict Liability[260]

The adoption of a due diligence standard poses certain standards. Due diligence is the conduct "to be expected from a good government;" one "mindful of its international obligations."[261] The vagueness of this definition does little to clarify the requirements of due diligence. Instead, "ecostandards," or norms laid out in agreements have been looked to for possible indication of the standards required for due diligence. It may be difficult to develop a common standard of due diligence when states are held to different obligations regarding the same issue-area.

Divergent standards also prevent the evolution of these rules into customary law since state practice will differ, as it is difficult to frame a common duty when standards remain uncommon. In addition, a due diligence standard, precisely because it is undefined and subjective, illustrates "the paradox of creating a universalist system from a radically subjective concept."[262] Because nations have "cultural, political, and economic dissimilarities," the definition of due diligence will vary, as states take into account their subjective interests.[263] Indeed, this standard-setting has evolved in some areas into the principle of "common but differentiated responsibility," whereby states are held responsible in direct proportion to their contribution to the harm.[264]

While, however, holding a state strictly or absolutely liable for environmental harm caused by breach of an obligation without proof of fault may avoid the difficulties of defining due diligence, this standard of care presents its own problems. Strict liability restrains international consensus for both developed and developing states, each of whose interests are at odds with the principle. Developing states will often not have adequate technical resources to foresee harm and high costs of prevention may frustrate economic development.[265] Developed states, on the other hand, mistrust "this automatic right to redress,"[266] without consideration of the specific situation at hand. In addition, the instances to which strict liability will be applied requires subjectivity in choosing which activities will trigger the standard.[267]

Academics generally support due diligence rather than strict or absolute liability, although there is no consensus on the matter.[268] The case law does not provide much guidance either. In *Trail Smelter*, Canada had accepted responsibility for the harm caused by the smelter, thus obviating the need to choose a standard[269] and in *Corfu Channel*, no definitive ruling on standards of responsibility was made.[270] Most agreements require due diligence from parties, although some do provide for strict or absolute liability.[271]

Whatever standard is chosen, the question as to what degree of harm must occur before states will be held liable is not clear; nor is the issue of an equitable balancing of interests expressly addressed under either standard. While there may not be strong customary support for a balancing of interests,[272] it is becoming increasingly obvious that economic and development interests must be taken into account in the international legal order, where these issues are becoming critical to the law-making process and more substantive obligations.[273]

Problems of proof can also occur, both to the effects and source. This can be a particular problem in determining the link of causality concerning pollution. Distance and time may make it difficult to identify or trace the source as well.[274] Problems specific to the global commons also arise with regard to standing and the fact that remedies tend to focus on damages that have already taken place, rather than on prevention.[275]

The difficulties discussed in this section may signal that the traditional methods of attributing international liability is not the best technique for tackling global environmental harm.[276] It is suggested, then, that the debate over the standard of liability is not of much value. By engaging in such a polemic; "international legal scholars construct their systems from the sparse material of international tribunal decisions and charter declarations instead of proceeding from the basic building blocks of concordant state interests and aspirations."[277]

In determining state interests and aspirations from which to proceed, the focus should turn elsewhere.[278]

International Cooperation

Along with the principle of prevention of harm to the

environment, the principle of cooperation in the protection of the environment is also important in the context of global environmental change. The duties most often mentioned in regard to this obligation include the duties to inform, consult, and assess.[279] The extent to which these duties are accepted as obligations within international law is not a controversial matter:

> ...the basic principle that states must cooperate in avoiding adverse effects on their neighbors through a system of impact assessment, notification, consultation, and negotiation appears generally to be endorsed by the relevant jurisprudence, the declarations of international bodies, and the work of the ILC. ... [and] some support in state practice.[280]

However, the degree to which these duties have gone beyond generalities to specifics is not as clear.

Duty to Inform

The duty to inform of the risk of environmental harm finds its greatest support in emergency situations, and thus is "probably the least controversial principle of general international environmental law."[281] This principle was given support in the *Corfu Channel* case, which outlined the necessity for states not to knowingly allow its territory to be used for acts contrary to the rights of other states.[282] This statement of the Court allows the case to be taken as authority for the obligation to inform of known environmental hazards.[283] The 1982 Law of the Sea Convention and the 1989 Basel Convention on the Control of Transboundary Movement of Hazardous Wastes also have provisions dealing with the duty to warn of known environmental hazards.[284] The 1992 Rio Declaration on Environment and Development also takes account of the duty to warn of environmental emergencies, thus contributing to the shaping of expectations notwithstanding its soft law status.[285]

Regarding non-emergency situations, the tribunal held in the *Lac Lanoux Arbitration* that France was required to inform Spain of its intent to divert a shared watercourse, but it is unclear whether this requirement was the result of the treaty at hand or a customary duty.[286] The General Assembly, in adopting the Charter of Economic Rights and Duties of States, reinforced the duty to cooperate "on the basis of a system of information and prior consultations" in the exploitation of shared natural resources.[287] This principle of cooperation regarding the exploitation and conservation of natural resources was upheld in the *Fisheries Jurisdiction* cases.[288] In addition, treaties covering nuclear installations near borders, continental shelf operations, long-range transboundary air pollution and marine pollution from land-based sources or dumping call for some degree of prior notification (and consultation).[289] The non-binding Rio Declaration also calls for timely notification.[290]

Defining the degree of risk which sets this principle in motion is not clearcut, however. Grave dangers and catastrophes such as nuclear accidents are not controversial,[291] but situations where a sense of imminent crisis is missing create uncertainty as to when the duty to inform of environmental risk actually arises. Thus, as Springer argues:

> One could hardly speak at present of an existing rule in *positive* international law which could impose the duty upon States to inform those who could be concerned, of activities which can be prejudicial to their sovereignty or affect environmental quality (emphasis added).[292]

Even if one takes the duty to exist, Springer adds that its content is ambiguous: when should it be enforced (ie what is the threshold of harm to be crossed and does it apply to areas beyond national jurisdiction); how far in advance of the activity should notice be given; what information should be supplied; and to whom should the notice be given?[293]

Duty to Consult

The duty of a potential polluter state to consult with a potential victim state finds support in the *Lac Lanoux Arbitration*.[294] Thus: "there does exist a duty of consultation and of bringing into harmony the respective actions of the two States when general interests are involved in matters concerning waters."[295] Yet:

> ...Because consultation can involve extensive discussions and further consequences if the discussions prove unsuccessful in

> satisfying the concerned state, it is a duty to which a state may be even less willing to commit itself than that of simply supplying information. For this reason, there is even greater doubt [than that surrounding the duty to inform] about the existence of a general duty to consult.[296]

Thus, to ensure that the duty is not questioned, agreements must specifically provide for consultation.[297] For example, the Geneva Convention on Long-Range Transboundary Pollution[298] states that consultations shall be held upon request between the polluting state and the state affected by pollution or in danger of being so damaged.[299] Non-binding agreements such as the UNEP Principles of Conduct Concerning Natural Resources Shared By Two or More States, adopted by the General Assembly,[300] requires in Principle 6 that states sharing natural resources, in addition to notifying other states of plans that may significantly affect the environment of an other state, enter into consultations concerning those plans when requested by that other state.[301] The Rio Declaration also calls for consultation regarding activities potentially harmful to the environment.[302] In addition, provisions calling for parties to promote and cooperate in research, included in many treaties such as the FCCC, also implicitly require consultation.[303] Requirements of communication of information also include the duty to consult.[304] Communication and promotion are difficult to achieve without consultations.

Duty to Assess

The duty of a state to assess environmental harm is a logical extension of the duty to inform another state of that harm; a state must assess before it can inform. As a result, it suffers from the same lack of criteria as does the duty to inform.

Assessment is best carried out through environmental impact assessments. UNEP has adopted non-binding "Goals and Principles of Environmental Impact Assessment."[305] An Environmental Impact Assessment (EIA) is, according to UNEP, "an examination, analysis and assessment of planned activities with a view to ensuring environmentally sound and sustainable development."[306] The EIA guidelines stated that the "environmental effects of... activities should be fully taken into account" before such activities are authorized.[307] Under these Principles, an EIA should include: (1) A description of the proposed activity; (2) A description of the potentially affected environment; (3) A description of practical alternatives and (4) An assessment of the likely or potential environmental impacts of the activity and alternatives.[308]

As with the duties to notify and consult, the safest way to ensure that states have a duty to carry out assessments is to include them in the agreement under consideration. The 1991 Convention on Environmental Impact Assessment in a Transboundary Context is the most advanced in its application of these assessments, requiring Parties to utilize assessments in proposed activities, taking into account the views of states likely to be affected.[309] The FCCC requires that Parties, "to the extent feasible," "employ appropriate methods, for example impact assessments," for taking climate change considerations into account in their social, economic and environmental policies and actions.[310] While the Vienna Ozone Convention does not specifically refer to impact assessments, it does require its Parties to cooperate through observations, research and information exchange "in order to better understand and assess the effects of human activities on the ozone layer."[311]

Articles 204, 205 and 206 of the Law of the Sea Convention, address monitoring of the risks of effects of pollution, publication of reports of monitoring, and assessment of potential effects of [state] activities.[312] The non-binding Rio Declaration also calls for environmental impact assessments.[313]

"NEW CONCEPTS" IN INTERNATIONAL LAW

In addition to the established principles of international law, new concepts have begun to develop. These new concepts include (1) the precautionary principle; (2) intergenerational equity; (3) common heritage and common concern; and (4) the polluter pays principle. While these concepts may not have acquired the status of principles of international law, their legal significance is important in the shaping of shared expectations, which are critical to international law-making in the view of this author.[314]

Precautionary Principle

The precautionary principle has begun to appear frequently in various declarations and international agreements, attracting the interest of legal scholars in the process.[315] The Second International North Sea Conference was the first forum to explicitly enunciate the precautionary principle: "In order to protect the North Sea... a precautionary approach is necessary which may require action to control inputs of such substances even before a causal link has been established by absolutely clear scientific evidence."[316]

But, the 1987 Declaration states only that pollution emissions should be reduced through use of the best available technology, and did not provide for a total ban on potentially harmful emissions, so that it is unclear how broadly the principle can be interpreted in that document.[317]

Interpretations of the precautionary principle can involve a spectrum of possible obligations, ranging from the prevention of harm principle described above, to a complete reversal of the burden of proof whereby evidence of no harm must be shown before an activity can be carried out.[318]

A weak formulation can be found in the 1990 Bergen Ministerial Declaration on Sustainable Development, which, in linking the principle with sustainable development, states that:

> In order to achieve sustainable development, policies must be based on the precautionary principle. Environmental measures must anticipate, prevent and attack the causes of environmental degradation. Where there are threats of serious or irreversible damage, lack of full scientific certainty should not be used as a reason for postponing measures to prevent environmental degradation.[319]

Stronger formulations can be found in the Oslo Commission Prior Justification Procedure, which allows dumping of industrial wastes in the North Sea only if it can be shown that no harm will be caused to the marine environment.[320]

Thus, the level of risk, the level of precaution and the economic factors to be considered are not clear, nor does it resolve the arduous regulatory difficulties facing international decision-makers.[321]

Precautionary language was used in both the Vienna Ozone Convention and the FCCC. The Vienna Ozone Convention refers to the "precautionary measures" already taken for the protection of the ozone layer,[322] while the FCCC states that the parties "should take precautionary measures to anticipate, prevent or minimize the causes of climate change and mitigate its adverse effects."[323] While the Vienna Convention does not address the "principle" as such, the FCCC refers to "precautionary measures" in Art. 3 entitled "Principles."[324] Although Art. 1 states in a footnote that "titles of articles are included only to assist the reader," the footnote does not state that titles are thus without legal significance and so leaves interpretation of the footnote unclear.[325]

The potential legal implications of Art. 3 are, however, reduced. The article states that (1) the principles are to guide the Parties in their actions to achieve the Convention and implement its provisions and (2) the Parties are to be guided "inter alia" by the principles, ie other principles than those listed may be taken into account in the implementation of the Convention. In addition, "states" was replaced by "Parties".[326] These wordings were intended to "forestall arguments that the principles listed in Article 3 are part of customary international law and bind states generally. Instead, the principles clearly apply only to the Parties and only in relations to the Convention, not as general law."[327]

Nevertheless, Art. 3 does take account of precautionary measures, while taking into account also that policies and measures should be cost-effective so as to ensure global benefits at the lowest possible cost.[328] The application of precautionary measures, if not the name "precautionary principles," is thus accounted for in the FCCC.

In addition, the Second World Climate Conference[329] addressed precautionary measures: "where there are threats of serious or irreversible damage, lack of full scientific certainty should not be used as a reason for postponing cost-effective measures to prevent such environmental degradation."[330] This passage is also included in Principle 15 of the Rio Declaration.[331]

The precautionary principle, however, is not yet an accepted principle of international law,[332] and is largely limited to non-binding declarations. This is due in part to lack of a definitive interpretation and due in part to the fact that it is also at odds with a "no-regrets" policy, which advocates taking action only when action is also justified on other grounds.[333]

Because there is no accepted definition of the precautionary principle, it is difficult to assess its significance if it was an accepted principle of international law. If it was to be so accepted, then it will have changed the requirements of foreseeability and due diligence, described above, to one whereby:

> a state which has participated in the endorsement of the precautionary principle in a particular sector would be held liable in the future for causing harm (whether to neighbors or commons) for activities in that sector which today are strongly suspected (but not proven) to cause substantial harm.[334]

Intergenerational Equity

Another progressive concept in international environmental law is the idea of intergenerational equity. The theory of intergenerational equity "assumes that each generation receives a natural and cultural legacy in trust from previous generations and holds it in trust for future generations."[335] The FCCC states that the Parties "should protect the climate system for the benefit of present and future generations of humankind..."[336]

While it is difficult to refute a *moral* obligation for the present generation to pass on to the next an environment in good condition, the prospect of a *legal* obligation to do so is somewhat distant.[337] Perhaps more importantly, such a concept does not aid in "determin[ing] the content of current regulations," and the appointment of an "Ombudsmen" to care for these future rights is "surely an impractical suggestion."[338] Put another way, concentrating efforts on the rights of future generations does not necessarily aid in promulgating regulations for today's citizens. Yet such an approach could help shape expectations as to future behavior of states.

Common Heritage, Shared Resources and Common Concern

Another concept introduced into international law is the idea of the common heritage of mankind. This principle suggests that the resources of an area "cannot be appropriated to the exclusive sovereignty of states but must be conserved and exploited for the benefit of all, without discrimination."[339]

This concept has been applied in Part XI of the 1982 Law of the Sea Treaty and the 1979 Moon Treaty.[340] However, the concept was not adopted in either the Vienna Ozone Convention nor the FCCC, where it was deliberately replaced by the concept of common concern, discussed below. Thus, other concepts must be considered for determining the legal status of the atmosphere.

The legal concept of shared resources is not appropriate for application to the atmosphere. It is impossible to treat the atmosphere as a resource that can be "shared" equally, as it cannot be divided. In addition, the atmosphere and climate do not have proprietary connotations, not being subject to appropriation, reducing the relevancy of the concept of shared resources. The atmosphere also cannot be considered as, or part of, simple airspace, nor does it fit into the concept of common property.[341]

The UN General Assembly in 1988 took a very different approach, declaring that the global climate was the "common concern of mankind."[342] The legal significance of common concern is not yet clear, however. The Executive Directorate of the UN Environment Programme sponsored in 1990 The Meeting of the Group of Legal Experts to Examine the Concept of The Common Concern of Mankind in Relation to Global Environmental Issues.[343] While the opinion was expressed there that the concept was not yet a rule of general international law, it was agreed that the concept was an evolving rule.

Birnie and Boyle state that the Vienna Ozone Convention confers the status of common concern or interest on the ozone layer, since the definition given to "ozone layer" by the Convention regards the ozone layer as a "global unity, without reference to legal concepts of sovereignty, shared resources, or common property."[344] As such, all Parties maintain a common legal interest in protecting the ozone layer, whether directly injured or not, and in enforcing rules for protection of the ozone layer.[345] The FCCC states that "change in the Earth's Climate and its adverse effects are a common concern of humankind."[346] Thus, it may not be too problematical to draw the conclusion that the FCCC treats climate change, if not he climate per se, as a common concern of mankind, and thereby bestowing the same legal interest on the Parties to protect against climate change and to enforce rules for doing so.

Whether the concept of common concern has been legally conferred on the atmosphere as a whole is still unsure, however. In addition, its consequences is still unclear. One possible interpretation is the implication that states' obligations towards that "concern" would be *erga omnes*.[347] Any state, then, would have legal standing to bring a claim against another in that area, without having to show that it was uniquely harmed.[348]

Polluter Pays Principle

The polluter pays principle places responsibility on the entity causing or likely to cause damage to the environment to pay compensation for restoration.[349] In so doing, "the cost of these measures should be reflected in the costs of goods and services which cause pollution in production or in consumption."[350] The consequence of a full application of this principle is that liability is in effect unlimited.

The OECD has promoted the use of the polluter pays principle.[351] The EEC also endorsed the principles in a programme of action adopted in 1973, and the Single European Act of 1986[352] provided a legal basis.[353] In addition, this principle can be found in various documents, including the 1990 Convention on Oil Preparedness, Response and Co-operation,[354] the Meeting on the Protection of the Environment of the Conference on Security and Cooperation in Europe (CSCE),[355] Principle 16 of the Rio Declaration,[356] and a UNEP Governing Council Decision.[357]

The polluter pays principle, as stated above, would require compensation in full; unlimited liability in effect. This approach has been largely incorporated in the 1990 US Oil Pollution Act (OPA) enacted in reply to the 1989 Exxon Valdez grounding in Alaska which caused extensive environmental damage.[358] Under OPA, liability is unlimited in circumstances including gross negligence, wilful misconduct and violations of federal regulations.[359] As a result of such an approach, OPA could increase the cost of tanker transportation of crude oil to the United States by approximately US$450 million per year, based on current shipping volumes and patterns.[360] The estimated cost passed on to the American consumer is a $2.00 per year increase in gasoline and utility bills.[361] Thus, the consumer will pay some of the costs involved in the good and services which cause pollution.

The OPA can be contrasted with the approach taken under the 1969 Convention on Civil Liability for Oil Pollution Damage, where the owner is entitled in most cases to limit his liability under a formula related to tonnage and to an overall total.[362]

The polluter pays approach has been subject to criticism, however. One scholar states that the approach is not appropriate as a principle of liability between states:

> Liability in international law has been traditionally concerned with compensating for damage, although it is nearly impossible to compensate states fully for environmental damage. Moreover, if the goal of those who argue for a polluter-pays liability principle is to discourage polluting behavior, the amount needed to deter such behavior is unlikely to be the same as that needed to compensate for damage. Moreover, the polluter-pays principle as an economic approach suggests that a party could be liable only for negligent behavior, not strictly liable, in international law. Finally, the emphasis on liability is questionable. There is virtually no instance in public international law when states have admitted liability for environmental damage to another country in the absence of treaty provisions. Indeed, the trend has been directly opposite — some countries have paid for the installation of proper pollution control in polluting countries because the costs of doing so were less than the costs of continuing to suffer pollution damage.[363]

Such an argument places the polluter pays approach in a dubious position, then, particularly in light of the argument that there should be burden-sharing on the part of consumers of the goods involved as well, and not have the burden of pollution placed solely on the polluters. Developing states also are not convinced of the merits of the principle, insisting that developed states help defray the cost of pollution. This approach is followed by the Montreal Protocol to the Vienna Ozone Convention, *infra*, Chapter 5, whereby financial aid is offered to developing states for environmental protection.

Accordingly, as one scholar points out, the principle remains at the international level a political and economic principle,[364] but which will, however, influence the future application of the legal principle in the shaping of expectations regarding future behavior of states.

CONCLUSION

This chapter has outlined the main approaches to international law, and in particular, the policy-oriented approach, which will be utilized with respect to regime theory, *infra*. The policy-oriented approach illustrates the process of decision-making as more than just application of rules, although it does not require a rejection of sources of international law. Therefore, the policy-oriented school is most conducive to the development of thought necessary to understand and respond to the particularly serious environmental challenges in question here, and is also able to incorporate the study of regimes and the regime process.

From the above discussion, it is evident that the duty not to cause harm as well as the duty to cooperate are general principles that are long on hope and short on specifics. Standing on their own, they do not provide much guidance for either ozone layer depletion or climate change. The "new" concepts introduced into international law, while progressive components of legal theory, are of little benefit to international law at the present time as "they affect the timing of development rather than its content."[365] They can, however, help shape expectations as to the future behavior of states and thus contribute to international law-making.

Faced with such a lack of applicable law, the response of states has been to form regimes of cooperation within the international legal order. Examining such modes of cooperation within the international legal order might prove beneficial to the overall development of the legal order.

In order to understand how and when this might occur, a new approach should be undertaken, one that focuses on the common interests of states in creating and maintaining legal rules, rather than attempting to force conformity to abstract international legal principles such as the duty to prevent harm or duty to cooperate. The development of progressive concepts of law within the international legal order as described above also favors such an approach, since "this step forward does not depend upon itself, but rather upon its principal participants."[366] It is to a discussion of the concept of international regimes that we now turn.

NOTES

1. L.F.E. Goldie, "Special Regimes and Pre-emptive Activities In International Law," *International And Comparative Law Quarterly* Vol. 11 (July 1962), p. 677.

2. See, *infra*, Chapters 5 and 6, for descriptions of each regime.

3. GI Tunkin, "On the Primacy of International Law in Politics," in *Perestroika and International Law*, ed. WE Butler (Dordrecht: Martinus Nijhoff Publishers, 1990), pp. 6–7.

4. Oscar Schachter, *International Law In Theory and Practice*, 2d ed. (Dordrecht: Martinus Nijhoff, 1991), p. 18.

5. See, *infra*, Chapter 2, Policy-Oriented School. In so doing, the disciplines of international and international relations are overcoming their "two-culture problem" in a collaboration involving the discovery of legal sources of obligation, as suggested by Oran Young, "Remarks," *American Society of International Law: Proceedings of the 86th Meeting*, Washington, DC (1992), p. 175.

6. Rosalyn Higgins, "International Law and the Avoidance, Containment and Resolution of Disputes" in *Recueil des Cours* Vol. 230, 1991-V (Dordrecht: Martinus Nijhoff Publishers, 1993), p. 23.

7. J.L. Brierly, *The Law of Nations* 5th ed. (Oxford: Oxford University Press, 1961), p. 42.

8. Higgins, "International Law," *supra*, n. 6.

9. Samuel Pufendorf, *On the Law of Nature and Nations* (1672), can be said to exemplify the naturalist school.

10. See, for example, Brierly, *The Law of Nations*, *supra*, n. 7, p. 114, and Arthur Nussbaum, *A Concise History of the Law of Nations* (NY: Macmillan, 1947).

11. See, G.J.H. van Hoof, *Rethinking the Sources of International Law* (Deventer: Kluwer, 1983), p. 32.

12. Ibid.

13. Malcolm Shaw, *International Law*, 3rd ed. (Cambridge: Grotius Publications Ltd, 1991), p. 25.

14. Martti Koskenniemi, *From Apology to Utopia* (Helsinki: Finnish Lawyers' Publishing Company, 1989), p. 70.

15. van Hoof, *Rethinking the Sources of International Law*, *supra*, n. 11, pp. 33–34.

16. See, *infra*, Chapter 2, Intergenerational Equity.

17. Shaw, *International Law*, *supra*, n. 13, p. 50 and van Hoof, *Rethinking the Sources*, *supra*, n. 11, p. 33.

18. Thus, the idea that "jus cogens is a form of natural law of nations... continues to enjoy support in modern legal theory." G.M. Danilenko, *Law-Making in the International Community* (Dordrecht: Martinus Nijhoff Publishers, 1993), pp. 214–215.

19. Myres S. McDougal, Harold D. Lasswell, Lung-Chu Chen, *Human Rights and World Public Order* (New Haven: Yale University Press, 1980), pp. 68–71.

20. John Austin, *The Province of Jurisprudence Determined* (London: Weidenfeld and Nicolson, 1954).

21. John Austin, *Lectures on Jurisprudence or the Philosophy of Positive Law*, Vol. I, 5th ed. (London, 1913), p. 34.

22. van Hoof, *Rethinking the Sources*, *supra*, n. 11, p. 36.

23. Hans Kelsen, *Principles of International Law* (NY: Rinehart, 1952), pp. 307–317.

24. Ibid., pp. 317–365.

25. Ibid., pp. 22–23.

26. Ibid., pp. 124–139.

27. H.L.A. Hart, *The Concept of Law* (Oxford: Clarendon Press, 1961).

28. Ibid., p. 92. Dworkin finds fault with Hart's rule of recognition, or what Dworkin refers to as "pedigree,"disagreeing that pedigree can identify all legal rules. For Dworkin, the law consists not just of rules, but of principles as well, which play a role in judicial decisions and which cannot be dismissed as extra-legal. Principles cannot be identified simply by consulting sources, but only through a moral or political discussion of which principles should be used to justify black-letter law. *Taking Rights Seriously* (London: Duckworth & Co., 1977). As such, Dworkin's view of law has been called a "natural law of political institutions," as well as legal idealism. van Hoof, *Rethinking the Sources*, *supra*, n. 11, p. 50.

29. van Hoof, *Rethinking the Sources of International Law*, *supra*, n. 11, p. 49.

30. Hart, *The Concept of Law*, *supra*, n. 27, pp. 225–230. Dworkin also disagrees with Hart's claim that a lack of clarity in legal rules is a result of the "open texture" of rules requiring the exercise of discretion to assist in the invention of new rules: "The truth may be that when courts settle previously unenvisaged questions concerning the most fundamental rules, they *get* their authority to decide them accepted after the questions have arisen and the decision has been given." Ibid., pp. 149–150. Instead, Dworkin argues that courts *discover*, and not invent, the proper principle to determine pre-existing rights and obligations. For Dworkin, the fundamental right to which everything can be reduced is the right to equal concern and respect. For this, he is criticized for

resembling too closely a form of legal idealism, as it could be open to various interpretations. van Hoof, *Rethinking the Sources*, *supra*, n. 11, p. 53.

31. van Hoof, *Rethinking the Sources*, *supra*, n. 11, p. 45. van Hoof prefers the label "structural positivism."

32. Lung-Chu Chen, *An Introduction to Contemporary International Law* (Yale University Press: New Haven, 1989), pp. 11–12.

33. The legal realists were skeptical about claims of legal objectivity: "the question of whether the action of the courts is justifiable calls for an answer in nonlegal terms. To justify or criticize legal rules in purely legal terms is always to argue in a vicious circle." F. Cohen, Transcendental Nonsense and the Functional Approach, *Columbia Law Review*, Vol. 35 (1935), p. 810. The Realists also claimed that the study of law must make use of the social sciences, as it does in practice. Karl Llewellyn, "A Realistic Jurisprudence—The Next Step," *Columbia Law Review* Vol. 30 (1930), p. 431.

34. Myres S. McDougal and Harold D. Lasswell, "The Identification and Appraisal of Diverse Systems of Public Order," *American Journal of International Law*, Vol. 53, No. 1 (January 1959), p. 28. See, also, *infra*, Chapter 3, Definition of Regimes.

35. So-called due to its association with Yale Law School and Myres McDougal.

36. McDougal and Lasswell, "Systems of Public Order," *supra*, n. 34, p. 6.

37. This is a representative and not an exhaustive list. See, Eisuke Suzuki, "The New Haven School of International Law: An Invitation to a Policy-Oriented Jurisprudence," *Yale Studies in World Public Order* Vol. 1 (1974), p. 23.

Power: making and influencing community decisions; *enlightenment*: gathering, processing and disseminating information and knowledge; *wealth*: production, distribution and consumption of goods and services, control of resources; *well-being*: safety, health and comfort; *affection*: intimacy, friendship, loyalty, positive sentiments; *respect*: freedom of choice, equality and recognition; *rectitude*: participation in forming and applying norms of responsible conduct. Myres McDougal and Michael Reisman, "International Law in Policy-Oriented Perspective," in *The Structure and Process of International Law* ed. McDonald and Johnston (1986), p. 118, W. Michael Reisman, "The View From the New Haven School of International Law," in *American Society of International Law: Proceedings of the 86th Annual Meeting*, by the American Society of International Law, Washington, DC (1992), p. 122.

38. McDougal and Lasswell, "Systems of Public Order," *supra*, n. 34, p. 8. See, also, *infra*, Chapter 3, for similarity to the international relations concept of "regime."

39. McDougal and Lasswell, "Systems of Public Order," *supra*, n. 34.

40. Ibid., pp. 8–9.

41. Myres McDougal and Associates, *Studies in World Public Order* (New Haven: Yale University Press, 1960), pp. 1006–1007.

42. Reisman, "New Haven School," *supra*, n. 37, p. 120.

43. See, Chen, *Contemporary International Law*, *supra*, n. 32, pp. 18–19.

44. Myres McDougal, "The Impact of International Law Upon National Law: A Policy-Oriented Perspective," in M. McDougal & Associates, *Studies in World Public Order*, 2d ed. (New Haven: New Haven Press, 1987), pp. 169–170. See, also, Harold D. Lasswell and Myres S. McDougal, *Jurisprudence For A Free Society*, Vols. I and II (New Haven: New Haven Press, 1992).

45. Reisman, "New Haven School," *supra*, n. 37, p. 121.

46. Ibid., p. 121. See, also, Rosalyn Higgins, "Integrations of Authority and Control: Trends in the Literature of International Law and International Relations," in *Toward World Order and Human Dignity*, ed. W. Michael Reisman and Burns H. Weston (NY: The Free Press, 1976).

47. Chen, *Contemporary International Law*, *supra*, n. 32, p. 17.

48. The sources of obligation in international law, as opposed to Art. 38 sources of law, have been the center of debate within the discipline as there is no agreement on what exactly establishes a source of obligation. This can best be understood by examining Oscar Schachter's well-known "baker's dozen" list of the proposed sources of obligation in international law: 1) consent of states, 2) customary practice, 3) a sense of "rightness"— the juridical conscience, 4) natural law or natural reason, 5) social necessity, 6) the will of the international community 7) direct (or "stigmatic") intuition, 8) common purposes of the participants, 9) effectiveness, 10) sanctions, 11) "systematic" goals, 12) shared expectations as to authority, 13) rules of recognition. Oscar Schachter, "Towards a Theory of International Obligation," *Virginia Journal of International Law,* Vol. 8, No. 2 (1968), p. 301.

49. Ibid., p. 311.

50. Ibid., p. 308.

51. Ian Brownlie, *Principles of Public International Law*, 4th ed. (Oxford: Clarendon Press, 1990) pp. 7–9.

52. Consent or recognition carries the risk that an established rule of law will be seen as subject to rejection by an individual state which claims that it no longer agrees to it or that it had never expressly manifested its agreement. Perception also does not necessarily involve an act of consensual acceptance since one can perceive and recognize authority and control without accepting it in the sense in which a party accepts an agreement. Behavior, while an indicator of opinio juris, does not imply the elimination of a psychological test. Schachter, "Theory of International Obligation," *supra*, n. 48, pp. 312–314.

53. Ibid., p. 314.

54. W. Michael Reisman, "International Lawmaking: A Process of Communication," in *American Society of International Law: Proceedings of the 75th Annual Meeting*, by the American Society of International Law, Washington, DC (1981), pp. 108–113.

55. McDougal and Lasswell, "Systems of Public Order," *supra*, n. 38, p. 11.

56. Ibid.

57. Chen, *Contemporary International Law*, *supra*, n. 32, p. 21.

58. Schachter, *International Law in Theory and Practice*, *supra*, n. 4, p. 22. Recent research attempted to "bridge the theories" of the positivist and policy-oriented schools in order to appraise the influence of international law on decision making in the context of conflict resolution. See Joaquin Tascan, *The Dynamics of International Law in Conflict Resolution* (Dordrecht: Martinus Nijhoff Publishers, 1992).

59. Higgins, "International Law," *supra*, n. 6, p. 34. Higgins is a disciple of the policy-oriented school, having studied under McDougal.

60. *Ibid.*

61. Myres McDougal, "A Footnote," *American Journal of International Law* Vol. 57, No. 2 (April 1963), p. 383.

62. Schachter, "A Theory of International Obligation," *supra*, n. 48, pp. 302–303.

63. See *infra*, Chapter 4, Scientific Uncertainty.

64. See *infra*, Chapter 4, Critical Issue of Economics, and Critical Issue of Development.

65. See discussion of role of the General Assembly-created International Negotiating Committee in climate change negotiations, *infra*, Chapter 6, International Action Regarding Climate Change.

66. McDougal, "The Impact of International Law," *supra*, n. 44, p. 140.

67. Higgins, "Integrations of Authority and Control," *supra*, n. 46, p. 83.

68. See, for example, Clarence Jenks, *Law in the World Community (London: Longmans,* 1967), Wolfgang Friedmann, *The Changing Structure of International Law* (NY: Columbia University Press, 1964). Legal functionalism builds on the work of David Mitrany, *A Working Peace System: An Argument for the Functional Development of International Organization* (1943).

69. See, Richard Falk, *The Status of Law in International Society* (Princeton: Princeton University Press, 1970) p. 463.

70. Richard Falk, "New Approaches to the Role of International Law," *American Journal of International Law* Vol. 61, No. 2 (April 1967), p. 492.

71. Lasswell and McDougal, *Jurisprudence, supra*, n. 44, p. 335. See, also, W. Michael Reisman, "The New Haven School," *supra*, n. 37, pp. 118–125. The policy-oriented school, however, does not digress into the realm of critical legal theory, as the school believes choice is necessary because rules are incomplete or missing, not because rules are contradictory.

72. Higgins, "Integrations of Authority and Control," *supra*, n. 46, p. 90.

73. There is also a movement within international law to reveal the systemic basis of international law. This approach attempts to investigate the effect of the international system on the role of international law. Richard Falk and Saul Mendlovitz have attempted to use systems analysis to analyze the prospects and obstacles of transition from one international system to another, in order to provide a set of universal values for the decision-maker. See, Morton Kaplan and Nicholas Katzenbach, *The Political Foundations of International Law* (1961). However, this does not remove the problem of choice that the decision-maker faces, which the systems method advocates through "universal values." See, Higgins, "Integrations of Authority and Control," *supra*, n. 46, p. 91.

74. Higgins, "International Law," *supra,* n. 6, pp. 28–29.

75. See, Ian Brownlie, *Basic Documents in Public International Law*, 3rd ed. (Oxford: Clarendon Press, 1983), p. 397.

76. Brownlie, *Public International Law, supra*, n. 51, p. 12.

77. Clive Parry, *The Sources and Evidences of International Law* (Manchester: Manchester University Press, 1965), p. 29.

78. Reprinted in *International Legal Materials* Vol. 8, No. 4 (1970), pp. 679–735. Provisions of the Convention such as the rules on interpretation, material breach and fundamental change of circumstances are considered to be customary law. Shaw, *International Law, supra*, n. 13, p. 561.

79. Vienna Convention, *supra*, n. 78, Art. 31, 32.

80. Ibid.

81. Ibid.

82. Ibid., Art. 19–23. See, also, Shaw, *International Law*, supra, n. 13, pp. 570–576; Brownlie, *Public International Law*, *supra*, n. 51, pp. 608–610, and *Reservations to Genocide Convention Case*, *ICJ Reports* (1951), p. 15.

83. Patricia W. Birnie & Alan E. Boyle, *International Law & the Environment* (Oxford: Clarendon Press, 1993), p. 14.

84. Ibid.

85. See, *infra*, Chapter 4.

86. Brownlie, *Public International Law*, *supra*, n. 51, p. 513, citing prohibition on the use of force, genocide, racial non-discrimination, crimes against humanity, and prohibition against slavery and piracy.

87. Vienna Convention, *supra*, n. 78, Art. 53.

88. Brownlie, *Public International Law*, *supra*, n. 51, pp. 514–415.

89. Rebecca M.M. Wallace, *International Law*, 2d ed. (London: Sweet & Maxwell, 1992), p. 33.

90. Higgins, "International Law," *supra*, n. 6, pp. 48–49.

91. See, *infra*, chapters 3, 5, 6 for norm development within regimes.

92. See, *North Sea Continental Shelf Case*, *ICJ Reports* (1969), p. 41. Baxter argues that the idea of "norm-creating" is redundant, since if a rule does pass into international law, it is norm-creating. *Recueil des Cours* I Vol. 129 (1970), p. 62.

93. Vienna Convention, *supra*, n. 78, Art. 34, 35, 36. Certain treaties creating rights and duties for third states have been labelled "objective regimes,"such as treaties for international waterways, demilitarization, and those creating organizations. The International Law Commission, however, rejected this concept. Brownlie, *Public International Law*, *supra*, n. 83, p. 633.

94. van Hoof, *Rethinking the Sources of International Law*, *supra*, n. 11, p. 120.

95. Birnie and Boyle, *International Law & The Environment*, *supra*, n. 83, p. 12.

96. See, *infra*, Chapters 5 and 6. Other examples include the 1979 Convention on Long-Range Transboundary Air Pollution and the UNEP Regional Seas Conventions.

97. See, *infra*, Chapter 4, for a discussion of the critical issues and catalysts that may determine this sense of "urgency" for global environmental change, as well as future protocols.

98. See, *infra*, Chapter 3.

99. *Case of Nicaragua v. United States* (Merits), *ICJ Reports*, (1986), p. 14.

100. American Law Institute, *Restatement (Revised) Foreign Relations Law of the United States* (St. Paul, MN: American Institute Publishers, 1987), section 102(2), p. 24.

101. Proponents of this view include Lazare Kopelmanas, "Custom as a Means of the Creation of International Law," *British Yearbook of International Law* Vol. 28 (1937), pp. 127–151, and Kelsen, *Principles of International Law, supra*, n. 128.

102. See, Bin Cheng, "United Nations Resolutions on Outer Space: 'Instant' International Customary Law?" *Indian Journal of International Law* Vol. 5 (1965), pp. 23–48.

103. *Nicaragua, supra*, n. 99, *North Sea Continental Shelf Cases* (FRG v Denmark, FRG v Netherlands) *ICJ Reports* 1969, p. 3.

104. Brownlie, *Public International Law, supra*, n. 51, pp. 10–12, Mark E. Villiger, *Customary International Law and Treaties* (Dordrecht: Martinus Nijhoff Publishers, 1985), stating that objections must be maintained from the early stages of the rule, through formation and beyond, and must be maintained consistently, p. 16. But see Jonathan I. Charney, *British Yearbook of International Law* Vol. 56 (1985), pp. 1–24, who claims that while states "in theory or in a court of law... may invoke the persistent objector rule, the realities of the societal pressure will require either that they conform to the new rule or that a new accommodation be reached."

105. Higgins, "International Law," *supra*, n. 6, p. 48.

106. Brownlie, *Public International Law, supra*, n. 51, p. 5.

107. Michael Akehurst, "Custom as a Source of International Law," *British Yearbook of International Law* Vol. 47 (1975), pp. 1–53.

108. Ibid., pp. 6–7.

109. *Restatement, supra*, n. 100, Section 102, Comment B, p. 25.

110. AA D'Amato, *The Concept of Custom in International Law* (Ithaca: Cornell University Press, 1971), pp.89–90, 78–79, although, for D'Amato, resolutions can constitute the "element of articulation" for a customary rule, see, *infra*, for discussion on opinio juris.

111. Akehurst, "Custom as a Source," *supra*, n. 107, p.10.

112. See, *infra*, Chapter 4, International Organizations.

113. See, *infra*, Chapter 2, Prevention of Environmental Harm.

114. *Supra*, n. 103, regarding the Truman Proclamation of 1945.

115. PCIJ, Series A, No. 10 (1927), p. 28. See, also discussion *infra*, on *opinio juris*.

116. *Nicaragua, supra*, n. 99, para 202–205.

117. *Fisheries Jurisdiction* (UK v. Iceland) *ICJ Reports* 1974, 23–26.

118. *North Sea Continental Shelf Cases, supra*, n. 103, p. 43.

119. Brownlie states that the "International Court does not emphasize the time element as such in its practice," *Public International Law, supra*, n. 51, p. 5.

120. H.C.M. Charlesworth, "Customary International Law and the Nicaragua Case,"*Australian Yearbook of International Law* Vol. 11 (1983-87), p. 7.

121. *North Sea Continental Shelf* cases, *supra*, n. 103, p. 43.

122. *Anglo-Norwegian Fisheries* case, *ICJ Reports* (1951) pp. 131, 138.

123. *Asylum* (Columbia v Peru), *ICJ Reports* (1950), p. 277.

124. See, Brownlie, *Public International Law, supra*, n. 51, p. 5–6 where he cites the *Asylum* case in which the Court could not find any constant and uniform usage.

125. *Nicaragua, supra*, n. 99 p. 98.

126. *Supra*, n. 115, p. 28.

127. *Supra*, n. 103, pp. 44–45.

128. Charlesworth, "Customary International Law," *supra*, n. 120, p. 10.

129. Ibid. See, also, Brownlie, *supra*, *Public International Law*, n. 51, pp. 7–10.

130. D'Amato, *Concept of Custom*, *supra*, n. 110, pp. 74–75.

131. Akehurst, "Custom as a Source," *supra*, n. 107, p. 37, giving the example of the Truman Declaration.

132. *Nicaragua, supra*, n. 99, pp. 99–100.

133. Ibid., p. 100.

134. Higgins considers herself part of the middle of the spectrum, see, "International Law," *supra*, n. 6, p. 52.

135. Charlesworth, "Customary International Law," *supra*, n. 120, p. 170.

136. Anthony D'Amato, "Trashing Customary International Law," *American Journal of International Law* Vol. 81, No. 1 (January 1989), p. 102

137. See, Brownlie, *Public International Law, supra*, n. 51, pp. 4–11. and DJ Harris, *Cases and Materials on International Law*, 4th ed. (London: Sweet & Maxwell, 1991), pp. 25–46.

138. Kirgis offers an interesting description of how customary law is established. He views the elements of custom as interchangeable along a sliding scale. Thus, "as the frequency and consistency of the practice decline in any series of cases, a stronger showing of *opinio juris* is required. At the other end of the scale, a clearly demonstrated *opinio juris* establishes a customary rule without much (or any) affirmative showing that governments are consistently behaving in accordance with the asser-

ted rule. Exactly how much state practice will substitute for an affirmative showing of an *opinio juris*, and how clear a showing will substitute for consistent behavior, depends on the activity in question and on the reasonableness of the asserted customary rule." Frederic L. Kirgis, Jr., "Custom on a Sliding Scale," *American Journal of International Law* Vol. 81, No. 1 (January 1987), p. 149.

139. Ian Brownlie, "A Survey of International Customary Rules of Environmental Protection", *Natural Resources Journal* Vol. 13, No. 2 (April 1973), p. 179.

140. Ibid.

141. See, *infra*, Chapters 5 and 6 for the development of international law in the area of ozone layer depletion and climate change.

142. See, *infra*, Chapter 2, New Concepts.

143. Myres McDougal, "Editorial Comment," *American Journal of international Law* Vol. 49, No. 3 (July 1955), pp. 357–358.

144. K. Venkata Raman, "The Role of the International court of Justice in the Development of International Customary Law," in *Proceedings of the American Society of International Law* (1965), Washington, DC, p. 171.

145. Antonio Cassese, *International Law in a Divided World* (Oxford: Clarendon Press, 1986), pp. 170–171.

146. Brownlie, *Public International Law*, *supra*, n. 51, p. 15.

147. Louis Henkin, Richard Crawford Pugh, Oscar Schachter and Hans Smit, *International Law: Cases and Materials*, 2d ed., (St, Paul, Minn.: West Publishing Co., 1987), pp. 117–129.

148. R.Y. Jennings, *Recueil des Cours* II (1967), p. 339.

149. Ibid., p. 340.

150. *Restatement*, *supra*, n. 100, section 102, pp. 24–25.

151. Antonio Cassese, *International Law In A Divided World*, (Oxford: Clarendon Press, 1986), pp. 173–174 quoting A. Verdross, "Les principles generaux du droit dans la systeme des sources du droit international public," in *Hommage Guggenheim* (Geneva, 1968), p. 530.

152. Alexandre Kiss and Dinah Shelton, *International Environmental Law* (New York: Transnational Publishers, Inc., 1991), p. 107.

153. Birnie and Boyle note that the most prevalent use of principles concern procedure, evidence and jurisdiction, *International Law & The Environment*, *supra*, n. 83, p. 24.

154. Brownlie, *Public International Law*, *supra*, n. 51, p. 21.

155. *ICJ Reports* (1955), p. 4.

156. *Reparation for Injuries Suffered in the Service of the United Nations* Case *ICJ Reports* (1949), pp. 174.

157. *Reservations to the Genocide Convention Case, ICJ Reports*, (1951), p. 15.

158. *Supra*, n. 122, p. 131.

159. Brownlie, *Public International Law*, *supra*, n. 51, pp. 21–24.

160. See, *infra*, Chapter 4, Domestic Regulations.

161. Schachter, *International Law in Theory and Practice*, *supra*, n. 4, p. 40.

162. Brownlie, *Public International Law*, *supra*, n. 51, p. 25.

163. Ibid., pp. 24–25.

164. van Hoof, Rethinking the Sources, *supra*, n. 11, p. 178, quoting J. Watson, "Legal Theory, Efficacy and Validity in the Development of Human Rights Norms in International Law," 3 UILF (1979), p. 637.

165. Shaw, "International Law," *supra*, n. 13, pp. 92–93.

166. *Restatement*, *supra*, n. 100, Section 103, Reporters Notes 3, p. 38.

167. Ibid. See, also, Brownlie, *Public International Law*, *supra*, n. 51, p. 25.

168. Birnie & Boyle, *International Law & the Environment*, *supra*, n. 83, p. 26.

169. Pierre Dupuy, "Soft Law and the International Law of the Environment," *Michigan Journal of International Law* Vol. 12, No. 2 (Winter 1991), p. 420.

170. Gunther Handl, "A Hard Look at Soft Law," *American Society of International Law: Proceedings of the 82nd Meeting*, by the American Society of International Law, Washington, DC (1988), p. 371.

171. Joseph Gold,"Strengthening the Soft International Law of Exchange Arrangements," *American Journal of International Law* Vol. 77, No. 3 (July 1983), p. 483.

172. Tadeusz Gruchalla-Wesierski, "A Framework for Understanding 'Soft Law,'" *Revue De Droit De McGill*, vol. 30 (1984), p. 44. See also, generally, Seidl-Hohenveldern, "International Economic Soft Law," *Recueil des Cours* (1979), pp. 173–175 and W. Riphagen, "From Soft Law to Ius Cogens and Back," *Victoria University of Wellington Law Review* Vol. 17 (1987), pp. 81–99.

173. C.M. Chinkin, "The Challenge of Soft Law: Development and Change In International Law," *International and Comparative Law Quarterly* Vol. 38, Part IV (October 1989), p. 851,

174. See, *infra*, Chapters 3 and 4.

175. Birnie and Boyle, *International Law & The Environment*, *supra*, n. 83, p. 27.

176. Dupuy, "Soft Law and the International Law of the Environment," *supra*, n. 169, p. 432, Chinkin, "The Challenge of Soft Law," *supra*, n. 173, pp. 857–858, Gruchalla-Wesierski, "Soft Law" *supra*, n. 172, p. 53–54.

177. See, *supra*, Chapter 2, Customary Law.

178. Gruchalla-Wesierski, "Soft Law," *supra*, n. 172, pp. 53–54 who states that "as a result of its abstract nature, soft law cannot be held to provide the state practice that the wording of the norm describes."

179. Robert Y. Jennings, "What is International Law and How Do We Tell It When We See It?" *Annuaire Suisse De Droit International* Vol. XXXVII (1981), p. 67.

180. Chinkin, "The Challenge of Soft Law," *supra*, n. 173, p. 856.

181. Hiram E. Chodosh, "Neither Treaty Nor Custom: The Emergence of Declarative International Law," *Texas International Law Journal* Vol. 26, No. 1 (Winter 1991), p. 97.

182. Ibid.

183. Gruchalla-Wesierski, "Soft Law," *supra*, n. 172, pp. 49–50. The author describes two types of escape clauses: 1) allowing the party to subjectively interpret the norm, ie "consistent with their needs," 2) weak command, ie "should" as opposed to "must".

184. Birnie & Boyle, *International Law & the Environment*, *supra*, n. 83, p. 27.

185. Prosper Weil, "Towards Relative Normativity in International Law," *American Journal of International Law*, Vol. 77, No. 3 (July 1983), pp. 413–442 where the author claims the international legal order is faced "with a pathological phenomenon of international normativity."

186. Dupuy, "Soft Law," *supra*, n. 169, p. 422.

187. W. Michael Reisman, "Remarks," in *American Society of International Law: Proceedings of the 82nd Meeting*, by the American Society of International Law, Washington, DC (1988), p. 374.

188. Dupuy, "Soft Law," *supra*, n. 169, p. 433.

189. See, *infra*, Chapter 2, Liability for Environmental Harm.

190. Dupuy, "Soft Law," *supra*, n. 169, pp. 434–435.

191. Chinkin, "Soft Law," *supra*, n. 173, p. 865. See, also, "expectations" with regard to the policy-oriented school, *supra*, Chapter 2, Policy-Oriented School.

192. Michael Bothe, "Legal and Non-Legal Norms —A Meaningful Distinction in International Relations?" *Netherlands Yearbook of International Law*, Vol. 11 (1980), pp. 85–86.

193. See, Patricia Birnie, "Legal Techniques of Settling Disputes: The 'Soft Settlement' Approach," in *Perestroika and International Law*, ed. W.E. Butler (Dordrecht: Martinus Nijhoff, 1990), p. 184.

194. R.R. Baxter, "International Law in 'Her Infinite Variety'," *International and Comparative Law Quarterly*, Vol. 29, Part 4 (October 1980), p. 557. See, also, Chapters 5 and 6, *infra*.

195. Birnie, "Soft Settlement," *supra*, n. 193, p. 183.

196. Patricia Birnie, "International Environmental Law: Its Adequacy For Present and Future Needs," in *The International Politics of the Environment*, ed. Andrew Hurrell and Benedict Kingsbury, (Oxford: Clarendon Press, 1992), p. 53.

197. See, *infra*, Chapter 3, Dispute Settlement Mechanisms.

198. Chinkin, "The Challenge of Soft Law," *supra*, n. 173, p. 866.

199. Baxter, "Her Infinite Variety," *supra*, n. 194, p. 564.

200. Ibid., p. 565.

201. See, *infra*, Chapters 5 and 6.

202. See, *infra*, Chapter 3.

203. Schachter, "Theory of International Obligation," *supra*, n. 48, p. 311.

204. Schachter, "Theory of International Obligation," *supra*, n. 48, pp. 310–311.

205. McDougal et al, *Human Rights and World Public Order*, *supra*, n. 19, 167–179.

206. See, *infra*, Chapter 4, International Non-state Actors.

207. Chen, *Contemporary International Law*, *supra*, n. 32, pp. 56–57, quoting C. Alexandrowicz, *The Law-Making Function of the Specialized Agencies of the United Nations* (1973), p. 161.

208. See, *infra*, Chapter 4, and application to ozone layer depletion and climate change in Chapters 5 and 6.

209. Chen, *Contemporary International Law*, *supra*, n. 32, p. 81.

210. Reisman, "International Lawmaking," *supra*, n. 54, p. 107–108.

211. Schachter, "Theory of International Obligation," *supra*, n. 48, pp. 314–319.

212. Higgins, "International Law," *supra*, n. 6, p. 34.

213. Kiss and Shelton, *International Environmental Law*, *supra*, n. 152, p. 129.

214. Stockholm Declaration of the United Nations Conference on the Human Environment, *International Legal Materials* Vol. 11, No. 6 (1972), pp. 1416–1469.

215. See text *infra*.

216. "You should not use your property in such a way so as to harm others."

217. *American Journal of International Law* Vol. 33, No. 1 (January 1939) pp. 182–212; Vol. 35, No. 4 (October 1941) pp. 684–736.

218. Ibid., p. 716.

219. Brownlie, "Survey of International Customary Rules," *supra*, n. 139, p. 180.

220. *Trail Smelter*, *supra*, n. 217, p. 716.

221. Birnie and Boyle, *International Law & The Environment*, *supra*, n. 83, p. 100. The authors point out that the tribunal was required to follow US law on that issue.

222. Patricia Birnie, "The Development of International Environmental Law," *British Journal of International Studies*, Vol. 3, No. 2 (July 1977), p. 176.

223. John E. Read, "The Trail Smelter Dispute," *The Canadian Yearbook of International Law*, Vol. 1, (1963), pp. 224–225. This underscores the importance of economics in environmental issues. Economics as a critical issue in the climate change and ozone layer depletion regimes will be described, *infra*, Chapter 4.

224. See, for instance, Alfred P. Rubin, "Pollution By Analogy: The Trail Smelter Arbitration," *Oregon Law Review* Vol. 50, No. 3, Part I (Spring 1971), pp. 259–282.

225. Lynton Keith Caldwell, *International Environmental Policy*, 2d ed., (Durham: Duke University Press, 1990), p. 123.

226. Rubin, "Trail Smelter Arbitration," *supra*, n. 224, p. 281.

227. Ibid, pp. 281–282. See, *infra*, Chapter 4, for the critical issue of development in the climate change and ozone layer depletion regimes.

228. *Corfu Channel* case, *ICJ Reports* (1949), pp. 4–38.

229. Ibid., p. 22.

230. Brownlie "Survey of International Customary Rules," *supra*, n. 139, p. 180.

231. Birnie, "Development of International Environmental Law," *supra*, n. 222, p. 176.

232. *International Law Reports* Vol. 24 (1957), pp. 101–142.

233. "Thus, while it is admitted there is a principle prohibiting the upper riparian State from altering the waters of a river in circumstances calculated to do serious injury to the lower riparian State, such a principle has no application to the present case, since it was admitted by the Tribunal... that the French project will not alter the waters of the Carol." *Yearbook of the ILC* Vol. II, Part II (1974), p. 197. The main significance of this case will be discussed below regarding the duty of cooperation.

234. *ICJ Reports* (Interim Measures) 1973 (Australia v. France), pp. 99–106, (New Zealand v. France), pp. 135–142. *ICJ Reports* (Jurisdiction) 1974 (Australia v. France), pp. 253–272, (New Zealand v. France), pp. 457–478. The plaintiffs also sought to prevent interference with territorial sovereignty (from nuclear fallout) and ensure freedom of the high seas.

235. Brownlie cautions that when a unilateral declaration is not directed to a specific state, but is expressed *erga omnes* as here, the facts must be carefully examined when determining the intention to be bound. Brownlie, *Public International Law*, *supra*, n. 51, pp. 638–639.

236. Patricia Birnie, "The Role of International Law in Solving Certain Environmental Conflicts," in *International Environmental Diplomacy*, ed. John E. Carroll (Cambridge: Cambridge University Press, 1988), p. 112.

237. See, *supra*, n. 214.

238. John McCormick, *The Global Environmental Movement: Reclaiming Paradise*, (London: Belhaven Press, 1989), p. 97.

239. Louis B. Sohn, "The Stockholm Declaration on the Human Environment," *Harvard International Law Journal* Vol. 14, No. 1 (Winter 1973), pp. 423–424, who notes that the success of the Conference was due to a complex *preparatory process* where agreement on most issues was reached prior to the Conference, leaving few questions to be resolved at the Conference itself (emphasis added). Regimes incorporate this process.

240. See text, *supra*.

241. Allen Springer, "United States Environmental Policy and International Law: Stockholm Principle 21 Revisited" in *International Environmental Diplomacy*, ed. John E. Carroll (Cambridge: Cambridge University Press, 1988), p. 51.

242. Sohn, "Stockholm Declaration," *supra*, n. 239, p. 493.

243. Ibid., p. 492. For example, Professor Sohn states that it was unfortunate that the proposal of the Holy See, calling for a "just environmental policy" in states' exploitation of natural resources, was not considered.

244. UN Resolution A/Res/3281, 15 January 1975, reprinted in *International Legal Materials* Vol. 14, No. 1 (1975), pp. 251–265.

245. *International Legal Materials* Vol. 19, No. 6 (1979), pp. 1442–1455, where Principle 21 is expressed verbatim in the introduction.

246. *International Legal Materials* Vol. 21, No. 6 (1982), pp. 1245–1354, where Art. 194(2) states that "States shall take all measures necessary to ensure that activities under their jurisdiction or control are so conducted as not to cause damage by pollution to other states and their environment, and that pollution arising from incidents or activities under

their jurisdiction or control does not spread beyond the areas where they exercise sovereign rights in accordance with this Convention."

247. *International Legal Materials*, Vol. 26, No. 6 (1987), pp. 1516–1540, where the Preamble recalls and recites Principle 21 verbatim.

248. *International Legal Materials*, Vol. 31, No. 4 (1992), pp. 849–873, where Principle 21 is repeated in the Convention's Preamble.

249. See, in addition, the 1980 Memorandum of Intent between the US and Canada, *International Legal Materials* Vol. 20, No. 3 (1981), pp. 690–695; the 1972 Convention on the Prevention of Marine Pollution by Dumping of Waste and Other Matter (London Dumping Convention), *International Legal Materials* Vol. 18, No. 2 (1979), pp. 499–529; and the 1982 UN Resolution on a World Charter for Nature, *International Legal Materials* Vol. 22, No. 2 (1983) pp. 455–460.

250. *International Legal Materials* Vol. 31, No. 4 (1992), pp. 874–880.

251. Marc Pallemaerts, "International Environmental Law From Stockholm to Rio: Back to the Future?" in Philippe Sands, ed. *Greening International Law* (London: Earthscan, 1993), p. 6. See, also, Willem Kakebeeke, "Transboundary Air Pollution," *Yearbook of International Environmental Law* Vol. 3 (1992), p. 223.

252. Pallemaerts, "From Stockholm to Rio," *supra*, n. 251, p. 5.

253. Ileana Porras, "The Rio Declaration: A New Basis for International Cooperation," in Philippe Sands, ed. *Greening International Law* (London: Earthscan, 1993), p. 31.

254. See, *infra*, Chapters 4, 5 and 6, Development Uncertainty.

255. See, *supra*, Chapter 2, Soft Law.

256. Porras, "The Rio Declaration," *supra*, n. 253, p. 26. See also, *Environmental Protection and Sustainable Development: Legal Principles and Recommendations*, adopted by the Experts Group on Environmental Law of the WCED (London: Graham & Trotman, 1987).

257. Porras, "The Rio Declaration," *supra*, n. 253, pp. 26–27. The Principle addresses developed states when referring to the need to "reduce and eliminate unsustainable patterns of production and consumption,"and addresses developing states when it refers to the need to "promote appropriate demographic policies."

258. *International Law & The Environment*, *supra*, n. 83, p. 91.

259. Schachter, *International Law in Theory and Practice*, *supra*, n. 4, p. 368, since prohibition of environmental risk cannot be absolute. See, also, Johan G. Lammers, "Balancing The Equities In International Environmental Law," in *The Future of the International Law of the Environment*, ed. Hague Academy (Dordrecht: Martinus Nijhoff, 1985),

pp. 153–163.

260. Birnie and Boyle point out that strict liability is sometimes interpreted as a reversal of the burden of proof, and due diligence remains a relevant consideration. Sometimes it is interpreted to imply that a failure of due diligence is not required, but other defenses are available. The distinction between strict and absolute liability is then made on the basis of strict liability permitting more defenses to liability. Birnie and Boyle, *International Law & The Environment*, *supra*, n. 83, p. 142. For the purposes of this book, strict liability follows the second interpretation above, and thus no distinction will be made between it and absolute liability.

261. Pierre Dupuy, "Due Diligence in the International Law of Liability," in *OECD Legal Aspects of Transfrontier Pollution*, ed. OECD (Paris, 1977), p. 369.

262. Harvard Law Review, ed., "Developments In The Law: International Environmental Law," *Harvard Law Review*, Vol. 104, No. 7 (May 1991), p. 1509.

263. Ibid., p. 1510.

264. For example, the Vienna Ozone Convention and its amended Protocol attempt to lay out standards regulating emissions of CFCs and other ozone-depleting gases. Yet, there are exceptions to these requirements for developing states. See *infra*, Chapter 5. There are divergent reporting standards in the FCCC as well. *Infra*, Chapter 6.

265. "Developments in the Law," *supra*, n. 262, pp. 1510–1511. See also, *infra*, Chapter 4, Critical Issue of Development.

266. Pierre Dupuy, "International Liability for Transfrontier Pollution," *Trends in Environmental Policy and Law*, ed. Michael Bothe (Gland, Switzerland: IUCC, 1980), pp. 373–374.

267. "Developments in the Law," *supra*, n. 262, p. 1511.

268. Birnie and Boyle, *International Law & The Environment*, *supra*, n. 83, p. 144. See also, Alan Boyle, "Nuclear Energy and International Law: An Environmental Perspective," *British Yearbook of International Law: An Environmental Perspective* Vol. 60 (1989), pp. 291–292.

269. See, *supra*, n. 217. The *Gut Dam Arbitration, International Legal Materials*, Vol. 8, No. 1 (1968), pp. 118–143, is also not helpful, since it was concerned with interpretation of a bilateral treaty.

270. See, *supra*, n. 228.

271. For example, the 1972 Convention on International Liability for Damage Caused by Space Objects, *International Legal Materials* Vol. 18, No. 5 (1971), pp. 965–972.

272. Boyle, "Nuclear Energy," *supra*, n. 268, pp. 275–276, where the author points out that *Trail Smelter* did not utilize a balancing of interests in determining whether Canada was in breach of its obligation. However, Canada accepted fault without a finding as such, thus not requiring the tribunal to balance activity versus effect regarding that obligation.

273. See *infra*, Chapter 4, Critical Issues of Economics and Development.

274. See, Kiss and Shelton, *International Environmental Law*, *supra*, n. 152, pp. 352–353. There is the additional question of whether local remedies should be exhausted first. Alan E. Boyle, "State Responsibility for Breach of Obligations to Protect the Global Environment," in *Control Over Compliance With International Law*, ed. William E. Butler (Dordrecht: Martinus Nijhoff Publishers, 1991), p. 72. Boyle dismisses the issue of exhausting legal remedies where the global commons is concerned, since there is usually no obvious plaintiff to exhaust such remedies.

275. Boyle, "State Responsibility," *supra*, n. 274, pp. 72–74. Ozone layer depletion and climate change do not per se violate the rights of any one state. Ibid., p. 73. Attempts to gain standing by invoking responsibility on behalf of the international community, on the basis of an international crime or by virtue of a treaty even though there is no direct effect of the breach on the party bringing the suit or the suit is brought by a non-party state, are of uncertain outcome. Ibid., pp. 73–74.

276. See Birnie, "International Environmental Law," *supra*, n. 196, p. 66 where the author states that "there are serious difficulties with the effective application of state responsibility in the field of environmental law."

277. "Developments in the Law," *supra*, n. 262, p. 1509.

278. The suggestion of this author is regimes. See, *infra,* Chapter 3.

279. See, Schachter, *International Law In Theory and Practice*, *supra*, n. 4, p. 373 and Allen Springer, *The International Law of Pollution* (Westport: Quorum Books, 1983), p. 145.

280. Birnie and Boyle, *International Law & The Environment*, *supra*, n. 83, p. 103.

281. Schachter, *International Law In Theory and Practice*, *supra*, n. 4, p. 373.

282. See, *Corfu Channel*, *supra,* n. 228, p. 22.

283. Birnie & Boyle, *International Law & The Environment*, *supra*, n. 83, p. 108.

284. Convention on the Law of the Sea, *supra*, n. 246, Art. 198 states that "When a state becomes aware of cases in which the marine environment is in imminent danger of being damaged or has been

damaged by pollution, it shall immediately notify other States it deems likely to be affected by such damage, as well as the competent international organizations". Basel Convention on the Control of Transboundary Movement of Hazardous Wastes, Art. 13, *International Legal Materials*, Vol. 28, No. 3 (1989), pp. 649–686.

285. Principle 18, *supra*, n. 250.

286. *Lac Lanoux*, *supra*, n. 232, p. 138.

287. Charter of Economic Rights and Duties of States, Art. 3, *supra*, n. 244.

288. *Fisheries Jurisdiction* Cases *ICJ Rep.*, (1974), (UK v. Iceland), pp. 3–35; (FRG v. Iceland), pp. 175–206.

289. Birnie and Boyle, *International Law & The Environment*, *supra*, n. 83, p. 104.

290. Principle 19, *supra*, n. 250.

291. See, Boyle, "Nuclear Energy," *supra*, n. 268, p. 281, Kiss and Shelton, *International Environmental Law*, *supra*, n. 152, pp. 132–134, and Schachter, *International Law In Theory and Practice*, *supra*, n. 4, p. 373.

292. Springer, *International Law of Pollution*, *supra*, n. 279, p. 147, quoting Alexandre Kiss, *Survey of Current Developments in International Environmental Law*, IUCN Environmental Policy and Law Paper, No. 10 (Morges, Switzerland:IUCN, 1976), p. 31.

293. Ibid., pp. 147–148.

294. Birnie & Boyle, *International Law & the Environment*, *supra*, n. 83, p. 103. The authors state that France had complied with its obligations under a treaty and customary law to consult and negotiate in good faith.

295. See, *Lac Lanoux*, *supra*, n. 232, p. 133.

296. Springer, *International Law of Pollution*, *supra*, n. 279, pp. 148–149.

297. See, *supra*, Chapter 2, Duty to Inform.

298. See, *supra*, n. 245.

299. Ibid.

300. Cooperation in the Field of the Environment Concerning Natural Resources Shared by Two or More States, *International Legal Materials* Vol 17, No. 5 (1978), pp. 1091–1098. This document is noted in UN General Assembly Resolution 34/186.

301. Ibid. In addition, Principle 1 states that "it is necessary that consistent with the concept of equitable utilization of shared natural resources, States co-operate with a view to controlling, preventing, reducing or eliminating adverse environmental effects which may result from the utilization of such resources". Equitable utilization may,

moreover, be of little value for tackling global environmental change, since the underlying concept is one of shared resources between two states, not of a global resource such as the atmosphere. See Alan E. Boyle, "International Law and the Protection of the Global Atmosphere: Concepts, Categories and Principles," in *International Law and Global Climate Change*, ed. Robin Churchill and David Freestone, (London: Graham & Trotman, 1991), p. 8.

302. Principle 19, *supra*, n. 250.

303. FCCC, *supra*, n. 248, Art. 4(1)g, See, also, Vienna Ozone Convention, *supra*, n. 247, Art. 3, and Montreal Protocol to the Vienna Convention on Substances that Deplete the Ozone Layer, *International Legal Materials* Vol. 26, No. 6 (1987), pp. 1541–1561, Art. 9.

304. FCCC, *supra*, n. 248, Arts. 4, 12. Montreal Protocol, *supra*, n. 303, Art. 7.

305. UNEP, *Environmental Impact Assessment*, Environmental Law Guidelines and Principles, No. 9, (Nairobi: UNEP, 1987), p. 1.

306. Ibid.

307. Ibid.

308. Ibid., p. 2.

309. *International Legal Materials* Vol. 30, No. 3 (1991), pp. 800–819. Other activities not listed can be subject to assessment should the parties agree.

310. FCCC, *supra*, n. 248, Art. 4(f).

311. Vienna Ozone Convention, *supra*, n. 247, Art. 2(a). The Montreal Protocol also provides for cooperation of the parties regarding reporting of data, exchange of information and technical assistance, Arts. 6, 9 and 10, *supra*, n. 303.

312. Law of the Sea, *supra*, n. 246.

313. Principle 17, *supra*, n. 250. A US Federal Appeals Court, however, has ruled that under the National Environmental Policy Act, an EIA is not required for the North American Free Trade. Public Citizen; Friends of the Earth, Inc.; Sierra Club, Appellees v. United States Trade Representative, No. 93-5212, US Court of Appeals for the District of Columbia, 1993 US APP. LEXIS 24660. While this is a US case, the catalytic effect of leader states and domestic regulations is important to regime formation and development. See, *infra*, Chapter 4, Catalysts for Climate Change and Ozone Layer Depletion Regimes.

314. See, *supra*, Chapter 2, Policy-Oriented School and Policy-Oriented Lawmaking.

315. See, for example, Lothar Gundling, "The Status in International Law of the Principle of Precautionary Action," in *The North Sea; Perspectives on Regional Environmental Cooperation* ed. D.

Freestone and T. Ijlstra, pp. 23–30 (Dordrecht: Martinus Nijhoff, 1990), Ellen Hey "The Precautionary Concept in Environmental Policy and Law: Institutionalizing Caution," *Georgetown International Environmental Law Review* Vol. 4, No. 2 (1992), pp. 303–318, David Freestone, "The Precautionary Principle," in *International Law and Global Climate Change*, ed. R. Churchill and D. Freestone (London: Graham & Trotman, 1991), p. 30, and Daniel Bodansky, "Scientific Uncertainty and the Precautionary Principle," *Environment* Vol. 33 (1991), p.4.

316. Robin Churchill, "Hard or Soft Law in International Environmental Law-Making? Some Reflections on the International North Sea Conferences," speech delivered at meeting of the British International Law Association, 22 January 1992. See, also, Freestone, "The Precautionary Principle," *supra*, n. 316, p. 23.

317. Birnie, "International Environmental Law," *supra,* n. 196, p. 80.

318. See, Freestone, "The Precautionary Principle," *supra*, n. 315, p. 30, and Edith Brown Weiss, "International Environmental Law: Contemporary Issues and the Emergence of a New World Order," *Georgetown Law Journal* Vol. 81 (March 1993), p. 690, where the author points out that "there is no agreement on the content of this principle, or even as to whether an actual principle has emerged or only an approach to address a problem."

319. Ministerial Declaration on Sustainable Development in the ECE Region, United Nations Economic Commission for Europe Conference on Action for a Common Future, Bergen, Norway, 15 May 1990, UN Doc. A/CONF.151/PC10.

320. Remi Parmentier, "Radioactive Waste Dumping At Sea," in Philippe Sands, ed. *Greening International Law* (London: Earthscan, 1993), pp. 150–151.

321. See, Daniel Bodansky, "New Developments in International Law: Remarks by Daniel Bodansky," *American Society of International Law: Proceedings of the 85th Annual Meeting*, by the American Society of International Law, Washington, DC (1991), pp. 413–417.

322. Preamble, *supra*, n. 247.

323. Art. 3(3), *supra*, n. 248.

324. Ibid.

325. Daniel Bodansky, "The United Nations Framework Convention on Climate Change," *Yale Journal of International Law* Vol. 18, No. 2 (Summer 1993), p. 502, fn 308. The author also notes that the dispute settlement procedure of the FCCC, Art. 14, does not contain an express limitation that parties could not be found in violation of Art. 3 under Art. 14.

326. Ibid.

327. Ibid., p. 502.

328. FCCC, *supra*, n. 248, Art. 3(3).

329. See, *infra*, Chapter 6, International Action Regarding Climate Change.

330. Ministerial Declaration, Paragraph 7, *Environmental Policy and Law* Vol. 20, p. 220.

331. Rio Declaration, *supra*, n. 250.

332. Birnie and Boyle, *International Law & The Environment*, *supra*, n. 83, p. 98. See, also Weiss, "Environmental Law," *supra*, n. 318.

333. It is so-called because the measures to be taken are "chosen for broad-based reasons and no one would regret having taken them even if, as the science became clearer, [the problem] turned out not to be a serious threat." R. A. Reinstein, "Climate Negotiations," *The Washington Quarterly* Vol. 16, No. 1 (Winter 1993), p. 86. The best-known advocate of the "no-regrets" policy is the United States. See James A. Baker III, "Diplomacy for the Environment," speech given to the National Governors Association, 26 February 1990. (Washington, DC: US Dept of State, Bureau of Public Affairs).

In addition, a recent US government report concluded that over the last 15 years, US environmental policy has evolved largely in reaction to popular panics and not in response to sound scientific analyses of which environmental hazards present the greatest risks. See, Keith Schneider, "New View Calls Environmental Policy Misguided," *The New York Times*, 21 March 1993, p. 1. The article quotes Richard D. Morgenstern, acting administrator for policy planning and evaluation at the US EPA as saying: "Our society is very reactive, and when concerns are raised people want action. The problem in a democracy is you can't easily sit back and tell people it would be better to learn more. We're now in the position of saying in quite a few of our programs, 'Oops, we made a mistake [and overreacted to the degree of harm expected].'"

334. Freestone, "The Precautionary Principle," *supra*, n. 315, p. 37.

335. See, Edith Brown Weiss, "Intergenerational Equity in International Law," *Proceedings of the American Society of International Law*, by the American Society of International Law, Washington, DC (1987), p. 127, and Catherine Redgwell, quoting Weiss, "Intergenerational Equity and Global Warming," in *Intergenerational Law and Global Climate Change*, ed. Robin Churchill and David Freestone (London: Graham & Trotman, 1991), p. 42.

336. FCCC, *supra*, n. 248, Art. 3(1).

337. See, Boyle, "The Protection of the Global Atmosphere," *supra*, n. 301, p. 16. In addition, the concept of vesting such rights in future generations appears to be inconsistent with certain rights accorded to individuals, particularly in the domestic law of western democracies,

such as the greater right of the living individual over the unborn fetus on the issue of abortion.

338. See, Birnie, "International Environmental Law," *supra*, n. 196, p. 79. Professor Birnie points out that the only model for such an approach is the Supervisory Authority mechanism of the 1974 Nordic Convention, a mechanism not activated by any of the concerned Parties. Art. 4 of that Convention provides that "Each State shall appoint a special authority (supervisory authority) to be entrusted with the task of safeguarding general environmental interests..." Convention on the Protection of the Environment Between Denmark, Finland, Norway and Sweden, *International Legal Materials*, Vol. 13, No. 3 (1974), pp. 591–597. See, also, Gary P. Supanich, "The Legal Basis of Intergenerational Responsibility: An Alternative View — The Sense of Intergenerational Identity," *Yearbook of International Environmental Law* Vol. 3 (1992), pp. 94–107, where the author questions Weiss' theory of intergenerational equity.

339. Birnie & Boyle, *International Law & The Environment*, *supra*, n. 83, p. 120. See also Arvid Pardo and Carl Q. Christol, "The Common Interest: Tension Between the Whole and the Parts," in *The Structure and Process of International Law*, ed. R. St. McDonald and Douglas Johnston (Dordrecht: Martinus Nijhoff, 1983), pp. 643–660.

340. Law of the Sea, *supra*, n. 246, Art. 136, and the 1979 Agreement Governing the Activities of States on the Moon and Other Celestial Bodies, Art. 11(1) and (5), *International Legal Materials* Vol. 18, No. 6 (1979), pp. 1434–1455. The concept of common heritage is of doubtful legal status. See, Birnie and Boyle, *International Law & The Environment*, *supra*, n. 83, p. 121.

341. Boyle states that the atmosphere is not the same as airspace since the atmosphere is not a spatial dimension subject to national sovereignty, but is a moving airmass and not subject to any national boundaries. He also rejects the concept of common property, since the atmosphere falls only partly into areas of common property or areas open for use to all states, and partly into areas of sovereign airspace. See Boyle, "Protection of the Global Atmosphere," *supra*, n. 301, pp. 7–9.

342. UN General Assembly Resolution 43/53, Protection of Global Climate for Present and Future Generations of Mankind, UN General Assembly Official Records of the General Assembly, 43rd Session, Supplement No. 49 (A/43/49), p. 133. That view was also taken in the Noordwijk Declaration on Atmospheric Pollution and Climate Change, Ministerial Conference on Atmospheric Pollution and Climatic Change, 5-7 November 1989, *Environmental Policy and Law* Vol. 19, No. 6 (1989), pp. 229–231, as well as by the UN Environment Programme Governing Council Decision 15/36, 25 May 1989, UN General Assem-

bly, *Official Records, 44th Session, Supplement No. 25 (A/44/25)*, p. 164. The 1989 Ottawa Meeting of Legal and Policy Experts for the Protection of the Atmosphere also stated that the atmosphere "constituted a common resource of vital interest to mankind." Statement reprinted in "Selected Materials," *American University Journal of International Law and Policy*, Vol. 5, No. 2 (Winter 1991), pp. 529–542.

343. David J. Attard, ed., *The Meeting of the Group of Legal Experts to Examine the Concept of The Common Concern of Mankind in Relation to Global Environmental Issues* (Nairobi: UNEP, 1991). The Group of Experts have met once since that time. David J. Attard, facsimile correspondence, 17 May 1993.

344. Birnie and Boyle, *International Law & The Environment*, *supra*, n. 83, p. 391.

345. Ibid.

346. Preamble, *supra*, n. 248.

347. See Frederic L. Kirgis, Jr., "Standing To Challenge Human Endeavors That Could Change The Climate," *American Journal of International Law* Vol. 84, No. 2 (April 1990), p. 527.

348. Ibid., pp. 527–529. Boyle suggests two other meanings. One is that it creates rights for future generations. A second interpretation is that it contributes to already existing obligations of customary international law, and that the atmosphere is already protected by international law. Boyle, "Protection of the Global Atmosphere," *supra*, n. 301, pp. 11–13.

349. Kiss and Shelton, *International Environmental Law*, *supra*, n. 152, p. 67.

350. Birnie & Boyle, *International Law & the Environment*, *supra*, n. 83, p. 109, citing OECD definition.

351. OECD Council Recommendation on the Implementation of the Polluter Pays Principle, OECD and the Environment (Paris: OECD, 1986), OECD Council Recommendation on Application of the Polluter-Pays Principle to Accidental Pollution, *International Legal Materials* Vol. 28, No. 5 (1989), pp. 1320–1325.

352. Art. 130R(2), *International Legal Materials* Vol. 25, No. 3 (1986), pp. 506–518.

353. Birnie and Boyle, *International Law & the Environment*, *supra*, n. 83, p. 110.

354. *International Legal Materials* Vol. 30 (1991), p. 735.

355. See Birnie and Boyle, *International Law & The Environment*, *supra*, n. 83, pp. 110–111.

356. Principle 16, *supra*, n. 250.

357. SS.II/4/B, 3 August 1990. It can also be found in sectoral pollution control regimes, such as the 1992 Oslo/Paris Convention, Art. 2(2b), the 1992 Helsinki Convention, Art. 3(4), and the 1992 ECE Convention on International waterways, Art. 2(5b).

358. See, Peter Wetterstein, *Environmental Impairment Liability in Admiralty* (Finland: Abo Akademi University Press, 1992) for a good account of liability under OPA.

359. Birnie & Boyle, *International Law & the Environment*, *supra*, n. 83, p. 296.

360. This is due to increasing vessel operating costs due to OPA pressure on manning and maintenance expenditures, increasing insurance costs, increasing construction costs, and increasing overhead costs for intensified safety training and response plans. See, John M. Ellis, "Impact of Environmental Taxation on Consuming Countries and the Economic of Shipping," paper presented at the Oil & Money Conference, London, 26 October 1993.

361. Ibid. The $450 million implementation cost does not include any impact OPA may have on transportation costs to other countries, however, and as ships trade globally and OPA standards become more common worldwide, costs will increase.

362. Birnie and Boyle, *International Law & the Environment*, *supra*, n. 83, pp. 293–295. A Protocol not yet in force would require shipowners to bear full costs up to the limit of their own liability.

363. Weiss, "Environmental Law," *supra*, n. 318, p. 705, fn 180.

364. Birnie, "International Environmental Law," *supra*, n. 196, p. 80. The author points out that there are ad hoc examples of application of the principle, including the US Superfund and the IMO's International Oil Pollution Compensation Fund.

365. Ibid., p. 83. In addition to these concepts, there is a movement toward bringing environmental protection under the rubric of international human rights law. See, for example, Dinah Shelton, "What Happened in Rio to Human Rights?" *Yearbook of International Environmental Law* Vol. 3 (1992), pp. 75–93, and Symposium, Earth Rights and Responsibilities: Human Rights and Environmental Protection, *Yale Journal of International Law* Vol. 18, No. 1 (Winter 1993), pp. 212–413. This may not be the best route at present, however, in view of the Asian and Chinese animosity toward the imposition of what they perceive as western human rights on their cultures displayed at the recent International Conference on Human Rights, Vienna, June 1993. See, Thomas Hammarberg, "Vienna Will Be Remembered for What Wasn't Said," *International Herald Tribune*, 29 June 1993, p. 4. The writer is a former secretary-general of Amnesty International and is currently with the UN Committee on the Rights of the Child.

366. Wallace, *International Law*, *supra*, n. 89, p. 33.

CHAPTER 3

International Regimes

Once established, that expectation becomes a culture.[1]

INTRODUCTION TO INTERNATIONAL REGIMES

The concept of international regimes[2] is proposed to provide a middle ground between the two extremes of anarchy and world government[3] through the creation of legal obligations in specific issue-areas. Regimes remain, of course, part of the larger legal order and thus subject to its rules, and it is important "not to lose sight of the interconnections and coherence of the larger whole [legal order]."[4] Regimes, then, serve to fill gaps in the international legal order with regard to a specific issue-area.[5]

But what exactly is a regime? Although regimes were addressed initially by international law as a means of describing the prospect of legal regulation in unregulated areas,[6] the theory has gained prominence primarily within the discipline of international relations. Within that discipline, four different theoretical approaches have evolved, but which, however, are not mutually exclusive. These have been labelled structural, game-theoretic, functional, and cognitive.[7]

The structural approach attempts to connect the existence of regimes with the existence of a dominant power. Thus, this theory, in its simplest form, maintains that the presence of a dominant power or coalition is necessary for regime formation and for the regime to remain stable. Hegemonic stability theory has been criticized, however, for several reasons. These include the presence of enough empirical evidence to argue that the existence of a hegemon may be neither sufficient or necessary for regime formation; that the mere existence of a hegemon is probably not enough to facilitate regime formation and maintenance (there must be the will to take on the leadership role); and that there is confusion as to what a hegemon is and what type of hegemonic structure is advantageous under what circumstances for what type of regime.[8]

The game-theoretic or strategic approach attempts to determine, from a given set of rules, the most likely strategy to be used by each player, in effect, this approach studies the logic of interdependent decision-making. It is difficult, however, to specify the preferences of the players, and domestic processes are frequently ignored. Applying formal game theory to a large number of actors can become unmanageable, and reducing the number of choices to two (cooperation or defection) could become an oversimplification. Game theory also is not helpful in predicting whether regimes will come into existence, as well as what norms and rules the regime will consist of.[9]

The functional approach attempts to explain behavior in terms of benefits or rewards which motivate behavior. However, knowing the function of a regime does not help explain why regimes exist in some issue-areas, but not in others. This is important since regimes may not always be convergent, but may be divergent and institutionalize inequalities.[10]

Finally, the cognitive theory's "core ... insight is that cooperation cannot be completely explained without reference to ideology, the values of actors, the beliefs they hold about the interdependence of issues, and the knowledge available to them about how they can realize specific goals."[11] Thus, regimes are conditioned by ideology and consensual knowledge, and evolve as the actors learn.

The above theories reveal the different strands within regime theory. While there is no coherent set of propositions to be gleaned from the above, this does not mean that international legal scholars cannot proceed in the area of regime theory. This also does not mean that the divisions within regime theory are underplayed, but that there is an awareness of them. Methodological difficulties, while not to be ignored in the "two-culture problem" between international law and international relations, does not mean that there are no intellectual opportunities for collaboration. Oran Young, a leading international relations regime specialist has stated that:

> there are good grounds for concluding that the development of a more effective working relationship between the legal community and the social science community is a necessary condition for the articulation of a comprehensive and fully satisfactory account of the nature and roles of regime in international society.[12]

It is only recently that regime theory has again become the focus of legal scholars' search for methods to induce greater international cooperation.[13] Writing with regard to environmental problems, one scholar noted that regimes bring to light the:

> strong dependence on economic and political factors, ... on the relative strength and bargaining power of competing... lobbies,... on scientific evidence (certainty versus uncertainty), and on public opinion.[14]

This book expands upon the preliminary research done by these legal scholars and seeks to answer their calls for further investigation of regimes. This requires the integration of the work of international relations specialists in this area. Until recently, the relations between these two disciplines has been one of "mutual neglect."[15] As noted by Hurrell and Kingsbury:

> Regime theorists have tended to neglect the particular status of legal rules, to downplay the links between specific sets of rules and the broader structure of the international legal system, and to underrate the complexity and variety of legal rules, processes, and procedures. On the other hand, theoretical accounts of international... law have often paid rather little explicit attention to the political bargaining processes that underpin the emergence of new norms of international... law, to the role of power and interest in inter-state negotiations, and to the range of political factors that explain whether states will or will not comply

> with rules.[16]

This pushes regime research in the direction of an interdisciplinary approach.[17]

DEFINITION OF REGIMES[18]

There is no complete agreement on what exactly comprises a regime.[19] Goldie, in his earliest work on regimes identified them as:

> (1) the acceptance, amongst a group of States, of a community of laws and of legal ideas; (2) the mutual respect and recognition accorded by certain States to the unilateral policies of others acting in substantial conformity with their own, enmeshing all the States concerned in a regime with respect to those policies; (3) a common loyalty, among a group of States, to the principle of abstention regarding a common resource.[20]

Goldie added:

> when this is mutually and equitably administered in the light of scientific knowledge, the participation of these States within a regime of this kind most clearly illustrates the possibility of restraining pre-emptive acts which might otherwise be permitted under international law.[21]

So for Goldie, regimes provide an intermediate stage of formulation for rules which may eventually become part of the general system of international law as acceptance widens to include more states within the regime.[22]

Over a decade after Goldie's writing on international regimes, international relations scholars began to further explore the concept. Within that discipline, the most frequently cited definition of regimes is that of Stephen Krasner. He states that international regimes are "principles, norms, rules and decision-making procedures around which actor expectations converge in a given issue-area."[23]

Although it is difficult for an international legal scholar not to notice the influence of international law within Krasner's definition, Krasner does not explicitly take account of international law.

His definition differs substantially from Goldie's, where the development of a legal conscience by the regime members leading to rules of law is regarded to be critical.[24] While the language of Krasner's structural approach to regimes was probably used so as to avoid the confines of traditional treaty-based law as well as to avoid equating regimes with formal treaties or international organizations, his use of norms, rules and decision-making procedures brings his definition of regimes precariously close to, if not within, the process-oriented account of the international legal order.

Within Krasner's framework, principles are defined as "beliefs of fact, causation, and rectitude," norms are "standards of behavior defined in terms of rights and obligations," rules are "specific prescriptions or proscriptions for action," while decision-making procedures are "prevailing practices for making and implementing collective choice."[25] A comparison to the work of leading international legal scholars following the policy-oriented approach reveals a similarity in meanings of these terms, particularly to those theorists adopting a "cognitive theory" approach to regimes, notwithstanding the different labels.

Oscar Schachter, while applying different labels to these terms, offers similar definitions for their application within international law. He describes three types of legally relevant "norms": rules, principles and objectives. These are analogous to Krasner's rules, norms and principles. For Schachter, "rules" dictate a specific result, such as the rule that nine votes are required to adopt a Security Council resolution.[26] This equates with Krasner's definition of "rules" (specific prescriptions). His description of "principles" is similar to Krasner's use of "norms" (standards of behavior) in that interpretations of these "principles" will vary with respect to the circumstances as with non-use of force versus self-defence.[27] Finally, Schachter describes "objectives," which do not give rise to claims of entitlement but become relevant when making choices between opposing "rules" or "principles" (as he defines those terms).[28] Schachter's use of "objective" is loosely analogous to Krasner's use of "principles."[29]

Rosalyn Higgins' description of the meaning of rules and norms within international law also does not differ dramatically from Krasner's (or Schachter's, except perhaps in labelling, where Higgins' use of "norm" is analogous to Schachter's use of "principle"):

> A 'rule' is an obligation of law which in its terms cannot be gainsaid: For example, the requirement that the Security Council be composed of 15 members; or that an important vote in the General Assembly requires a two-thirds vote. A norm, by contrast, is an authoritative provision of law that continues to command significant community expectations as to its contemporary validity and which may be appropriately invoked and applied in the particular factual context. But our appreciation of that very context can give rise to debate as to whether that norm, or another different (indeed, competing) norm, should be applied. The prohibition against the use of force is thus a norm. Recent events... have illustrated graphically the diverse views that may be advanced as to whether that norm is applicable to the fact situation; or rather the norm permits the use of force in self-reliance; or perhaps permits reprisals.[30]

While there is disagreement among regime analysts regarding the precise meanings of these terms,[31] the degree of similarity between Krasner's terms and international legal concepts is striking, notwithstanding the different labels used. Rules are basically obligations that cannot be put aside, while norms are behavior standards. This suggests more of a presence of a legal order encompassing regimes than international relations scholars have implied, as well as more of a role for the concept of regimes within international law than legal specialists have acknowledged.[32]

While Krasner's definition may not appear to have explicitly addressed the presence of international law surrounding regimes (although as pointed out earlier it appears to implicitly address law) this is not surprising as Krasner was defining regimes in the political context of international relations. Eckart Klein's definition, on the other hand, can be seen to have gone to the opposite extreme. More in line with traditional legal thinking,[33] Klein states that regimes "refer to treaty-based settlements which are intended, by defining the status of a certain area, to form part of the international order," and the purpose of which is to stabilize a contentious situation or to regulate common use of an area.[34] Under this view, an international regime consists of: 1) a treaty between states, or between states and international organizations regulating an issue-area; 2) a general interest underlying the regulation; and

3) the intention of the parties to serve the general interest by endowing the area with a general status *erga omnes*.[35] This definition, however, is too narrow in that it *requires* a treaty, thus incorporating one of the difficulties some regimes attempt to evade (at least in their early existence): legal formalism. As will be argued below, regimes may come into existence long before a treaty is negotiated, and could arguably exist without a formal treaty.

Thomas Gehring offers a more integrated work in this area by more closely linking international law and regimes. He explains regimes as the regulations, developed within the context of a Diplomatic Conference of Parties (which addresses both political and technical issues) to a convention, governing a specific area of international relations. However, some regulation occurs outside of the body of formal law, such as through recommendations of working groups.[36] Gehring asserts that regimes so defined maintain a tight relationship between "their normative substance and their decision-making procedures to implement, administer and develop prescriptions to meet the demand for quick legal action."[37] This definition expands upon Klein's, but still provides for the presence of international law which Krasner neglects, albeit in the confines of a Conference of Parties.

Within Gehring's framework of the Conference of Parties, law-making is the search for consensus among the states involved on the need for international action and the basis for doing so. As Gehring correctly points out, the lack of a centralized authority for the international legal system requires consensus for the creation of new rules of international law.[38] Regimes organize the process for shaping consensus. Thus, agreement on the priorities and strategies for international action is reached through consensus-building. A body of technical knowledge, accumulated from expert opinions, gives rise to what Gehring calls "cognitive expectations," or expectations based on knowledge. Prescriptions for behavior or "normative expectations" evolve, based on the cognitive expectations of the actors involved.[39] Normative expectations can also induce changes in cognitive or knowledge expectations, for example, through requiring ongoing research. Thus, regimes provide the building block for norms and rules, eventually commanding a much larger commitment as the norms and rules evolve.

Gehring also maintains that norms and rules may be only partially articulated in formal legal instruments. Thus, differing degrees of formal law are utilized in regimes.[40] Indeed, there may be reasons why the parties to a regime might desire an informal agreement instead of a more formal undertaking, such as when states are uncertain about the future benefits and wish then to remain easily and quickly open to adjustment.[41] Informal agreements may also be necessary to give effect to controversial concepts such as "sustainable development" or "differentiated responsibility," which have imprecise meanings.

Dispute settlement functions are also internalized within Gehring's concept of regimes. Since states rarely use third-party dispute settlement procedures to resolve critical issues of policy, internalizing such procedures is a practical reflection of the present state of international affairs. Yet there is an additional benefit in that such internal dispute settlement procedures can utilize not only international law to guide decisions, but also incorporate the normative expectations developed within the regime. This method of dispute settlement ensures optimal cooperation and is of great importance since the "legal relations would be based on more highly articulated rules and standards... than those generally obtaining [within international law]."[42]

One international lawyer undertaking a preliminary examination of regimes states that "grasping the concept of a regime can be a bit of a challenge."[43] Goldie, however, has set out the relevant parameters in that regimes encompass the acceptance of legal ideas in the regulation of an issue-area; a minimal set of limitations (which may evolve) on a state's policies to ensure conformity with certain standards.[44] Most of the other definitions described above either ignore the presence of law or require it in traditional, formal methods. However, some sort of legal obligation, not necessarily formal, is needed within a regime.[45] Indeed, to qualify as legally binding, it must satisfy the sources test.[46] In addition, a legal obligation supplies a minimum standard for distinguishing regimes from ordinary political or administrative arrangements, provides a gauge for judging the effectiveness of a regime, and allows for comparison of the rules at different moments in time.[47]

Gehring's view of regimes appears to be the most fluid, allowing for the presence of law in informal as well as formal methods. Nevertheless, Gehring's regime requires as a starting point a Conference of Parties to a convention. Regimes, however, may be formed prior to a diplomatic conference.

The definition used in this book is that a regime constitutes the development of legal regulations ("normative expectations") by both state and non-state actors through collective decision-making ("cognitive expectations"), governing a specific issue-area and creating a legal obligation among the actors. Since regimes may eventually deal with more than one issue-area, however, the "simple" regime described above can evolve into a "complex regime." This can occur as the "international community, or major portions of it, adopts a series of interlocking measures... toward a common... goal, bolstered by shared values, norms, or fears."[48]

Notwithstanding the fact that international law and international relations have been working in relative isolation in general and in the area of regimes specifically, the two disciplines may be drawing closer together in their "mutual concerns." Hurrell illustrates this point by drawing comparisons between an international relations regime theorist and an international lawyer.[49] The former defines regimes as "institutions with explicit rules, agreed upon by governments, that pertain to particular sets of issues in international relations."[50] The latter describes the purpose of international agreements as providing a framework for the facilitation of on-going negotiations for the development of rules of law.[51] The international relations viewpoint appears to be moving towards a greater rule-oriented view of order, while the international legal view is moving away from its traditional view of rule-making. Although these are just two viewpoints, they reflect a gradual movement of the two disciplines towards each other regarding state behavior.[52] This development can only be encouraged; it is my view that, just as it is important for the international relations specialist to take account of international law when studying regimes, so also is it important for international lawyers to take account of extralegal aspects of law-making in the formation and development of regimes, and not just the final result.[53]

FORMATION OF REGIMES

Just as there is a dispute concerning the definition of regimes, there is also a dispute concerning when regimes come into existence.[54] Within international relations, a widely used taxonomy regarding regimes identifies three different models: structural or realist, modified structural or modified realist, and Grotian.[55] The realist model argues that regimes are created when cooperation is desired among self-interested actors and are merely "arenas for acting out power relationships."[56] The modified realist model argues that states enter into regimes to coordinate state behavior in order to achieve desired outcomes in certain issue-areas.[57] Finally, the Grotian model argues that regimes exist in all areas of international relations and that states are "constrained by principles, norms, and rules that prescribe and proscribe varieties of behavior."[58] Grotians consider regimes subjective, existing "primarily as participants' understandings, expectations or convictions about legitimate, appropriate or moral behavior."[59] This model takes account of domestic and transnational actors as well, although agreeing that the state is the main actor.[60] For Grotians, these regimes range from "an empty facade that rationalizes the rule of the powerful" to "codified international law or morality."[61]

Research within international law is more convergent regarding regime formation. Goldie maintains regimes are dependent on the existence of shared values (independent of the legal order).[62] Gehring attributes the formation of a regime to consensus among a conference of parties to a convention on the necessity of international action, thus arguably depending on the shared values or interests of states regarding a certain issue-area.[63] Williamson states that regimes arise as states adopt a series of measures toward a common goal, "bolstered by shared values, norms, or fears."[64] He stresses that while the perception of the problem and goal may be widespread, it is not universal. Instead, it is the work of common efforts by states which make the goal more universally accepted, transforming practical arrangements into normative constraints on behavior.[65]

In these analyses, shared values provide normative structures for the formation of these regimes, which do not arise solely from self-interest. In the language of the policy-oriented school of international law, these shared values are called shared expectations.[66]

This type of analysis is anathema to a realist model of regimes within international relations.[67] But, as Hurrell points out, "this rigor has been bought at a significant cost," including a downplaying of the sense of community and the necessity of ethics.[68]

But realist self-interest and moral idealism can be mutually supporting in the sense that a minimal sense of equity must enter into the formation of regimes, no matter how great the self-interest that lies behind the regime formation: "[a] collaboration that is perceived by a participant as blatantly unfair cannot be a durable arrangement in international society."[69] In another sense, this is also a realization that a "responsible" view of sovereignty, whereby absolute sovereignty is limited, is necessary within the international system.[70]

The policy-oriented international law perspective of regime formation mirrors closely the Grotian model discussed above. Indeed, their view of regimes as value-biased is very similar to the policy-oriented view that law-making reflects choices and thus is not neutral:

> All regimes are biased. They establish hierarchies of values, emphasizing some and discounting others. They also distribute rewards to the advantage of some and the disadvantage of others, and in so doing they buttress, legitimize, and sometimes institutionalize patterns of dominance, subordination, accumulation, and exploitation.[71]

However, the Grotian model appears to limit the presence of international law somewhat, since the Grotians consider regimes to be particularly prevalent in the broad range "between the limits of major-power hegemony and legal or moral order,"[72] whereas this author advocates regimes as being part of the international legal order notwithstanding their (sometimes) lack of legal formalism.

For the formation of a regime to take place, there must be present shared expectations of future behavior regarding the regulation of an issue-area.[73] Formation of a regime is an important aspect since it may indicate that the legal order is present before a rule-oriented approach to international law would acknowledge its presence. It is difficult to pinpoint the exact moment when formation occurs, but the attempt is critical if anything is to be learned about when and why states will cooperate in the regulation of a previously unregulated area. In the words of the policy-oriented school, the identifying characteristic of a regime or what the school labels an "arena" is:

> a structure of expectations shared among the members of a community. The identifying characteristic of an arena is a structure of expectations shared among the members of a community; that is, choices affecting the community are made which, if opposed, will in all probability be enforced against opposition.[74]

MAINTENANCE OR DEVELOPMENT OF REGIMES

From the perspective of answering the skeptic's question, "do regimes matter?", formation pales in significance with comparison to the maintenance or development of a regime.[75] Maintenance or development depends upon the extent to which critical issues have been resolved and cognitive expectations shaped.[76] Thus, the stronger the regime through critical issue agreement, the stronger the cognitive expectations, and the stronger the rules and norms or normative expectations flowing from that regime.[77] Thus, the shared or normative expectations are shaped just as in the formation of the regime. In addition, there are catalysts that, if present, can aid the formation and development of a legal regime, although their presence is not critical to either.[78]

Regarding regime development, it is argued that because of the internalizing of the making and application of law, and by virtue of "dispute settlement procedures consistent with the consensus-building process of communication, regimes can develop into comparatively autonomous sectoral legal systems."[79] Schachter agrees that a regime may eventually achieve a significant degree of autonomy. Indeed, he believes that international law is shifting away from its focus on state sovereignty, and that regimes will form "new centers of authority," due to the inability of states to deal unilaterally with such complex problems as global environmental change.[80] Birnie supports this view of states' shift towards "responsible" sovereignty, at least within the area of environmental regulation, as a necessity for self-preservation.[81] Others, however, see regimes as something short of formal law or a legal order, but somewhat more structured than an arrangement based solely on power politics.[82]

THE LEGAL STATUS OF REGIMES

Theorists disagree as to how valuable the concept is within the international order.[83] Within international law, a critical question must be to what extent can a regime be considered part of the legal order.

A great deal would depend, of course, on the definition of what exactly comprises international law, or indeed, as some realist skeptics would question, whether international law exists at all. This work incorporates the policy-oriented approach to international law, which was described above.[84] This school views international law-making as a continuous process. In this process, shared expectations creating legal obligations are sustained or changed by the continuation or abatement of streams of communications regarding the authority and credible control intentions of those whose support is needed for the norms' efficacy.[85]

A similar view states that the difference between legal and non-legal norms and rules can be attributed to the interpretation or construction of norms and rules, "a skill transmitted through a socialization process which people undergo when they become 'rule handlers.'"[86] These rule handlers rely on the expectations perceived as legitimate and expected to be complied with.

Critics counter this reliance on "shared expectations" by arguing that legal obligation may be dissolved by having it depend on expectations, perceptions and compliance, and thus risk turning law into politics. Support for the relevance of "expectation," however, comes (for international law!) from strange places. International relations specialists argue that cooperation is facilitated by law and regimes "because of the functional benefits which they provide in the form of an order based not on coercion, but on the coordination of interests and of patterned expectations."[87]

Schachter adds that when deciding whether or not an obligation exists, the decision will need to be made on the basis of the relevant variables (perceptions, expectations, and compliance):

> to impose hard-and-fast categories [of sources of law] on a world filled with indeterminacies and circularities can only result in a pseudo-realism which does justice neither to our experience nor to our higher purposes.[88]

Regimes establish legal obligations, where those obligations are made by those having authority to prescribe them and the target audience will perceive (have shared expectations) that those norms and rules have are authoritative (legitimate) and effective (control intention). Normative or shared expectations evolve as cognitive expectations or knowledge develop, which grows as the uncertainty surrounding critical issues is overcome. These shared expectations, then, are a source of obligation. Admittedly, the obligation may at times be weak, but as the knowledge grows, so will the strength of the shared expectations and thus the obligations. This process can be shown through analyses of existing regimes.[89]

During this process of "obligating," regimes succeed in the area Oscar Schachter calls "international legal craftsmanship."[90] For Schachter, a legal mechanism should be created to meet environmental or other objectives, other than through the techniques of commands and prohibitions, which will advocate positive acts and provide incentives for having them.[91] The process of regime building, which assimilates policy, law, and management,[92] can accomplish this. Regimes, through consensus-building, can succeed in inducing states to behave in ways they may not at first prefer.[93] In an international legal system which lacks a supranational law-making body, this process of consensus-building "in a specific and often narrowly defined area of international relations is the most important function of an international regime."[94]

EFFECTIVENESS OF REGIMES: PROSPECTS FOR COMPLIANCE

The degree to which a regime can ensure compliance with its regulations is, on a practical basis, the most important factor to consider in the evaluation of legal regimes.[95] Within international law, compliance has been addressed in some detail,[96] although not within the area of regimes. Identifying sources of law may not be all that helpful, however, in answering the question "Do regimes matter?", since "the force of a rule's compliance pull cannot be gauged solely or primarily by examining its source."[97] Thus, it will be argued below that a regime will be able to provide an effective level of compliance through the evolution of norms and rules, dispute-settlement mechanisms, accountability and transparency, as well as conditional cooperation and exclusion.[98]

Evolution of Norms and Rules

The evolution of normative or shared expectations within regimes is an important process, as these norms and rules create legal obligations.[99] Thus, Oscar Schachter refers to regimes as "clearly part of the process by which international law develops," since regimes create "rules binding on... large groups of States,"[100] rules which evolve from the normative expectations agreed upon within the regime. Or, as Goldie has suggested, regimes provide a

> development of a legal consciousness and moral awareness and sensitivity concerning the self-seeking and exclusionary qualities of pre-emptive activities and following from that consciousness and that sensitivity, the making of legal rules limiting and channelling its drives, in brief, the 'detailed shaping of legal consciousness into manageable rules of law'.[101]

This evolution of normative expectations can be examined in two parts: the first being the actual physical process of evolution, and the second being the legal status of the norms themselves. While the two may appear to be separate strands of thought, it is through the evolution process that the norms and rules acquire legal status. The first strand has been explored more within international relations, while the second strand has been a concern of international law, although not within the concept of regimes.

The legal status of the shared or normative expectations created within regimes was discussed above.[102] Regarding the evolution of norms and rules, as cognitive expectations or knowledge are shaped by member States of the regime, normative expectations will develop.[103] The ozone layer depletion regime discussed below is particularly good evidence of this.[104] However, normative or shared expectations within the regime may change even without new technical knowledge as a result of discussion and negotiation among regime members.[105] Prescriptions are not final and are not permanent. Shared expectations may change as the elements of authority and control may cease to be communicated, perhaps because of changes in global authority structures or reassessment by the relevant participants as to the degree or intensity of their interest in supporting the prescription.[106]

Within the regime, the common effort to solve a problem results in the underlying goal or purpose of the regime being "more universally accepted, gradually transforming pragmatic arrangements into normative constraints on behavior."[107] In achieving this common effort through the shaping of shared expectations, "the passing of 'binding decisions' under traditional law-creating methods is not the only way in which law development occurs. Legal consequences also can flow from acts which are not, in the traditional sense, 'binding'."[108] Thus, regimes can aid in norm development as critical issues are resolved.[109] More importantly, because these norms and rules evolve within the regime through collective decision-making,[110] the prospect for compliance is higher. Schachter affirms the probability of achieving high compliance within a regime, attributable in part to a representative decision-making body, which "tend to limit the sphere of autointerpretation by the states of their obligations."[111]

Dispute Settlement Mechanisms

Traditional dispute settlement mechanisms, such as arbitration or resort to the ICJ, seem out of place when dealing with global problems. These disputes will involve more than the traditional complainant and respondent, since all states are affected by adverse actions. In addition, traditional settlement procedures do not usually take place until there is a formal legal dispute, with the parties assuming an adversarial relationship.

> From the standpoint of... effectiveness, it may not matter whether state A or state B has the better legal argument; what is needed is a process that identifies the impediments to full implementation and seeks to overcome them.[112]

This process can be achieved within a regime, where disputes are normally resolved among the states themselves. This internal judicial system, which allows for settlement without the constrictions of formal international law, can either "confirm or modify authoritatively, ...the normative structure of the regime," thereby "shaping consensus on the interpretation of norms in light of the factual circumstances", and "reinforc[ing] the stability of the sectoral legal system as a whole."[113] This method of oversight, however, has been criticized as "a political body," since the dispute settlement mechanism is composed of party-states, rather than independent experts.[114] This may be so, but dispute settlement is better accommodated within the regime, than not accommodated at all, as the relative non-use of the ICJ reveals,[115] although use of the Court is on the increase.

Accountability and Transparency[116]

The absence of a world government means that regime members will need to find a "substitute for coercion" that a domestic system can usually provide. In most regimes, this is accomplished through "the exploitation of *accountability* of states by rendering their performance *transparent* to scrutiny by the international community."[117] In other words, despite state sovereignty, states are accountable for their actions: to their own populations, to other states, and the international public. States are held accountable through the information available about their actions, generated by the regime itself.

Various means have been noted for accountability and transparency within a regime. They include reporting and monitoring, target setting and surveillance. "Pledge and review" systems whereby states undertake unilateral pledges, whether legally binding or not, for action to be reviewed by a body of experts, are also a means of accountability.[118]

Accountability between international regimes and state practice is essential. Although some legal scholars advocate an international supervisory mechanism to integrate the two and ensure compliance,[119] it would still seem that the most effective type of accountability would take place, at least in the beginning, within a regime where the states provided their own supervisory functions. This can eventually develop into involving the authority of an international organization. But while normative expectations are still being resolved and obligations are still weak, there is no need for the involvement of an international supervisory mechanism.

It is important to distinguish between the two concepts of regimes and organizations, particularly within international law.[120] In viewing the legal order, regimes are a conceptual part of the legal order, while organizations form a tangible contribution. Regimes are a necessary part of the legal order. Organizations can strengthen regimes,[121] but only once the regime has taken hold. At that point, organizations may be useful to avoid a proliferation of independent, isolated regimes.

Conditional Cooperation and Exclusion

States may hinge their cooperation within a regime on the conditional cooperation or reciprocity of other members of the regime. Violations are thus likely to be limited by self-interest, as many "regimes involve concrete benefits and reciprocal restraints."[122] Goldie describes this aspect of compliance as:

> the mutual respect and recognition accorded by certain States to the unilateral policies of others acting in substantial conformity with their own, enmeshing all the States concerned in a regime with respect to those policies.[123]

This phenomena of respect and recognition is linked to "reputation", whereby "the focus of public concern is less on what an actor has done in the past (as in a formal legal system) than on what he is likely to do in the future."[124] Thus, states may adhere to the rules of a regime for the sake of reputation.

States may also find it in their best interests to adhere to regime regulations for fear of exclusion. Exclusion from the regime could mean a loss of benefits to the state concerned.[125] This could occur, for example, through trade restrictions levied upon non-Parties to a regime.

In the area of the environment, however, such trade restrictions have recently been called into doubt. A GATT Panel[126] recently ruled that Contracting Parties to GATT could not enact trade measures for the purpose of environmental protection outside their individual jurisdictions or to restrict imports or exports based on the *method* of production of a traded product (as opposed to the end product), as both procedures interfered with free trade, a cornerstone of the world trading system which GATT seeks to protect.[127] The Panel ruling resulted from Mexican objections to US trade sanctions placed on Mexican tuna to protect dolphins being killed when caught up in tuna nets.[128] Although limited to examination of the matter in light of existing GATT regulations, if upheld by the GATT Council, the ruling could affect environmental treaties such as the Montreal Protocol to the Vienna Convention on Substances that Deplete the Ozone Layer,[129] which imposes trade bans on non-party states who refuse to phase out ozone depleting substances.[130] Environmentalists fear such a ruling will be a setback to the prospects for sustainable development. Developing states on the other hand, fear that strong environmental provisions in trade agreements could "facilitate or provide easy justification to countries to apply environmental measures for political and other coercive measures."[131] GATT fears protectionist devices from such a precedent, resulting in obstruction of free trade.[132]

During the negotiations for the Montreal Protocol, it was determined that, since the trade sanctions could only be applied against those violating the Protocol's trade provisions, and since the sanctions were neither arbitrary nor unjustifiable, the trade sanctions would not violate GATT.[133] However, when trade sanctions are applied against non-Parties who are Parties to GATT, then GATT obligations are violated, making the sanctions potentially illegal.[134] The attempt to reconcile trade issues with environmental protection will not be easy.[135]

CONCLUSION

Edith Brown Weiss, a leading international lawyer, recently stated that:

> ...it is not clear to me that we will have been able to sustain the really extraordinary level of negotiating new international agreements that we have seen in the past decade. Governments are stressed today just trying to keep up with international negotiations and making sure that they have delegates who are fully informed attending these negotiations. The need places a big strain on industrialized countries, and more strain, on nonindustrialized countries. That suggests that legal instruments other than formal conventions may also increasingly

become an important component of how we manage the international arena.[136]

While Professor Weiss did not provide any examples as to what kind of "legal instruments" she was referring to, it is suggested here that regimes may be able to provide some degree of "management" until conventions can evolve. As outlined above, the formation of regimes entails a legal obligation. This legal obligation is met when there exists a shared expectation sustained by authority and a control intention. As such, a regime is not "soft law" (although it may contain some soft law) but is legally binding. Formed from shared expectations, regimes develop normative or shared expectations and obligations as cognitive expectations or knowledge evolve. The shaping of cognitive expectations depends on the degree of certainty regarding the critical issues within a particular regime.

This is an exciting prospect for a discipline long beleaguered by claims of ineffectiveness.[137] In the following chapter, an analysis of the issues critical to the maintenance or development of the climate change and ozone regimes will be examined.

NOTES

1. Paul Tsongas, "Convince These Americans That Bush Is Their President Too," *International Herald Tribune*, 18 May 1992, p. 4.

2. See *supra*, Chapter 1, n. 1.

3. See, Richard Williamson, "Building The International Environmental Regime: A Status Report," *Inter-American Law Review* Vol. 21, No. 2 (1990) p. 740. See also, Lynne M. Jurgielewicz, "Long Lines At Disney World Reduced By Sunstroke! Or Can International Law Control Climate Change?" *Revue Generale de Droit* Vol. 22, No. 2 (1991), pp. 468–470.

4. Oscar Schachter, *International Law in Theory and Practice* (Dordrecht: Martinus Nijhoff Publishers, 1991), p. 1.

5. See *supra*, Chapter 2, for the gaps in applicable international law for climate change and ozone layer depletion prior to the FCCC and the Vienna Ozone Convention.

6. See, L.F.E. Goldie, "Special Regimes and Pre-Emptive Activities in International Law," *International and Comparative Law Quarterly* Vol. 11, (July 1962), pp. 670–700. Goldie thus introduced the concept of

regimes into international law over a decade before it was introduced into the international relations literature by Ernst Haas, "On Systems and International Regimes," *World Politics* Vol. 27, No. 2 (January 1975), pp. 147–174. The international relations literature, however, has made little more than a passing reference to international legal research on regimes thus far.

7. See, Stephan Haggard and Beth A. Simmons, "Theories of International Regimes," *International Organization* Vol. 41, No. 3 (Summer 1987), pp. 491–517. This book's concept of regimes falls predominately, but not exclusively, within the cognitive approach. See also, Helen Milner, "International Theories of Cooperation Among Nations," *World Politics*, Vol. 44, No. 3 (April 1992), pp. 466–96, Stephen Krasner, *International Regimes* (Ithaca: Cornell University Press, 1983), Oran Young, *International Cooperation: Building Regimes For Natural Resources and the Environment* (Ithaca: Cornell University Press, 1989), Robert Keohane, *After Hegemony: Cooperation and Discord in the World Political Economy* (1984), and Oran Young and Gail Osherenko, *Polar Politics: Creating International Environmental Regimes* (Ithaca: Cornell University Press, 1993).

8. Thomas Bernauer, *The Chemistry of Regime Formation* (Geneva: UNIDIR, 1993), p. 321, Another broad criticism used against this approach is that it tends to look only at the distribution of power within the international capitalist system. Simmons and Haggard, "International Regimes," *supra*, n. 7, p. 503. See also, Stephen D. Krasner, "Structural Causes and Regime Consequences: Regimes as Intervening Variables," in *International Regimes*, ed. Stephen D. Krasner (Ithaca: Cornell University Press, 1983), p. 1. and Keohane, *After Hegemony*, *supra*, n. 7.

9. Haggard and Simmons, "International Regimes," supra, n. 7, pp. 504–506, Bernauer, *The Chemistry of Regime Formation*, supra, n. 479, pp. 208–209, and Milner, "International Theories of Cooperation Among Nations," *supra*, n. 7, where the author outlines the weaknesses of the game theoretic approach to regimes.

10. Haggard and Simmons, "International Regimes," *supra*, n. 7, pp. 506–508. The functional approach is somewhat similar to that of legal functionalism, described earlier, *supra*, Chapter 2.

11. Haggard and Simmons, "International Regimes," *supra*, n. 7, pp. 509–513. Cognitive approaches cannot, however, predict at what point consensual values or knowledge will bring about cooperation. This book's concept of regimes falls predominately, but not exclusively, within the cognitive approach. See, also, Bernauer, *The Chemistry of Regime Formation*, *supra*, n. 8, pp. 348–373, "Cognitive Factors," where the author argues that cognitive approaches can contribute to closing the explanatory gap.

12. Oran Young, "Understanding International Regimes: Contributions from Law and the Social Sciences," paper presented at the annual meeting of the American Society of International Law, Washington, DC, 1-3 April 1992, p. 39. The paper was part of a panel examining methods to "build bridges" between international law and international relations. In his comments, Young suggested that there might be opportunities for collaboration, notwithstanding the "two-cultures problem." "Remarks," in *American Society of International Law: Proceedings of the 86th Meeting*, by the American Society of International Law, Washington, DC (1992), p. 175.

13. See for instance, Douglas M. Johnston, "Systemic Environmental Damage: The Challenge To International Law and Organization," *Syracuse Journal of International Law and Commerce* Vol. 12, No. 2 (Winter 1985), pp. 255–282, Kenneth W. Abbott, "Modern International Relations Theory: A Prospectus for International Lawyers," *Yale Journal of International Law* Vol. 14, No. 2 (Summer 1989), pp. 335–411, Williamson, "International Environmental Regimes," *supra*, n. 2 and Thomas Gehring, "International Environmental Regimes: Dynamic Sectoral Legal Systems," *Yearbook of International Environmental Law* Vol. 1 (1990), pp. 35–56. These legal scholars are not just examining regimes to describe legal institutional arrangements and practices, as Goldie did, but have begun a preliminary look at the conceptual and theoretical issues underlying regime theory. There had been some collaboration between legal scholars and political scientists previous to this, for example, Seyom Brown, Nina A. Cornell, Larry L. Fabian and Edith Brown Weiss, *Regimes for the Ocean, Outer Space, and Weather* (Washington, DC: The Brookings Institution, 1977), and R. Michael M'Gonigle and Mark W. Zacher, *Pollution, Politics and International Law: Tankers at Sea* (Berkeley: University of California Press, 1979).

14. Winfried Lang, "The International Waste Regime," in *Environmental Protection and International Law*, ed. Winfried Lang, Hanspeter Neuhold and Karl Zemanek (London: Graham & Trotman, 1991), p. 148.

15. See, Andrew Hurrell and Benedict Kingsbury, ed., *The International Politics of the Environment* (Oxford: Clarendon Press, 1992).

16. Andrew Hurrell and Benedict Kingsbury, "The International Politics of the Environment: An Introduction," in *The International Politics of the Environment*, ed. Andrew Hurrell and Benedict Kingsbury (Oxford: Clarendon Press, 1992), p. 12.

17. Besides Hurrell and Kingsbury, others have advocated interdisciplinary work in this general area. See, Anne-Marie Slaughter Burley, "International Law and International Relations Theory: A Dual

Agenda," *American Journal of International Law* Vol. 87, No. 2 (1993), pp. 205–239. See also, Michael G. Schechter, "The New Haven School of International Law, Regime Theorists, Their Critics and Beyond," paper presented at the annual meeting of the International Studies Association, Acapulco, Mexico, March 1993, and Lynne M. Jurgielewicz, "International Regimes and Environmental Policy: An Evaluation of the Role of International Law," in *International Organizations and Environmental Policy*, ed. Robert Bartlett (Westport: Greenwood Press, 1995). Also, Abram Chayes and Antonia Chayes note in the abstract of their article that "a new dialogue is beginning between students of international law and international relations scholars concerning compliance with international agreements," "On Compliance," *International Organization*, Vol. 47, No. 2 (Spring 1993), pp. 175–205.

18. The definitions below were chosen to reflect the broad spectrum of the existing literature and are not inclusive.

19. See, for instance, Haggard and Simmons, "International Regimes," *supra*, n. 7. See also, Michael McGinnis and Elinor Ostrom, "Institutional Analysis and Global Climate Change: Design Principles For Robust International Regimes," where the authors concede lack of consensus on the meaning. Paper presented at the conference "Global Change,"sponsored by the Midwest Consortium for International Security Studies and Argonne National Laboratory, Chicago, Illinois (February, 1992), pp. 6–9, and Eckart Klein, "International Regimes," in R. Bernhard, ed., *Encyclopedia of Public International Law* Vol. 9, (Netherlands: Elsevier Science Publishers B.V., 1986), p. 202 where the author states that there is no generally accepted meaning of regimes. Regimes as defined in this book are distinct from the legal concept of "objective regimes," defined as treaties which create rights and duties for third states, such as treaty regimes for international waterways or demilitarization. While regimes as advocated in this book may eventually create third party duties or lead to formal treaties, they may not necessarily do so. Ian Brownlie, *Principles of Public International Law*, 4th ed. (Oxford: Clarendon Press, 1990), p. 633.

20. Goldie, "Special Regimes," *supra*, n. 6, p. 698.

21. Ibid.

22. Ibid., pp. 698–699. Goldie contrasted "special regimes" with regional arrangements by reason of the latter's geographical reference and because regional arrangements do not necessarily form a system reciprocating unilateral acts which lead to regimes, p. 676.

23. Krasner, "Structural Causes," *supra*, n. 8, p. 1.

24. Goldie, "Special Regimes," *supra*, n. 6, p. 698.

25. Krasner, "Structural Causes," *supra*, n. 8, p. 2.

26. *International Law in Theory and Practice*, *supra*, n. 4, p. 20.

27. Ibid.

28. Ibid., p. 21.

29. For example, Krasner lists reciprocity as an example of a principle. Krasner, "Structural Causes," *supra*, n. 8, p. 3. This seems similar to Schachter's definition of objective or policy. Decision-making procedures appear to mean the same.

30. Rosalyn Higgins, "The Role of Resolutions of International Organizations in the Process of Creating Norms in the International System," in *International Law and the International System*, ed. William E. Butler (Dordrecht: Martinus Nijhoff, 1987), p. 21.

31. See, Haggard and Simmons, "Theories of International Regimes," *supra*, n. 7, p. 494. Dissatisfaction with the meanings, however, can only lead to more research producing better understanding of regime theory.

32. This book is concerned with international law and thus the views of international legal scholars. For other general jurisprudential views see, Ronald Dworkin, *Taking Rights Seriously* (London: Duckworth and Co., 1977), who states that the law consists not just of rules, but of principles as well, which may conflict and must be weighed against each other. Principles cannot be identified simply by consulting sources, but only through a moral or political discussion of which principles should be used to justify black-letter law. For another view, see H.L.A. Hart, *The Concept of Law* (Oxford: Clarendon Press, 1961), who claims that law consists of a body of rules which emanate from certain sources, and that any lack of clarity results from the "open texture" of language. See, also, *supra*, Chapter 2, Positivists.

33. Not surprisingly, as Klein's definition appears in the *Encyclopedia of Public International Law*, *supra*, n. 19.

34. Ibid., p. 203. Lang similarly holds that regimes are established through framework conventions or protocols, Winfried Lang, "Diplomacy and International Environmental Law-Making: Some Observations," *Yearbook of International Environmental Law* Vol. 3 (1992), p. 120.

35. Still another definition states that although a regime "does not have any legal consequences *per se*," it is evidence of a "coherent subset of rules, subordinated to the universal system" forming "a framework bracket susceptible to recurring future application." Ingrid Detter De Lupis, *The Concept of International Law* (Stockholm: Norstedts, 1987), p. 40. This definition is at odds with the view of this author that regimes do have legal consequences.

36. Gehring, "International Environmental Regimes," *supra,* n. 13, p. 37.

37. Ibid.

38. Ibid., p. 38.

39. See, *supra*, Chapter 2, Policy-Oriented School and Policy-Oriented Lawmaking, where shared expectations give rise to legal obligations in the prescriptive process of lawmaking.

40. Gehring, "International Environmental Regimes," *supra*, n. 13, pp. 47–50.

41. Charles Lipson, "Why Are Some International Agreements Informal?", *International Organization*, Vol. 45, No. 4 (Autumn 1991), pp. 495–538. Lipson states that the choice between treaties and informal agreements is not based on whether it is "legally binding," which, for Lipson, is a misleading term since states must act for themselves to enforce their bargains. Rather, states choose treaties over informal arrangements when they wish to raise "the credibility of promises by staking national reputation on adherence." Ibid., p. 511. While agreeing with Lipson that states must decide for themselves whether to comply with their agreements, I do not agree that only formal treaties can raise the credibility of promises, since informal regimes can also create a source of legal obligation. See, *infra*, Chapter 3, The Legal Status of Regimes.

42. Goldie, "Special Regimes," *supra*, n. 6, p. 699. See, also, *supra*, Chapter 2, where the very general rules of international environmental law applicable to global environmental change are outlined.

43. Williamson, "International Environmental Regime," *supra*, n. 3, p. 739. He states that for the purposes of his paper, "it should be sufficient to note that nearly all regimes involve some use of international treaties and organizations (and thus international law), but have other critical elements which are not legal." Abbott did not pursue the "proper definition" of regime, alleging its relation to international law seemed likely to be sterile. Abbott, "International Relations Theory," *supra*, n. 13, p. 339.

44. Although Goldie saw regimes as more of an intermediate stage of formulation of rules while this book takes the view that norms and rules can evolve within the regime itself, his statement is still relevant here. See, "Special Regimes," *supra*, n. 6, pp. 80–81.

45. See, *infra*, Chapter 3, The Legal Status of Regimes.

46. See, *supra*, Chapter 2, Sources of International Law.

47. Gareth Porter and Janet Welsh Brown, *Global Environmental Politics* (Boulder, CO: Westview Press, 1991), p. 21. This argument is augmented by the ozone layer depletion regime, where the Vienna Ozone Convention and the adjustments and amendments to the Montreal Protocol allow for comparison of the norms at different points in the development of the regime, see, *infra*, Chapter 5. See also, Martin List and Volker Rittberger, "Regime Theory and International Environmental

Management," in *International Politics of the Environment*, ed. Andrew Hurrell and Benedict Kingsbury (Oxford: Clarendon Press, 1992), p. 89, where the authors state that regime identification "requires the observation of norm and rule guided behavior."

48. Williamson, "International Environmental Regime," *supra*, n. 3, p. 741. The author cites as an example the nuclear nonproliferation regime which includes two major treaties, an international organization, and other measures dealing with closely related issues such as export control, intelligence sharing and diplomacy.

49. Andrew Hurrell, "International Society and the Study of Regimes: A Reflective Approach," in *Regime Theory and International Relations*, ed. Volker Rittberger (Oxford: Clarendon Press, 1993), p. 54. See, also, List and Rittberger, "Regime Theory," *supra*, n. 47, pp. 89–90, and Porter and Brown, *Global Environmental Politics*, *supra*, n. 47, pp. 20–21.

50. Robert O. Keohane, *International Institutions and State Power* (Boulder, CO: Westview Press, 1989), p. 4.

51. Patricia Birnie, "International Environmental Law: Its Adequacy For Present and Future Needs," in *International Politics of the Environment*, ed. Andrew Hurrell and Benedict Kingsbury (Oxford: Clarendon Press, 1992), p. 57.

52. An examination of the recent texts dealing with the environment and cooperation may leave one feeling somewhat pessimistic, however. This is reflected in the scope of four recently published international relations books on the environment and cooperation: (1)Ian Rowlands and Malory Greene, ed., *Global Environmental Change and International Relations* (Basingstoke: Macmillan, 1991); (2)Porter and Brown, *Global Environmental Politics*, *supra*, n. 47; (3)Caroline Thomas, *The Environment in International Relations* (London: Royal Institute of International Affairs, 1992); and (4)Andrew Hurrell and Benedict Kingsbury, ed., *The International Politics of the Environment* (Oxford; Clarendon Press, 1992). Only Hurrell and Kingsbury give adequate space to the important linkage between international relations and international law in environmental cooperation, although Porter and Brown make a point of defining regimes in terms of legal instruments. Rowlands and Greene allot space only to a traditional analysis of the formal legal institutions involved in environmental cooperation, and Thomas does not allude to the role of law at all, except to formal legal instruments already in place. International legal scholars, of course, are in no position to cast the first stone, as their work has not often taken account of the work of international relations scholars.

53. This requires a policy-oriented approach to international law, see, *supra*, Chapter 2, Policy-Oriented School and Policy-Oriented Lawmaking.

54. See, Haggard and Simmons, "International Regimes," *supra*, n. 7.

55. Krasner, "Structural Causes," *supra*, n. 8, pp. 5–10. See also, Tony Evans and Peter Wilson, "Regime Theory and the English School of International Relations: A Comparison," *Millennium: Journal of International Relations* Vol. 21, No. 3 (Winter 1992), pp. 329–351.

56. Evans and Wilson, "Regime Theory," *supra*, n. 55, p. 330. See also, Susan Strange, "Cave! Hic Dragones: A Critique of Regime Analysis," in *International Regimes*, ed. Stephen D. Krasner (Ithaca: Cornell University Press, 1983), pp. 337–354.

57. Krasner, "Structural Causes," *supra*, n. 8, p. 7. See also, Robert O. Keohane, "The Demand For International Regimes," in *International Regimes*, ed. Stephen D. Krasner (Ithaca: Cornell University Press, 1983) pp. 141–171.

58. Krasner, "Structural Causes," *supra*, n. 8, p. 8. See also, Donald J. Puchala and Raymond F. Hopkins, "International Regimes: Lessons From Inductive Analysis," in *International Regimes*, ed. Stephen D. Krasner (Ithaca: Cornell University Press, 1983) pp. 61–91.

59. Puchala and Hopkins, "International Regimes," *supra*, n. 58, p. 62. This closely parallels what Haggard and Simmons have characterized as the cognitive approach, *supra*, n. 7.

60. Evans and Wilson, "Regime Theory," *supra*, n. 55, p. 331.

61. Puchala and Hopkins, "International Regimes," *supra*, n. 58, p. 86.

62. "Pollution From Nuclear Accidents," in *International Law and Pollution*, ed. Daniel Magraw (Philadelphia: University of Pennsylvania Press, 1991), p. 204. See also, Goldie, "Special Regimes," *supra*, n. 6, p. 698.

63. "International Environmental Regimes," *supra*, n. 13, p. 37.

64. "Building the International Environmental Regime," *supra*, n. 3, p. 741.

65. Ibid., p. 743. Although the author was referring to "complex regimes,"his analysis applies to simple regimes as well.

66. See, *supra*, Chapter 2, Policy-Oriented School. Emphasis on shared expectations does not mean that international legal specialists naively ignore the concept of power among states. Indeed, Schachter points out that"[n]early all... regimes are seriously affected by the differentiation in power among their members," *International Law in Theory and Practice*, *supra*, n. 4, p. 80. Indeed, power or control is

necessary under the policy-oriented school, along with an authority signal, if shared expectations are to be sustained. See, *supra*, Chapter 2, Policy-Oriented Lawmaking.

67. Put more bluntly, it is necessary to stress national [self] interest, "because [there's] not a lot of morality around." Professor Stuart Harris, "The Environment and International Relations," speech given at the Royal Institute of International Affairs, London, May 1992.

68. Hurrell, "International Society and the Study of Regimes," *supra*, n. 49.

69. Schachter, *International Law in Theory and Practice*, *supra*, n. 4, p. 61. See, also, Oscar Schachter, *Sharing the World's Resources* (NY: Columbia University Press, 1977) pp. 142–143.

70. Birnie, "International Environmental Law," *supra*, n. 51 p. 84.

71. Puchala and Hopkins, "International Regimes," *supra*, n. 58, p. 66.

72. Ibid., p. 87. See also, Evans and Wilson, "Regime Theory," *supra*, n. 55, p. 331, where the authors point out the Grotian claim "that a purely formal understanding of regimes-one that concentrates on bargaining and negotiating procedures, legal rules and concrete international organizations-does not take proper account of the prevailing social environment..." such as non-state actors.

73. See, *supra*, Chapter 2, Policy-Oriented Lawmaking for a description of the prescriptive process for identifying shared expectations.

74. Myres S. McDougal and Harold D. Lasswell, "The Identification and Appraisal of Diverse Systems of Public Order," *American Journal of International Law*, Vol. 53, No. 1 (January 1959), p. 8.

75. There is a hierarchy, then, among the aspects of a regime from the standpoint of utility. Most important is the maintenance or development of a regime (including compliance), the 2nd most important is the formation, and the 3rd is the definition. From the standpoint of legal theory, however, formation cannot be overlooked since the formation of a regime creates legal obligations. See, *supra*, Chapter 3, Formation of Regimes. See, *infra*, Chapter 4, for the discussion of the development of regimes with regard to critical issues and catalysts, and Chapters 5 and 6 for analyses of this development.

76. See, *supra*, Chapter 3, for discussion of cognitive expectations.

77. Ibid.

78. See, *infra*, Chapter 4, Catalysts.

79. Gehring, "International Environmental Regimes," *supra*, n. 13, p. 37.

80. *International Law in Theory and Practice*, *supra*, n. 4, p. 81. Schachter is referring to an advanced stage of development for regimes, after a treaty has evolved.

81. Birnie, "International Environmental Law," *supra*, n. 51, p. 84.

82. Williamson, "Building the International Environmental Regime," *supra*, n. 3, p. 740 and Puchala and Hopkins, "International Regimes," *supra*, n. 58, p. 87, advocating the Grotian model.

83. See Strange, "Cave! Hic Dragones: A Critique of Regime Analysis," *supra*, n. 56, p. 337, who claims that regimes have little impact on outcomes and behavior and subsequently should be dismissed as a passing academic fad.

84. See, *supra*, Chapter 2, Policy-Oriented School and Policy-Oriented Lawmaking.

85. W. Michael Reisman, "International Lawmaking: A Process of Communication," *Proceedings of the American Society of International Law* (1981), p. 113.

86. Friedrich V. Kratochwil, *Rules, Norms and Decisions* (Cambridge: Cambridge University Press, 1989), p. 205. In regimes, of course, the rule handlers are usually the regime members. Similarly, Gehring states that non-formalized regime norms and rules share the same "legally significant expectations" as formalized rules, as both types are based on consensus, "International Environmental Regimes," *supra*, n. 13, p. 55.

87. Hurrell and Kingsbury, "Introduction," *supra*, n. 16, p. 25. Although the authors were speaking about environmental law and environmental regimes, the point can be extrapolated to international law and international regimes.

88. Oscar Schachter, "Towards a Theory of International Obligation," *Virginia Journal of International Law* Vol. 8, No. 2 (1968) p. 322.

89. See, *infra*, Chapters 5 and 6 for analyses of the ozone layer depletion and climate change regimes.

90. *International Law In Theory and Practice*, *supra*, n. 4, p. 372.

91. Ibid.

92. See, Johnston, "Systemic Environmental Damage: The Challenge to International Law and Organization," *supra*, n. 13, p. 270.

93. Williamson, "Building the International Environmental Regime," *supra*, n. 3, p. 740.

94. Gehring, "International Environmental Regimes," *supra*, n. 13, p. 38.

95. For international relations specialists looking at compliance and effectiveness within regimes, see, for example, Peter M. Haas, Robert O. Keohane and Marc A. Levy, ed., *Institutions For The Earth* (Cambridge: MIT Press, 1993).

96. See, for example, Roger Fisher, *Improving Compliance with International Law* (Charlottesville, VA: University of Virginia Press, 1981) and William E. Butler, ed., *Control Over Compliance With International Law* (Dordrecht: Martinus Nijhoff, 1991).

97. Thomas M. Franck, *The Power of Legitimacy Among Nations* (New York: Oxford University Press, 1990), p. 206. For Franck, a rule is considered legitimate and therefore has a stronger compliance pull if it has been created in the correct "process," if there is adherence between the rule and the standards by which it is made, interpreted and applied, and the rule is determinate, has undergone symbolic validation and is coherent. In this respect, he uses a similar approach to the policy-oriented approach to lawmaking, which requires for legal obligation that the target audience view share expectations that have ben created in an authoritative manner and are likely to be complied with. While Franck is concerned with *compliance* and the policy-oriented school with *legal obligation*, their reasoning is similar in their different pursuits.

98. An effective level of compliance "will reflect the perspectives and interests of participants in the ongoing political process rather than some external scientific or market-validated standard," Abram Chayes and Antonia Chayes, "On Compliance," *International Organization* Vol. 47, No. 2 (Spring 1993), p. 202. Thus, an acceptable level of compliance rises as the regime strengthens, demanding more of its members. These compliance methods will be further examined in an analysis of the climate change and ozone layer depletion regimes, *infra*, Chapters 5 and 6.

99. See *supra*, n. 39.

100. *International Law in Theory and Practice, supra*, n. 4, p. 75. Although Schachter was referring to regimes that include a treaty, his comment still applies to regimes as defined in this book, see, *infra*, Chapters 5 and 6.

101. "Special Regimes," *supra*, n. 6, p. 698.

102. See *supra*, Chapter 2, Policy-Oriented Lawmaking.

103. See, *supra*, n. 39.

104. Chapter 5, *infra*.

105. Gehring, "International Environmental Regimes," *supra*, n. 13, p. 55.

106. Reisman, "International Lawmaking," *supra*, n. 85, p. 109.

107. Williamson, "Building the International Environmental Regime," *supra*, n. 3, p. 743.

108. Higgins, "Role of Resolutions," *supra*, n. 30, p. 23.

109. See, *infra*, Chapter 4.

110. See, *supra*, n. 39.

111. *International Law in Theory and Practice*, *supra*, n. 4, p. 75.

112. Joan E. Donoghue, "Legal Dimensions of Compliance and Dispute Resolution in a Global Climate Regime," paper given at the annual conference of the International Studies Association, Atlanta, Georgia (April 1992), pp. 9–11. The author is writing from her experiences as a legal adviser for the US State Department.

113. Gehring, "International Environmental Regimes," *supra*, n. 13, p. 54.

114. Jill Barrett, "The Negotiation and Drafting of the Climate Change Convention," in *International Law and Global Climate Change*, ed. Robin Churchill and David Freestone (London: Graham & Trotman, 1991), p. 200.

115. See, Lynne M. Jurgielewicz, "The Role of International Law in Non-Judicial Methods of Dispute Settlement," unpublished LLM thesis, London School of Economics and Political Science, 1989.

116. While dispute settlement mechanisms could technically be considered a method of accountability, they are treated separately in this work.

117. Abram Chayes and Antonia H. Chayes, "Adjustment and Compliance Processes in International Regulatory Regimes," in *Preserving The Global Environment*, ed. Jessica Tuchman Mathews (New York: W.W. Norton & Co., 1991), p. 290.

118. See, Glen Plant, "'Pledge and Review': A Survey of Precedents," in Michael Grubb and Nicola Steen, *Pledge and Review Processes: Possible Components of a Climate Convention* (London: Royal Institute of International Affairs, 1991), pp. V–XIV, where the author examines the pledge and review precedents of the IMO and IMF, among others.

119. See, for instance, Geoffrey Palmer, "New Ways To Make International Environmental Law," *American Journal of International Law* Vol. 86, No. 2 (April 1992), pp. 278–282; Glen Plant, "Institutional and Legal Responses to Global Warming," in *International Law and Global Climate Change*, ed. Robin Churchill and David Freestone, pp. 175–181, (London: Graham & Trotman, 1991); Elizabeth P. Barratt-Brown, "Building a Monitoring and Compliance Regime Under the Montreal Protocol," *Yale Journal of International Law* Vol. 16, No. 2 (Summer 1991), p. 569; and more generally, Fisher, *Improving Compliance With International Law*, *supra*, n. 96, esp. Chapter 10.

120. Haas, Keohane and Levy distinguish between regimes and bureaucratic organizations, with regimes being "rule-structures that do not necessarily have organizations attached." See, Peter M. Haas, Robert O. Keohane and Marc A. Levy, "The Effectiveness of International Environmental Institutions," in *Institutions For The Earth*, ed. Peter M. Haas, Robert O. Keohane and Marc A. Levy (Cambridge: MIT Press, 1993), p. 5.

121. See, *infra*, chapter 4, for a discussion of international organizations as catalysts for regime formation and formation.

122. Schachter, *International Law in Theory and Practice*, *supra*, n. 4, p. 75.

123. "Special Regimes," *supra*, n. 6, p. 698.

124. Keohane, *After Hegemony*, *supra*, n. 7, p. 106.

125. Keohane lists three examples: 1) only members of the International Energy Agency can receive oil under its emergency sharing program 2) only members of the International Monetary Fund are entitled to borrow funds from the IMF, and 3) GATT can exclude uncooperative members from its benefits, such as most favored nation status. Ibid., pp. 77–78.

126. General Agreement on Tariffs and Trade, 61 Statute A3, 55 United Nations Treaty Series 187. The US argued that Art. XX(b), which allows trade restrictions "necessary to protect human, animal or plant life or health" and Art. XX(g) which allows restrictions "relating to the conservation of exhaustible natural resources if such measures are made effective in conjunction with restriction or domestic production or consumption" permitted the trade restrictions placed on Mexican tuna.

127. Decision reprinted in *International Legal Materials*, Vol. 30, No. 6 (1991), pp. 1598–1623. See, GATT, "Trade and the Environment," *International Trade 90-91*, Vol. 1 (Geneva: GATT, 1992), p. 25.

128. The Panel suggested that if parties wanted to allow environmental trade restrictions, they would need to agree on limits to prevent abuse. Since GATT does not provide such limits, the Panel suggested that Parties amend or supplement the provisions of GATT or provide a waiver. GATT, "Trade and the Environment," *supra*, n. 127, p. 27.

129. *International Legal Materials*, Vol. 26, No. 6 (1987), pp. 1541–1561.

130. The Panel ruling may undermine the trade embargo provision of the Protocol, which discourages free-riders. Although the Panel had excluded from its opinion multilateral agreements where parties have agreed to waive their GATT rights, the trade embargo affects non-parties who have not waived any rights since they are not Parties to the Protocol. The panel decision also affects the Protocol's potential ban on products produced with ozone-depleting chemicals, since it would require states

to distinguish between products on the basis of production. See, Eric Christensen and Samantha Geffin, "GATT Sets Its Net On Environmental Regulation: The GATT Panel Ruling on Mexican Yellowfin Tuna Imports and the Need for Reform of the International Trading System," *University of Miami Inter-American Law Review* Vol. 23, No. 2 (Winter 1991-92), p. 598. However, there was (unusually) no request for adoption through Council confirmation, apparently for political reasons. Mexico, undergoing negotiations with the United States for the North American Free Trade Agreement, did not wish to hamper those negotiations. Mexico was also under pressure from environmentalists to remedy its own environmental laws, which it has since done, and thus now conforms with the US regulations for tuna-fishing.

131. "EFTA Members Press Convening of Working Party," *Focus: GATT Newsletter* No. 82 (July 1991), p. 2. See also, Charles Arden-Clarke, "South-North Terms of Trade-Environmental Protection and Sustainable Development," *International Environmental Affairs* Vol. 4, No. 2 (Spring 1992), pp. 122–138.

132. GATT, "Trade and the Environment," *supra*, n. 127, p. 21. See also, J. Owen Saunders, "Trade and Environment: The Fine Line Between Environmental Protection and Environmental Protectionism," *International Journal* Vol. XLVII, No. 4 (Autumn 1992), pp. 723–750.

133. Patricia Birnie and Alan Boyle, *International Law & The Environment* (Oxford: Clarendon Press, 1992), p. 408. The provision were deemed necessary to protect health.

134. The Vienna Convention on Treaties states that when two treaties conflict between a party to both treaties and a party to only one, then mutual rights and obligations are determined by the treaty to which both are parties. Art. 30, *International Legal Materials* Vol. 8, No. 4 (1969), pp. 679–735.

135. See, for instance, the Agora exchange between Thomas J. Schoenbaum, "Free International Trade and Protection of the Environment: Irreconcilable Conflict?" *American Journal of International Law* Vol. 86, No. 4 (October 1992), pp. 700–727 and Edith Brown Weiss, "Environment and Trade as Partners in Sustainable Development: A Commentary," *American Journal of International Law* Vol. 86, No. 4 (October 1992), pp. 728–735.

136. Comments of Edith Brown Weiss, "Issues Relating to the 1992 Brazil Conference on the Environment," in *American Society of International Law: Proceedings of the 86th Annual Meeting*, by the American Society of International Law, Washington, DC, 1992, p. 422.

137. It could also be considered a time of reckoning for international law in that if the discipline remains tied to its traditional positivist

past, then prospects for progress are dimmed, since the concept of regimes demands a non-traditional view of international law.

CHAPTER 4

Critical Issues and Catalysts for Effective Climate Change and Ozone Layer Depletion Regimes in the International Legal Order

The real longer-term challenge is not external to ourselves but is our own understanding and how we relate to one another.[1]

For regimes to "matter" in the international legal order, they need to be effective. This is measured in part by the strength of the regime's normative or shared expectations (norms and rules) adopted by the regime members.[2] These in turn are dependent on the degree to which cognitive expectations (knowledge) have been accepted regarding critical issues particular to the regime. These normative expectations, in order to maintain or develop the regime, must move beyond the basic expectations necessary to form the regime.[3] The degree of clarity regarding uncertainty is not as important as the degree of unity regarding the critical issues. In addition, there are catalysts that can help create and further develop the regime.

CRITICAL ISSUES

In the climate change and ozone layer depletion regimes, the critical issues are science, economics and development. Climate change and ozone layer depletion are both scientific based problems with economic ramifications and which need the full cooperation of all states, including developing states. Without substantial agreement on these issues, the climate change regime will flounder and the ozone layer depletion regime would have floundered.[4] The uncertainty beyond each of these issues will be examined, followed by an examination of how regimes can overcome this uncertainty. Finally, the secondary issues that may act as catalysts in the creation and/or maintenance or development of these regimes will be examined: leadership; international non-state actors; crisis; and domestic regulations.[5] These critical and catalytic issues will be applied to the climate change and ozone layer depletion regimes in the following chapters.

The Critical Issue of Science

Both climate change and ozone layer depletion were brought to the attention of the world by scientists. The certainty of the science, then, is a critical issue for both problems.

Scientific Uncertainty

In Chapter 1, the general scientific background concerning climate change resulting from global warming was explained. While much progress has been made concerning the causes of climate change, there still remains a significant amount of scientific uncertainty regarding potential effects, particularly on the extent and rate of change.[6] Because of this uncertainty, the debate continues as to whether abatement or adjustment through adaptation and mitigation techniques ("no regrets")[7] is the best approach to climate change.[8] Similarly, while scientific certainty is presently greater for ozone layer depletion than for climate change, that was not always the case.[9]

Because the prospect of damage on a global level arises from climate change and ozone layer depletion, the possibility of this "non-discrimination" among states can influence to a great extent the development of regimes. However, the greatest chance at influence may be not when there is greater scientific certainty, but when there is less.[10] At that point in time, when it is unclear as to where the damage will occur, more states would be willing to insure against a possible risk than if the risk were known to occur outside the individual state's jurisdiction.[11] This may not be a fair or equitable decision on the part of the non-affected state, but it will probably be the case that unaffected countries would be less willing to contribute to legal attempts to control global environmental change. When evidence surfaces that the global nature of the problem may in fact be more regional, then there is less likelihood that abatement will be stressed. Instead, an adaptative approach may be taken instead.[12]

But even if there was 100% scientific certainty as to effects, "science alone cannot save the environment. Political choice is required to translate the findings of the environmental sciences into viable policies."[13] It is important that the international legal order take into account this "politicization"[14] of scientific uncertainty, since it is necessary for cooperation between states.

Notwithstanding the need for political action, science is still called upon to provide evidence from which law and policy can be derived. One way to deal with scientific uncertainty is to utilize an economic cost-analysis calculation whereby states estimate the extent of damage that would occur from an environmental problem, and then multiply that amount by the probability that the damage will occur. A comparison is then made to the costs entailed in abatement or adaptation to the problem and an attempt is made to resolve the problem at minimal cost and with minimal damages.[15] This approach is often criticized, however, for failure to take adequately into account losses not traditionally viewed as economic, such as aesthetic value.[16] Nevertheless, regardless of how economically-oriented adaptation or abatement programs may be, the burden of scientific certainty ultimately returns to science and the production of sufficient evidence to create a need for policy action.

The degree of certainty that science is required to achieve before policy action is taken is in itself uncertain.[17] A former Administrator of the US Environmental Protection Agency has put the issue in quite clear perspective:

> The difficulty of converting scientific findings into political action is a function of the uncertainty of the science and the pain generated by the action.[18]

One researcher has attempted to develop a list of characteristics outlining when science is likely to have an impact on law and policy; in effect, when science has achieved a sufficient degree of certainty.[19] According to this finding, this is likely to occur when there is evidence of:

'Definite' or at least consensual conclusion;
Feasible 'cure' available;
Effects close in time and (social) space;
Problem affecting 'social center' of society;
Problem developing rapidly and surprisingly;
Effects experienced by or at least visible to the public;
Political conflict:low;
Issue linkage: none, or on substantive merits only;
Institutionalized setting, iterative decision-making.

Conversely, science is deemed to be too uncertain to have an impact when there is evidence of:

Tentative or contested hypothesis;
'Cure' unclear or not feasible;
Effects remote;
Problem affecting 'periphery' only;
Problem developing slowly and according to expectations;
Effects not (yet) experienced by or visible to the public;
Political conflict: high;
Tactical issue linkage, issue 'contamination';
Not institutionalized, ad hoc decision-making.

While lists such as the one above can be good indicators of determining a sufficient level of certainty for international action, interpretations will differ.[20] An acceptable level of certainty of science, however, cannot be determined solely on its own merits, by the science itself. The uncertainty will yield not to greater certainty, but to unity or the shaping of cognitive expectations regarding an acceptable amount of uncertainty. Achieving unity is due to some influence beyond pure scientific interpretation.

Overcoming Scientific Uncertainty

Scientific uncertainty may be overcome by the influence that the scientific community maintains with respect to policy-making.[21] For example:

> Science was not the driving force in the making of the Brundtland Report. Although some premises were delivered by scientists, generally they were not attributed much weight. Nor were the main conclusions scientifically founded. ...The report is a political document, not a scientific one.[22]

One of the studies examining the influence of the scientific community in environmental policy-making,[23] undertaken by Peter Haas, attributes the influence of scientists to their role as an "epistemic community," defined as "transnational networks of knowledge-based communities that are both politically empowered through their claims to exercise authoritative knowledge and motivated by shared causal and principled beliefs."[24] Members of an epistemic community share common values, a common body of facts, and interpret those facts or observations in the same manner.[25] Even though the members may belong to different scientific disciplines, they all share a common world view and concern about the same subject matter, and would offer similar advice if consulted.[26]

In order to create an international influence, a national epistemic community must eventually expand into an international epistemic community. This will enable the community to "infiltrate" government agencies of more than one state. The influence of these communities will be more pronounced if they are successful in the states that play a major role in regimes concerning the issues involved. The communities do not have to be large — what matters is that they are respected within their discipline and are able to extend their influence to those involved in decision-making.[27]

Haas maintains, however, that the influence of an epistemic community cannot always be generalized to all environmental problems. Nevertheless, Oran Young argues that science can play a role in placing certain issues on the international scene that might otherwise have never come to light without scientific research.[28] "Agenda setting," according to Young is most effective when scientists are able to reach consensus among themselves and "overcome [their] natural tendency... to exhibit extreme caution in the interests of avoiding any appearance of overstating the inferences to be drawn from the available evidence."[29] Scientists must have had some success in this regard; climate change and ozone layer depletion have surely reached a point of some priority on the international agenda of governments.[30]

But under what circumstances will scientists influence policy-making? It would seem that the most influential position of scientists would be inside government.[31] The Brookings Institution has undertaken a study of the effectiveness of scientific advisers within government agencies and has attributed successful integration to the following factors: 1) a clear charter or mandate; 2) an identifiable client or point of access to the government agency; 3) an active chairman; 4) a well-chosen and fairly balanced committee; and 5) adequate supporting resources from the agency and commitment of time from the members.[32] Without these factors present, an advisory committee can end up languishing within government bureaucracy instead of having their concerns heard.

The extent of influence may also depend on the familiarity of the government with the issue. If the government is unfamiliar with the issue, the advisers may be more influential in contributing to the choice of policy-making. If government is familiar with the issue, then the advisers may be involved in defending and promoting government policies rather than choosing them.[33]

Some scholars argue that putting the ultimate advisory burden on science has:

> allowed the decision-makers to divest themselves of the responsibility for the decisions which should be theirs, and theirs alone, to take and has pushed that responsibility onto the scientific method... [T]he scientific method cannot sustain such a responsibility.[34]

Nor should it — the responsibility of implementing legal regulations rests with governments, not scientists. Yet there probably is little choice regarding some degree of responsibility for scientists: the media will not wait for scientific certainty. All the scientist can do is to attempt to put the environmental risks in proper perspective for the public and the decision-makers, helping to shape cognitive expectations along the way. This is not easy, however, as one prominent scientist has pointed out:

> On the one hand, we are ethically bound to the scientific method...which means that we must include all the doubts, caveats, ifs and buts. On the other hand, we are not just scientists, but human beings as well. And like most people we'd like to see the world a better place... To do that we have to get some broad-based support, to capture the public's imagination. That, of course, entails getting loads of media coverage. So we have to offer up scary scenarios, make simplified, dramatic statements, and make little mention of any doubts we might have. This 'double ethical bind' that we frequently find ourselves in cannot be solved by any formula. Each of us has to decide that the right balance is between being effective and being honest. I hope that means being both.[35]

The Critical Issue of Economics

Economic concerns are always important in any international issue and climate change and ozone layer depletion are no exceptions. However, economic concerns can be overcome or alleviated through financial mechanisms.

Economic Uncertainty

Uncertainty regarding climate change resulting from global warming and ozone layer depletion does not lie exclusively within the realm of science; economic uncertainty will also have an effect on the successful implementation of these regimes, particularly climate change, as economists cannot be sure of the financial impact on global economies.[36]

Climate Change Economics

The most intensive studies of overall damage costs regarding climate change have been undertaken for the United States; studies for other countries are fragmentary, and general conclusions cannot be drawn from them yet.[37] Yet even the two major US studies differ in their projections of total damage costs to the

United States. The Cline study estimates the cumulative costs to the United States of a doubling of CO_2 equivalent concentrations of all greenhouse gases from preindustrial concentrations to be approximately five times greater than the estimate in the Nordhaus study. Cline estimated the damages to be approximately 1981 US$30 billion as opposed to approximately 1981 US$6 billion estimated by Nordhaus.[38]

Cline assumes greater risk from climate change in his calculation than does Nordhaus. For Cline, the "greenhouse effect poses major risks, especially over the very long term of two to three centuries, by which time temperature could rise by as much as 10-18ºC."[39] Nordhaus, on the other hand, is decidedly more optimistic about potential damage costs.[40]

These evaluations are specific to the United States and damages for other states may be larger or smaller. Cline estimates that developed countries at the mid-latitudes might expect to experience comparable damage, while states at higher latitudes might have less damage. For developing states, he estimates damage to be more costly since those states rely more heavily upon agricultural income, thought to be the economic sector likely to be most severely affected.[41] In addition, developing states are more limited in their capacity to absorb climate change damage from a financial perspective.[42]

It also must be remembered that these estimates, while consistent with the known facts of climate change, are at best two possible scenarios: "This is not science; it is metaphysics: value judgements and political goals will enter into the determination of whether [damage cost] exists."[43]

Economic uncertainty, then, is also subject to "politicization."[44]

Abatement vs. "No Regrets"[45]

In addition to cost related to damage, there is the cost of either abatement or a "no regrets" approach to climate change. Economics-based arguments for and against taking significant action to slow global warming abound. Climate stabilization or the abatement approach advocates cautionary safeguards against the risk of possibly severe future costs. Thus, climate stabilization at a tolerable level of temperature change arguably provides insurance against unknown risks.[46]

The opposing argument of "no regrets" suggest that states adapt to and mitigate climate changes, rather than to attempt to prevent these changes outright. In this area, the work of William Nordhaus is prominent in the relevant literature. He advocates adaptation to and mitigation of global warming as he estimates the economic benefits to be gained by abatement are not that great, at least for the industrialized states.[47] The most recent report of the National Academy of Sciences also advocates a policy of adaptation and mitigation rather than abatement of climate change, at least for the United States.[48] This is because only 3% of US gross domestic product is produced through agriculture and forest products, so the US economy would not be badly affected by a shift in agricultural zones caused by climate change.[49]

Nordhaus warns that reducing greenhouse gas emissions inefficiently or too quickly through strict emission caps will result in unnecessarily higher economic costs and lower economic growth than policies which are more efficient, such as taxes placed on carbon content of emissions,[50] and which are introduced gradually.[51]

Nordhaus points out that since the climate does not have a large economic impact upon the industrialized states, affecting under 1% of total national income, then adaptation would prove economically more beneficial than abatement for those states.[52] However, less developed and poorer countries, that are heavily dependent upon agriculture which is particularly sensitive to climate change, will be harder hit economically by global warming.[53] Although he recognizes this possibility, Nordhaus nevertheless advocates international cooperation, including aid to developing states, more research and development of new technologies, taxes on emissions of greenhouse gases, and a "no regrets" policy whereby mitigation measures that are *otherwise economically beneficial* are implemented.[54] These actions presumably would not have a detrimental impact on economic growth, thus allowing for a greater possibility of third-world aid as well as allowing for growth in less-developed states. This concern for the developing states is shared by others, including the British economist Wilfred Beckerman, who argues that the third world cannot afford to make economic sacrifices now in order to improve the future global environment.[55] As in the case of scientific uncertainty,[56] there is criticism of the above cost-benefit analysis of climate change, as opposed to a purely preventive or abatement approach, in that it fails to take certain factors into account. These include loss of species, global catastrophe or the fact that reducing fossil fuel consumption will aid in fighting other environmental problems such as acid rain and urban smog.[57] In addition, fears of a rapidly increasing global population contributing greater amounts of greenhouse gas emissions have added to the debate. A 1993 study estimates that global population will reach 8.5 billion by 2025, with most growth coming in the developed world.[58] While concerns over rapid population growth leading to increased greenhouse gas emissions include all of the developing world, there is a special concern regarding Asia, where more than half of the world's 5.4 billion population live. Asia's rise in population in addition to rapid economic growth is expected to cause a "massive increase in combustion of fossil fuels in the region over the next decade, dangerously raising levels of gases in the atmosphere that cause global warming."[59] This will raise the economic cost associated with climate change.

A compromise approach to the cost-benefit analysis is suggested by Professor David Pearce, a leading UK environmental economist. Pearce advocates pursuing the cost-analysis approach in general terms, because it is well-formulated for pursuing the optimal mix of adaptation to, and abatement of, global warming. He cautions, however, that the results will need to be examined very carefully since, inter alia, estimates for damage may be too low.[60] As an alternative to strict cost-benefit analysis, Pearce argues that a zone of unknown risk or warming threshold should be detected. Once that is detected, targets should be set to avoid moving beyond that threshold and incurring catastrophic impacts.[61] While these targets may be achieved through emission permits, Pearce follows Nordhaus in advocating carbon taxes for reaching targets.[62]

Methods to Control Greenhouse Gas Emissions: Carbon Taxes or a Quota System?

Carbon taxes face difficult implementation problems. These include choosing which gases to tax, as well as the amount of tax, which could place a burden on developing states.[63] One solution might be to tax various greenhouse gases at their differential rate of estimated contribution to global warming, or "global warming potential."[64] These estimated configurations must be used cautiously, however, in view of changing scientific knowledge regarding their global warming potential.[65]

Additionally, there are concerns over control and allocation of the accrued funds such as how they are to be levied and by whom.[66] Cline maintains that the tax should at first be levied and collected nationally, since revenues from carbon taxes sufficient to cause major emissions reductions would be so large as to make states unwilling to submit to an international tax authority. Eventually, the system might be harmonized on an international level.[67]

Also, carbon taxes cannot guarantee the amount of reduction of carbon emissions; that depends on the response of energy users and suppliers.[68] Nevertheless, Pearce maintains that economists advocate carbon taxes as the most economically efficient way to reduce emissions.[69]

A quota system is an alternative to a carbon tax. Cline maintains that the main reason for considering a quota system is income distribution equity. Thus, developing states may be more financially able to support a quota system than an outright tax. The difficulty is in setting the correct quotas of "carbon rights."[70]

Emission permits and subsequent trading of the permits may be able to make a quota system more economically efficient, if permits are set at the same price as a carbon tax generating an identical cut in emissions. These, however, present their own problems: the arrangements for allocation as well as trading will be difficult to create and maintain.[71] In addition, permit trading might lead to industries abandoning investment in compliance mechanisms or research and development, if purchasing permits proved cheaper than compliance. Nevertheless, advocates of permits stress the practicality of such a system since states retain sovereign control over transfers and most of the transfers will take place bilaterally rather than multilaterally, minimizing the need for international bureaucracy.[72] Permits also ensure that emissions do not exceed a certain level, although they cannot guarantee the costs as well as a carbon tax can and so are subject to energy price fluctuations.[73]

Ozone Layer Depletion Economics

The economic uncertainty behind ozone layer depletion is of a different nature than that for climate change described above. The rise in greenhouse gas emissions exacerbating the problem of climate change results mostly from fossil fuel combustion in connection with industrial production, needed for the maintenance of society.[74] While the total amount of these emissions can be scaled back, the sources of global warming cannot realistically be replaced, with the exception of CFCs and HCFCs.

Ozone depleting substances on the other hand, such as CFCs and HCFCs, can more realistically be substituted for, as their use is primarily confined to those sectors of industry that provide a higher standard of living, such as electronics, refrigeration, pesticides and computers.[75] While arguments could be made that these uses are necessary for society and that phasing out ozone depleting substances could lower a standard of living or prevent development, these substances are not as critical to society as fossil fuels. The focus of ozone layer depletion economics was, and remains, on the uncertain cost of substitutes and alternative processes.

The major obstacle to replacement is industries which make or utilize these substances, and who fear large economic costs for replacement as well as the costs for research and development of the replacements.[76] An additional concern is that replacements might be considered ozone depleting themselves, making them subject to replacement as well[77] and further driving up costs. For ozone layer depletion, then, economic uncertainty revolves around replacement costs. This will be examined in greater detail in an analysis of the ozone layer depletion regime.[78]

Overcoming Economic Uncertainty

As with scientists and scientific uncertainty, the economists are also divided as to the correct policy approach to resolving these problems.[79] Yet, if climate change and ozone layer depletion regimes are to be strengthened, economic uncertainties must be resolved.[80]

In order to help alleviate the economic concerns of climate change, William Cline has suggested a two stage approach whereby a first stage would include a "best-efforts," but not legally binding, international commitment to limit carbon emissions by 2000 to 1990 levels.[81] A second stage, if warranted by greater scientific certainty by the year 2000, would include stricter regulations, such as carbon taxes or tradeable permits.[82] Cline argues that this approach would be both economically attractive as well as risk-averse.

While Cline's approach to climate change may be economically efficient, the underlying concerns of economic uncertainty with respect to climate change still need to be addressed and developed. This includes the development of affordable technologies to help reduce the emissions of greenhouse gases. In addition, industries need to be convinced that using energy more efficiently can in fact be economically beneficial.[83] These issues, as well as the unknown costs concerning potential costs of damage, make economics a critical issue that must be addressed in the climate change regime.

Overcoming these economic concerns also needed to be addressed regarding ozone layer depletion. While at first, there had been warnings of severe economic consequences, by 1986 there was a more optimistic assessment.[84] At the present time, replacement availability looks particularly promising.[85]

The Critical Issue of Development

Traditionally, developing states have had little influence in matters of international concern, mostly due to lack of economic power. But in the area of the environment, the developing world has become "empowered" by its potential capacity for emitting greenhouse gases and contributing to climate change as well as ozone layer depletion. The development issue, then, has also become subject to politicization.[86] Their views must now be taken into account and their uncertain contribution to environmental problems addressed for a viable regime to evolve.

Development Uncertainty

"Intentional violations are not the norm in international law. Far more common are cases in which a country simply lacks the financial or technical capabilities needed to comply."[87] The extent to which developing countries will actually prosper economically and further their greenhouse gas emissions is unknown, and the exact degree to which such developing states will require technology and financing to implement international regulations regarding global warming is also unknown.[88] Such "development uncertainty" has played and will continue to play a large role in the negotiations of a climate change treaty, revealing the need for a flexible, responsive legal order.[89]

The majority of greenhouse gas emissions are at the present time attributed to the industrialized world. However, the less-developed states are poised to take the lead in overall emissions upon attaining a certain level of development and population. By 2100, it is projected that developing countries will account for 57% of world CO_2 emissions, compared with 29% today.[90]

Similarly, the longer term potential of developing states to use ozone layer depleting substances can not be ignored. A 1987 Rand Corporation report listed the 13 developing countries that would most likely have the highest demand for CFCs by the year 2000.[91] The concerns of these states need to be addressed, due to the size of their potential domestic markets.

Overcoming Development Uncertainty

In order to address the uncertainty associated with the unknown contribution of developing states to climate change, the underlying issue of economic development has to be addressed in tandem.[92]

International agreements can entice developing country membership through provisions for funding and transfer of technology. In addition, other efforts to alleviate the concerns of developing states when dealing with environmental problems have been made, for example, debt-for-nature swaps.[93] These swaps usually provide for loan forgiveness in return for environmental protection projects, such as the protection of rain forests. Since these forests serve as a natural sink for greenhouse gas emissions,[94] there is some potential for offsetting climate change. Between 1987 and 1990, 15 major swaps were carried out, involving 8 developing countries.[95] These "first generation" swaps[96] were carried out by private non-governmental organizations,[97] suggesting a role for non-state actors in regimes.[98]

The debt-for-nature swaps have been criticized, however, for failure to address the core causes of environmental degradation, including the lack of scientific and technological innovation within these debtor states. To address this problem, debt could conceivably be purchased in return for a pledge by the debtor state to further research and development. There is currently an attempt to establish such a debt-for-science swap between the United States and Mexico.[99]

These swaps, however, may involve an imposition of the environmental values of developed states on the developing world. While not necessarily a bad thing, reaching consensus on shared values is a better, albeit more difficult, approach. A "policy of inclusion" of developing states is necessary for the regime to develop.[100] This would ensure that the concerns of developing countries are heard, not just for egalitarian purposes but in order to assure that normative expectations will be adhered to by all. The odds of universal adherence would be significantly increased if developing states felt that they had a say in the outcome of the negotiations.

In addition, the developing world has long regarded the traditional legal order with suspicion, as it was largely brought into existence by the wealthier industrialized states. A legal system which recognizes and accommodates the need for increased interdependence among nations may persuade more developing countries to lower their suspicions that the legal order is biased in favor of the developed world. The traditional legal order is largely based on law that many of the newly created developing states had no or little say in, and therefore view with distrust.[101]

The uncertainty of the impact of development, then, is a critical issue in the climate change and ozone layer depletion regimes. Developing states wield great influence in this regard, since their involvement is critical to the implementation of substantive obligations and, therefore, the success of the regimes.[102]

Critical Issues Summary

Science, economics and development are, therefore, critical issues in the maintenance or development of the climate change regime, as they are in the ozone layer depletion regime. All of these issues maintain a degree of uncertainty that must be overcome if substantive normative expectations and obligations are to evolve and be maintained within the regimes. While these issues can never attain 100% certainty, there is still the possibility of achieving unity or shared expectations on these issues. As uncertainty is overcome, obligations become stronger.

CATALYSTS FOR CLIMATE CHANGE AND OZONE LAYER DEPLETION REGIMES

In addition to the critical issues, secondary issues can act as catalysts in both the creation and maintenance or development of a regime, and thus are important to a legal analysis of global environmental change. They include: leadership, international non-state actors; crisis; and domestic regulations. The selection of these catalysts is based on their importance as catalysts identified in the ozone layer depletion regime, a comparable environmental problem.[103] The selection of those catalysts relevant to climate change may not be the same, however, and other catalysts may surface in future research. An application of these catalysts to the respective regimes will be made in Chapters 5 and 6.

Leadership

Although ultimately the decision to enter into a regime remains with individual states, leadership by any one state is sure to aid the evolution of such an arrangement. Failure of a leader state to emerge can result in inaction regarding the regime. In addition, within states, individual negotiators may play a pivotal role in a state's leadership.[104]

State leadership has been defined as falling into one of three possible categories: leadership evolved from power, leadership evolved from skilful negotiation, and leadership evolved from intellectual contributions.[105] Since the concept of regimes in this book relies on shared values or interests, leadership evolved from power is not as important in this discussion as the other types.

International Non-state Actors

Although the sovereignty of states does not remain in doubt within the global system, states are certainly not the sole actors within the system. International organizations, non-governmental organizations, and transnational corporations are all actively involved in policy-making areas, including the environment and can contribute to regime formation and maintenance.

International/Intergovernmental Organizations

The involvement of international organizations within world politics is not new. Their influence within environmental affairs has increased as of late, as the environment in general has increasingly become a matter of international concern. International organizations can contribute to the creation and maintenance of regimes through having issues placed on their agendas and thus developing policies for action.

Of the many international organizations and specialized agencies dealing with environmental issues, the one predominately associated with such work is the United Nations.[106] Among its bodies and specialized agencies, the UN Environmental Programme (UNEP) is most closely involved in environmental affairs.[107]

UNEP's role as guardian of the global environment is often described as "catalytic" and its primary function that of a coordinating body vis-a-vis other UN agencies, as well as non-UN organizations concerned with the environment.[108] While UNEP admittedly has not received a formal mandate to develop international law,[109] the driving force of the legal activity of UNEP is drawn from the decisions of its Governing Council and documents such as the Report of the Ad Hoc Meeting of Experts held in Montevideo, 1981.[110]

Since it is not a specialized agency of the UN, UNEP's General Council reports to the General Assembly through the UN Economic and Social Council,[111] thus creating a "vertical chain of accountability".[112] This chain, however, may itself be so long that it prevents progress from being made quickly, thus creating more of a problem than it solves. In addition, this "chain" may be too far away from the immediacy of the problem in terms of decision-making.

Another international organization is the International Bank for Reconstruction and Development (IBRD)[113], which together with the International Development Association and the International Finance Corporation, make up the component parts of the World Bank.[114] In 1970, the World Bank established the post of Environmental Advisor and in 1973, the Office of Environmental Affairs, today called the Office of Environmental and Scientific Affairs.[115] Environmental Assessment Guidelines are utilized to ensure that both developing countries and the Bank "systematically take environmental interests into account at the earliest stage of designing development projects."[116] In its 1992 Annual World Development Report, the Bank outlined its strategy for reconciling its goal of economic growth with the need to conserve environmental resources: "The key is not to produce less, but to produce differently."[117]

The World Bank, in conjunction with UNEP and the United Nations Development Programme, established the Global Environmental Facility (GEF) which will aid projects that help to reduce ozone depletion, global warming, marine pollution and loss of biodiversity.[118] The Bank also plays a role in the funding mechanism for the Montreal Protocol.[119]

While the Bank attempts to take environmental concerns into consideration in its policy-making, there is still pessimism reserved for an institution whose primary concern is economic development.[120] In particular, the GEF has come under criticism from developing states as lacking transparency and for promoting the interests of the developed countries over the economic needs of developing states. Developed states as well have been critical, particularly the United States, which criticize the GEF's secrecy and bureaucratic slowness. However, the GEF has successfully passed from its interim, pilot stage and has become a permanent fixture, thus securing a valued place among international financial mechanisms.[121]

Another intergovernmental organization, the Organization for Economic Cooperation and Development (OECD), is widely regarded as a forum for economic development and international trade.[122] In 1970, the OECD established an Environment Committee for the analysis of environmental problems and the assessment of actions undertaken and contemplated by member states, with a special emphasis on the economic and trade ramifications, and to suggest solutions bearing in mind the cost benefits.[123] Perhaps the most interesting charge to the Committee was that the results of such work were to be effective within the broader spectrum of OECD work on economic policy and social development.[124] The linkage of these issue areas with the environment is important for the implementation of international law.[125]

Non-governmental Organizations (NGOs)

The role of NGOs within regimes as international actors cannot be overlooked.[126] These organizations help bring environmental issues to the attention of the public.[127] Caldwell distinguishes between three types of NGOs: professional organizations with restricted membership such as the International Council of Scientific Unions, institutes such as the World Resources Institute, and advocacy groups like Friends of the Earth International.[128]

The International Council of Scientific Unions (ICSU), composed of 20 member unions,[129] has taken an active role in the scientific aspects of the environment and climate change. The ICSU occasionally sets up various committees. Notable is the ICSU's Scientific Committee on Problems of the Environment (SCOPE), which concerns itself with furthering the awareness of the "influence of humans on their environment" and to function "as a non-governmental, interdisciplinary and international council of scientists", aiding governments, intergovernmental and non-governmental bodies with environmental concerns.[130] The ICSU, with the collaboration of UNEP, UNESCO and the WMO, established in 1986 the International Geosphere-Biosphere Program (IGBP). The IGBP embodies an integrated scientific approach to global environmental change, through the study of planetary processes and the effects of human activities on those processes.[131]

NGOs play a large role in raising public opinion. Although the origins of western environmentalism reach far back into the 17th century,[132] public opinion was effectively woken to the concerns of the environment with the publication of Rachel Carson's *Silent Spring* in 1962, first as a series of articles in the *New Yorker*, and then as a book in its own right.[133] By 1989, the extent to which the public believed environmental issues to be important was confirmed in a 14-country Harris Poll, reported in *Our Planet*, the magazine of UNEP.[134]

US Vice President Al Gore, Jr. alludes to the "environmentalism of the spirit" as a method of achieving environmental awareness within the general public.[135] While the union of science and religion may make some uncomfortable,[136] it is hard to separate the union of man and nature:

> Modern society will find no solution to the ecological problem unless it takes a serious look at its lifestyle. In many parts of the world, society is given to instant gratification and consumerism while remaining indifferent to the damage which these cause. As I have already stated, the seriousness of the ecological issue lays bare the depth of man's moral crisis.[137]

Whether or not one is inclined to see God in nature, it is difficult to dispute that "[t]he fate of mankind...depends upon the emergence of a new faith in the future."[138] The raising of public opinion by NGOs, then, can be a motivating factor in the formation and maintenance of legal regimes.

Transnational Corporations

Business has become an important factor in the environmental equation. With the realization that 500 companies control 70% of world trade,[139] it becomes fairly obvious that their influence on environment and development is considerable.[140] Transnational corporations (TNCs) have some very important assets: they only have to avert international action instead of trying to reach consensus on it; they have access to bureaucratic sectors in some governments; and sometimes may be able to propose technical alternatives that suit their interests.[141] All of these characteristics create a powerful role for business in the environment.

While the environment may not be the primary concern of industry, the responsibility lies with each sector to consider the other's perspective.[142] That being stated, it is also of some economic benefit for corporations to adopt "environmentally friendly" production and management techniques. Although criticized as a public relations gimmick, businesses are realizing the economic value of taking on environmental issues before the regulators.

Domestic Regulations

Domestic implementation of international agreements is obviously important for the successful implementation of a regime. What is not as obvious is the role of domestic regulations that precede the international agreement. These regulations can catalyze the formation of a regime, as well as the maintenance of similar regulations within a regime.

Crisis

The perception of an imminent crisis has always acted as a catalyst for international action; not least for international legal action on the environment. A crisis has the effect of propelling action before it is "too late." Such a crisis could help catalyze the formation and maintenance of a regime.

CONCLUSION

This chapter has outlined the issues critical to the development of the climate change and ozone layer depletion regimes. While these regimes can be formed on the basis of shared expectations; science, economics and development uncertainty must all be overcome for the regime to develop. As this process of overcoming uncertainty proceeds and cognitive expectations evolve, then the regime's normative expectations or obligations become stronger.[143] The catalysts discussed above can also play a role in the formation and development of regimes.

Even before the advent of such a complex problem as climate change, it was recognized that:

> No problem in international law, however, can be viewed realistically without its context of underlying political, economic, sociological, scientific, technical, and other factors, and no viable solution to an international law problem can be achieved which does not accommodate these contextual realities.[144]

Thus, "the challenge for global environmental management rests in identifying these interests and constructing a system based on them."[145]

NOTES

1. R.A. Reinstein, "Climate Negotiations," *The Washington Quarterly* Vol. 16, No. 1 (Winter 1993), p. 95. Mr. Reinstein was chief US negotiator for the UN Framework Convention on Climate Change.

2. Compliance with the regime norms and rules is another measure of effectiveness. See, *supra*, Chapter 3, Effectiveness of Regimes.

3. See, *supra*, Chapter 3, Formation of Regimes.

4. Analyses of both regimes will be undertaken in Chapters 5 and 6, *infra*.

5. See *infra*, Chapter 4, Catalysts.

6. See the discussion regarding the limitations of modelling in predicting the rate of climate change, Chapter 1, Climate Change.

7. See, *supra*, Chapter 2, n. 333, for an explanation of the "no regrets" policy. Adaptation and mitigation are considered together under this policy.

8. A third possibility of doing nothing or a "wait and see" is discarded since the formation of the climate change regime essentially nullifies that possibility; with the formation of the regime, "something" has already been done.

9. See, *supra,* Chapter 1, Ozone Layer Depletion, where the Ozone Trends Panel confirmed that chlorine monoxide was linked to ozone layer depletion.

10. Oran Young refers to this as the "window of opportunity," see, "Global Environmental Change and International Governance," *Millennium: Journal of International Studies* Vol. 19, No. 2 (Winter 1990), p. 342.

11. States' choice of action would be constrained by what Rawls refers to as a "veil of ignorance." This veil excludes knowledge that would distinguish one state from another, thus achieving impartiality when making choices. See, John Rawls, *A Theory of Justice* (Oxford: Oxford University Press, 1972).

12. See, for instance, the National Academy of Sciences Report recommending adaptation to and mitigation of climate change in lieu of prevention for the US and other similarly situated industrialized states, *Policy Implications of Greenhouse Warming* (Washington, DC: National Academy Press, 1991), p. 37.

13. Lynton Keith Caldwell, *Between Two Worlds: Science, The Environmental Movement and Policy Choice* (Cambridge: Cambridge University Press, 1990), p. 19. See also, William K. Stevens, "Biologists Fear Sustainable Yield Is Unsustainable Idea," *The New York Times*, 20 April 1993, p. C4, where the author quotes Dr. Donald Ludwig of the University of British Columbia as saying that policy makers must abandon the "pretence of scientific certainty."

14. See, *supra*, Chapter 1, n. 11.

15. Harvard Law Review, ed., "Developments in the Law: International Environmental Law," *Harvard Law Review* Vol. 104, No. 7 (May 1987), p. 1530. See, also, *infra*, Chapter 4, Abatement vs. No Regrets. There is proposed recent legislation within the US Congress advocating such an approach, William K. Stevens, "Congress Asks, Is Nature Worth More Than a Shopping Mall?" *The New York Times*, 25 April 1995, p. C4.

16. Developments in the Law, *supra*, n. 15, p. 1531. The reliability of the cost-analysis must also be taken into consideration.

17. While absolute certainty can never be reached on any scientific issue, scientists nevertheless attempt to achieve certainty in their search to solve the set of scientific problems referred to as "grand challenges," which includes modelling global climate changes.

18. William D. Ruckelshaus, "Toward A Sustainable World," *Scientific American* Vol. 261, No. 3 (September 1989), p. 166.

19. Arild Underdal, "The Politics of Science in International Resource Management: A Summary," in *International Resource Management: The Role of Science and Politics*, ed. Steinar Andresen and Willy Ostreng (London, Belhaven Press, 1989), p. 259.

20. On a domestic level, the US Supreme Court has set a new standard for how judges should decide when a scientific theory or process is sound enough to be admitted as evidence. The earlier (Frye) test requiring that the theory be "generally accepted as a reliable technique among the scientific community" was challenged on the grounds that the US Federal Rules of Evidence allow expert witnesses to present opinions that do not necessarily attain the level of "general acceptability." The Supreme Court in *Daubert v. Merrell Dow*, US Supreme Court Docket No. 92-102, held that the Federal Rules, not Frye, provide the standard for admitting scientific testimony in a federal trial, and that "judges should focus on the methodology behind the scientific testimony, rather than following an earlier standard [Frye] that concentrated on whether the experts' ideas or conclusions have won 'general acceptance'." "Birth-Defect Lawsuit That Set Science Standard Is Dismissed," *The New York Times*, 8 January 1995. The case was then sent back to the US Court of Appeals for the 9th Circuit, where a three-judge panel ruled that "the

plaintiffs' experts... had not followed a scientific method found to be valid by at least a minority of researchers..," and that "none of the experts' studies... had been reviewed by peers or published in scientific journals." Ibid.

21. See, Bruce L.R. Smith, *The Advisers: Scientists in the Policy Process* (Washington, DC: The Brookings Institution, 1992). The attempt to link scientific knowledge of advisers with the power of government creates a paradox for the adviser: "he or she must become a true insider to accomplish anything; but in doing so the adviser may lose the fresh view, detachment, and outsider qualities that are urgently required," p. 193.

22. Lloyd Timberlake, "The Role of Scientific Knowledge in Drawing Up the Brundtland Report," in *International Resource Management: The Role of Science and Politics*, ed. Steinar Andresen and Willy Ostreng (London: Belhaven Press, 1989), p.122, referring to the WCED Report on Sustainable Development (emphasis in the original).

23. Caldwell lists six possible sources of scientists contributing to policy: scientists employed 1)by government, 2)as government consultants, 3)as members of national academies, 4)as members of national commissions, 5)as part of legislative inquiry, and 6)particular to the United States, as participants in White House Conferences. *Between Two Worlds*, *supra*, n. 13, pp. 24–25.

24. Peter M. Haas, "Obtaining International Environmental Protection Through Epistemic Consensus," *Millennium: Journal of International Studies* Vol. 19, No. 3 (Winter 1990) p. 349. See also, Peter M. Haas, *Saving the Mediterranean: The Politics of International Environmental Cooperation* (New York: Columbia University Press, 1990), pp. 55–56. But see, Lawrence E. Susskind, *Environmental Diplomacy* (NY: Oxford University Press, 1994), where the author "doubt[s] very much whether the kind of epistemic community that Haas describes would have the clout to alter the balance of power between proponent coalitions and veto blocks," p. 74.

25. Haas, *Saving The Mediterranean*, *supra*, n. 24, p. 55.

26. Ibid.

27. See, Emanuel Adler and Peter M. Haas, "Conclusion: Epistemic Communities, World Order, and the Creation of a Reflective Research Program," *International Organization* Vol. 46, No. 1 (Winter 1992), pp. 378–381.

28. Oran Young, "Science and Social Institutions: Lessons For International Resource Regimes," *International Resource Management: The Role of Science and Politics*, ed. Steinar Andresen and Willy Ostreng (London: Belhaven Press, 1989), pp. 8–11.

29. Ibid., p. 10.

30. This can be seen from the gathering of world leaders at the UN Conference on Environment and Development. See, William K. Stevens, "Rio Raises Environment Issue To Lasting World-Class Status," *International Herald Tribune*, 15 June 1992, p. 2.

31. This is not to suggest that scientists do not have influence while working outside the government, but that advisory committees allow for more direct input into government decision-making.

32. Smith, *The Advisers*, *supra*, n. 21, pp. 189–191.

33. See Adler and Haas, "Epistemic Communities," *supra*, n. 27, p. 381.

34. "Developments in the Law," *supra*, n. 15, p. 1531, fn 52, quoting Heap, "The Role of Scientific Advice for the Decision-Making Process in the Antarctic Treaty System," in *Antarctic Challenge III*, at 21, 23 (R. Wolfrum ed. 1988).

35. Stephen Schneider, quoted by Patrick J. Michaels, "Benign Greenhouse," *Research and Exploration* Vol. 9, No. 2 (Spring 1993), p. 232.

36. See, David Pearce, "The Global Commons," in David Pearce et al, *Blueprint 2*, (London: Earthscan Publications, 1991). p. 13.

37. See, William D. Nordhaus, "Economic Approaches to Global Warming," in *Global Warming: Economic Policy Responses*, ed. Rudiger Dornbusch and James M. Poterba (Cambridge, Mass: MIT Press, 1991), p. 44. Thus, the emphasis in this chapter on US-based economic studies is not intentional. On the other hand, the importance of the United States as a major contributor of greenhouse gases may make a focus on the economic analysis of costs to the United States legitimate, since those costs will no doubt influence the US degree of commitment to resolving the problem.

38. Ibid. For Cline's estimate, see William Cline, *The Economics of Global Warming* (Washington, DC: Institute for International Economics, 1992), p. 131. Although Cline's estimate was in 1990 US$61 billion while Nordhaus was in 1981 US$6, Cline's can be converted using the following equation: (1990 US damage cost)/(1990 US national income)X(1981 US national income). See, R.A. Howarth and P.A. Monahan, *Economics, Ethics and Climate Policy*, Energy and Environment Division, Lawrence Berkeley Laboratory, November 1992, p. 24.

39. Cline, *The Economics of Global Warming*, *supra*, n. 38 pp. 376–377.

40. See, *infra*, Chapter 4, Abatement vs. No Regrets.

41. See, for example, Cynthia Rosenzweig and Daniel Hillel, "Agriculture in a Greenhouse World," *Research and Exploration* Vol. 9, No. 2 (Spring 1993), pp. 208–221.

42. William Cline, *Global Warming: The Economic Stakes*, (Washington, DC: Institute for International Economics, 1992), p. 50. Cline adds, however, that developing states tend to be clustered towards lower latitudes, where warming should be less than the global mean.

43. Howarth and Monahan, *Economics, Ethics and Climate Policy*, *supra*, n. 38, p. 27 quoting Carl J. Dahlman, "The Problem of Externality," *Journal of Law and Economics*, Vol. 22 (April 1979), p. 156. This may be partly the reason why Cline's and Nordhaus' estimates vary.

44. See, *supra*, Chapter 1, n. 11.

45. See, *supra*, Chapter 2, n. 333.

46. See, Charles Perrings, "Reserved Rationality and the Precautionary Principle: Technological Change, Time and Uncertainty In Environmental Decision Making," *Ecological Economics: The Science and Management of Sustainability*, ed. Robert Costanza (New York: Columbia University Press, 1991), pp. 153–166.

47. See, for example, "Hot Stuff," *The Economist*, 15 September 1990, p. 113. See also, Wilfred Beckerman, "Global Warming and International Action: An Economic Perspective," in *The International Politics of the Environment*, ed. Andrew Hurrell and Benedict Kingsbury (Oxford: Clarendon Press, 1992), where the author states that "once one looks at such estimates [of costs] as have been made,... one sees that the economic impacts hardly justify the alarm and the calls for dramatic action that characterize much public discussion of this issue," p. 260.

48. National Academy of Sciences, *Policy Implications of Greenhouse Warming*, *supra*, n. 12.

49. See, for example, William Nordhaus, "Greenhouse Economics," *Economist*, 7 July 1990, p. 20. The National Academy of Sciences report, *supra*, n. 12, states that while farming is sensitive to climate change, adaptation is possible, p. 43.

50. Different fossil fuels have different carbon content, making it important to tax the actual carbon content. Carbon taxes have been introduced in Finland, Norway, Sweden and the Netherlands. See, IUCC, Fact Sheet 230, "Why Carbon Taxes Are A Cost-Effective Way To Reduce Greenhouse Gas Emissions," *Climate Change Dossier* (Geneva: IUCC, March 1992).

51. Nordhaus, "Economic Approaches," *supra*, n. 37, pp. 50–51. See also, Nordhaus, "Greenhouse Economics," *supra*, n. 49, pp. 19–20, 22.

52. Nordhaus, "Greenhouse Economics," *supra*, n. 49, p. 20.

53. Ibid. See, also, Nordhaus, "Economic Approaches," *supra*, n. 37, pp. 45–46.

54. Nordhaus, "Economic Approaches," *supra*, n. 37, pp. 60–63. See, also Nordhaus, "Greenhouse Economics," *supra*, n. 49, p. 22.

55. See Wilfred Beckerman, *Pricing For Pollution*, 2d ed., (London: The Institute of Economic Affairs, 1990), p. 13.

56. See, *supra*, Chapter 4, Scientific Uncertainty.

57. "Hot Stuff," *supra*, n. 47.

58. The study, conducted by the Population Reference Bureau (Washington, DC), stated that UN and World Bank projections of an "ultimate" population growth of about 12 billion will only occur if birth rates fall as quickly as anticipated. Otherwise, population could rise to the 20-30 billion range. See, "PRB Population Survey," Inter Press Service (IPS) Newswire, Compuserve,14 May 1993. See, also, UN Population Fund, *Population and the Environment* (NY: UN Population Fund, 1991).

59. "Scientists Warn of Asia's Swelling Population," Inter Press Service Newswire, 14 May 1993.

60. David Pearce, "Economics and the Global Environmental Challenge," *Millennium: Journal of International Studies*, Vol. 19, No. 3 (Winter 1990), p. 372.

61. Pearce, "Global Commons," *supra*, n. 36, p. 16.

62. Ibid., p. 22.

63. Distribution of the revenue to developing states might rectify this. See, Scott Barrett, "Global Warming: The Economics of a Carbon Tax," in David Pearce, et al, *Blueprint 2* (London: Earthscan Publications Ltd, 1991), pp. 15–36. In addition, see, Christopher Flavin, *Slowing Global Warming: A Worldwide Strategy* (Washington, DC: World Resources Institute, 1989), pp. 53–54.

64. See, *supra*, Chapter 1, Climate Change.

65. Ibid.

66. See, Michael Grubb, *The Greenhouse Effect: Negotiating Targets* (London: Royal Institute of International Affairs, 1989), pp. 31–32. See also, William A. Nitze, *The Greenhouse Effect: Formulating A Convention* (London: Royal Institute of International Affairs, 1990), pp. 51–52.

67. Cline, *Global Warming: The Economic Stakes*, *supra*, n. 42, pp. 85–86.

68. Individuals and firms faced with a carbon tax of $100 per ton of carbon would seek to avoid this tax by spending up to, but not more than, $100 to abate a ton of carbon, thus assuring the cost does not rise over the set rate. See, IUCC, "Carbon Taxes," *supra*, n. 50. Grubb maintains that while carbon taxes can play a large role in limiting emissions, they fail to address broader issues of energy supply and demand. See, Michael Grubb, *Energy Policies and the Greenhouse Effect* (Dartmouth: Royal Institute of International Affairs, 1990).

69. David Pearce, "The Role of Carbon Taxes in Adjusting to Global Warming," *The Economic Journal* Vol. 101, No. 407 (July 1991), pp. 938–948.

70. Cline offers as an initial formula the following: 1/3 weight each on a state's base-year share in world emission total, current share in world GDP, and base-year share in world population. Eventually, there would be a phaseout of weights associated with past emissions and GDP ("realist" criteria) and an increase in weight on base-year population ("equity" criterion). Cline, *Global Warming: The Economic Stakes, supra*, n. 42, p. 86.

71. See, for example, Anil Markandya, "Global Warming: The Economics of Tradeable Permits," in David Pearce et al, *Blueprint 2* (London: Earthscan Publications Ltd., 1991), pp. 53–62. See also, Grubb, *Negotiating Targets, supra*, n. 66. pp. 32–41.

72. Grubb, *Negotiating Targets, supra*, n. 66, p. 41. See, also Joshua M. Epstein and Raj Gupta, *Controlling the Greenhouse Effect* (Washington, DC: The Brookings Institution, 1990), where the authors argue that only a market in carbon emission permits meets the criteria of effectiveness and efficiency, pp. 32–33.

73. See, IUCC, Fact Sheet 231, "Cutting Back Greenhouse Gases With Tradeable Permits," *Climate Change Dossier* (Geneva: IUCC, March 1992).

74. See, *supra*, Chapter 1, n. 22–26.

75. Even aerosols and fire-fighting equipment can be included in this category.

76. Most accounts of the ozone depletion issue allude to the reluctance of industry to develop replacements for ozone depleting substances. See, Richard Elliot Benedick, *Ozone Diplomacy* (Cambridge: Harvard University Press, 1991) and Sharon Roan, *Ozone Crisis* (NY: John Wiley & Sons, 1989).

77. For example, HCFCs, a replacement for CFCs, is now being phased out itself. See *infra*, Chapter 5, International Action Regarding Ozone Layer Depletion.

78. See, *infra*, Chapter 5, Economic Uncertainty.

79. Economists may not form a legitimate epistemic community with regard to global warming, however, as they do not share a common purpose to abate or adapt to climate change or ozone layer depletion. Rather, they are concerned with economic aspects of the issue, not the issue itself. See, *supra*, n. 24.

80. See, for example, Robert Repetto and Roger C. Dower, "Reconciling Economic and Environmental Goals," *Issues in Science and Technology* (Winter 1992-93), pp. 28–32.

81. Cline, *Global Warming: The Economic Stakes*, *supra*, n. 42, pp. 90–95. For a similar approach see, Nitze, *The Greenhouse Effect*, *supra*, n. 66, pp. 29–34.

82. Cline, *Global Warming: The Economic Stakes*, *supra*, n. 42, pp. 90–95.

83. See, for instance, Andrew Warren, "But Anti-Warming Can Be Big Business," *International Herald Tribune*, 25 Sept. 1991, p. 4. See, also, *infra*, Chapter 4, for a discussion of the catalytic role of transnational corporations.

84. See, *infra*, Chapter 5, Economic Uncertainty.

85. Ibid.

86. See, *supra*, Chapter 1, n. 11.

87. Lee A. Kimball, *Forging International Agreement: Strengthening Intergovernmental Institutions For Environment and Development*, (Washington, DC: World Resources Institute, 1992), p. 43.

88. An additional concern are those states with "economies in transition" from a state controlled market to a free market, for example, the former Soviet bloc.

89. See, the Kuala Lumpur and Tokyo Declarations addressing the financial arrangements for developing states, *The Earth Summit: The United Nations Conference on Environment and Development (UNCED)*, introduction by Stanley P. Johnson (London: Graham & Trotman, 1993), pp. 31–39.

90. Cline, *Global Warming: The Economic Stakes*, *supra*, n. 42, p. 82. In addition, the Tata Conference, one of several international meetings to discuss development concerns, announced that developing states could be responsible for 50% of carbon dioxide emissions by the middle of the next century. Tata Conference Statement, *American Journal Of International Law and Policy* Vol. 5, No. 2 (Winter 1990), p. 554.

91. China, India, Brazil, Saudi Arabia, South Korea, Indonesia, Nigeria, Mexico, Turkey, Argentina, Venezuela, Algeria and Iran. See, Benedick, *Ozone Diplomacy*, *supra*, n. 76, p. 151.

92. This is true not only so that developing states will be able to afford environmental protection, but also because to argue otherwise may be to suggest that imposing developed countries' environmental standards on the developing world is more important than eradicating poverty. See, "Pollution and the Poor," *Economist*, 15 February 1992, pp. 14–15.

93. The first swap, completed in 1987, entailed Conservation International paying $100,000 to Citicorp Bank in return for an outstanding debt of $650,000 owed by Bolivia to Citicorp. The remaining Bolivian debt was entirely forgiven by Conservation International on condition that Bolivia protect 4 million acres of tropical forest. See,

George E. Brown, Jr. & Daniel R. Sarewitz, "Fiscal Alchemy: Transforming Debt Into Research," *Issues in Science and Technology* (Fall 1991), pp. 72–73.

94. Forests, however, only absorb carbon during the lifetime of the trees. After the forest matures, it provides no further contribution for absorbing carbon dioxide. See, National Academy of Sciences, *Policy Implications of Greenhouse Warming*, *supra*, n. 12, p. 76.

95. Brown and Sarewitz, "Fiscal Alchemy," *supra*, n. 93, p. 73. See also, "Developments in the Law," *supra*, n. 15, p. 1570.

96. See, Michael S. Sher, "Can Lawyers Save the Rain Forest? Enforcing the Second Generation of Debt-For-Nature Swaps," *Harvard Environmental Law Review* Vol. 17, No. 1 (1993), p. 151.

97. The three major groups involved in these swaps are Conservation International, the World Wildlife Fund and the Nature Conservancy.

98. See, *infra*, Chapter 4, International Non-state Actors.

99. Brown and Sarewitz, "Fiscal Alchemy," *supra*, n. 93, p. 75. This proposal is an example of a "second generation" or public swap. It differs from the "first generation" or private swap in that governments are playing the central role and that greater amounts of debt are being reduced. Sher, "Second Generation of Debt-For-Nature Swaps," *supra*, n. 96, p. 151.

100. Lynne M. Jurgielewicz, "Development Issues and Global Environmental Change," *International Economic Law Society Bulletin* Vol. 4, No. 2 (Spring-Summer 1991), p. 30.

101. See, generally, Francis Snyder and Peter Slinn, ed. *International Law and Development* (Abingdon: Professional Books Ltd., 1987) and Mohammed Bedjaoui, *Toward A New International Economic Order*, in the series "New Challenges to International Law" (London: Holmes & Meier Publishers, 1979).

102. See, Shridath Ramphal, "In a North-South Gap, Seeds of Environmental Discord," *International Herald Tribune*, 24 January 1992. Mr. Ramphal is President of the World Conservation Union.

103. See *infra*, Chapter 5, Catalysts in the Ozone Layer Depletion Regime. These catalysts may play a part in lifting the level of acceptable compliance, *supra*, Chapter 3, Effectiveness of Regimes. See, also, Abram Chayes and Antonia Chayes, On Compliance, *International Organization* Vol. 47, No. 2 (Spring 1993), pp. 202–204.

104. International organizations and corporations may also play a role within the policy of a state and will be considered as a separate catalytic factor, *infra*, Chapter 4, International Non-state Actors.

105. Oran R. Young, "Political Leadership and Regime Formation: On the Development of Institutions in International Society," *International Organization* Vol. 45, No. 3 (Summer 1991), pp. 281–308.

106. Out of the three principal UN Councils, the Security Council, the Trusteeship Council and Economic and Social Affairs (ECOSOC), ECOSOC is the only council (at this time) primarily involved with environmental affairs, although both of the other councils have had some dealings concerning the environment. Lynton Keith Caldwell, *International Environmental Policy: Emergence and Dimensions*, 2d ed. (Durham: Duke University Press, 1990), p. 101.

107. Some of the other UN bodies and agencies also concerned with environmental issues include the Food and Agriculture Organization (FAO), the International Labour Organization (ILO), the International Maritime Organization (IMO), the UN Educational, Scientific, and Cultural Organization (UNESCO), the World Health Organization (WHO), the World Meteorological Organization (WMO), the International Bank for Reconstruction and Development (IBRD), the UN Conference on Trade and Development (UNCTAD) and the UN Development Programme (UNDP). Caldwell, *International Environmental Policy*, *supra*, n. 106, pp. 104–106. For an overview of UNEP's role in international environmental law, see Carol Annette Petsonk, "The Role of the United Nations Environment Programme (UNEP) in the Development of International Environmental Law," *The American University Journal of International Law and Policy* Vol. 5, No. 2 (Winter 1990), pp. 351–391.

108. Caldwell, *International Environmental Policy*, *supra*, n. 106, p. 75. For example, UNEP's coordinates and disseminates information through its Earthwatch Programme, which includes the Global Environmental Monitoring System (GEMS) for air and water quality, the International Registry of Potentially Toxic Chemicals (IRPTC), and an information referral system (INFOTERRA) which refers environmental questions to the correct forums.

109. See UNGA Res. 2997, *International Legal Materials* Vol. 12, No. 2 (1973), pp. 433–438 where UNEP was not explicitly given the directive to develop international law. But see, T.C. Bacon, "The Role of the United Nations Environment Programme in the Development of International Environmental Law," *Canadian Yearbook of International Law* Vol. 12 (1974), p. 255 where the author pointed out that "it was not intended that the Stockholm Conference [which established UNEP], should consider legal questions," and "it was merely a technical, scientific meeting."

110. UNEP, *Environmental Law in the United Nations Environment Programme*, (Nairobi: UNEP, 1990), p. 2.

111. Caldwell, *International Environmental Policy*, *supra*, n. 106, p. 102.

112. Glen Plant, "Institutional and Legal Responses to Global Climate Change," in *International Law and Global Climate Change*, ed. Robin Churchill and David Freestone (London: Graham & Trotman, 1991), p. 167.

113. Established in 1945, the World Bank resulted from the 1944 Bretton Woods Conference to finance development activities. D.W. Bowett, *The Law of International Institutions*, 4th ed. (London: Stevens & Sons, 1982), pp.109–110.

114. Paul Muldoon, "The International Law of Ecodevelopment," *Texas International Law Journal* Vol. 22, No. 3 (1987), p. 9.

115. Ibid., p. 33.

116. Barber B. Conable, "Development and the Environment: A Global Balance," *American Journal of International Law and Policy* Vol. 2, No. 2, (Winter 1990), p. 246.

117. *World Development Report 1992: Development and the Environment* (Oxford: Oxford University Press, 1992).

118. "Green Aid," *Our Planet: The Magazine of the UNEP* Vol. 2, No. 4, (1990), p. 9. See, also, *infra,* Chapters 5 and 6, International Non-state Actors.

119. See, *infra*, Chapter 5, International Non-state Actors.

120. The Bank itself appears to be cautious about its role in the "global commons." Listing "degradation of the global commons" as one of five problem areas requiring special attention from the Bank and its members, the Bank disclaims any recognition of international legal obligations regarding "commons" areas in the absence of treaty provisions. See, World Bank, *The World Bank and the Environment: Annual Report-Fiscal 1990* (Washington, DC: World Bank, 1990), p. 1. fn 1.

121. See, *International Legal Materials*, Vol 33, No. 5 (September 1995), p. 1273.

122. The OECD was the result of the reconstitution of the Organization for European Economic Administration, which was formed to administer Marshall Aid. Bowett, *The Law of International Institutions, supra*, n. 113, p. 189.

123. Caldwell, *International Environmental Policy*, *supra*, n. 106, p. 98.

124. Ibid.

125. See, *supra,* Chapter 4, Critical Issue of Economics and Critical Issue of Development.

126. NGOs are too many in number to be listed here; perhaps a mark of their growing proliferation, if not influence.

127. See, John McCormick, *The Global Environmental Movement* (London: Belhaven Press, 1989), pp. 143–148.

128. Caldwell, *International Environmental Policy, supra*, n. 106, pp. 111–112.

129. Ibid, p. 114.

130. Ibid.

131. Benedick, *Ozone Diplomacy, supra*, n. 76, p. 201.

132. See, Richard H. Grove, "Origins of Western Environmentalism," *Scientific American* Vol. 267, No. 1 (July 1992), pp. 22–27.

133. Rachel Carson, *Silent Spring* (New York: Houghton Mifflin, 1962).

134. *Our Planet* Vol. 1, No. 2/3 (1989), pp. 14–15. But see, Keith Schneider, "Big Environment Hits a Recession,"The New York Times, 1 January 1995, p. 4, where the author cites the study "Restructuring Environmental Big Business," carried out by the Center for the Study of American Business which cites the loss of declining revenue and membership of environmental interest groups.

135. Al Gore, Jr., *Earth in the Balance* (London: Earthscan, 1992), pp. 238–265.

136. For example, recently, Dr. George F. Smoot of the Lawrence Berkeley Laboratory (US) detected density fluctuations in the afterglow of radiation from the Big Bang, which scientists theorize was the beginning of time and space.. Reflecting on his discovery, Smoot said: "[i]f you're religious, it's like looking at God." "It really is like finding the driving mechanism for the universe, and isn't that what God is?" Later, true to the vein of separation of science and religion, Smoot said "[w]hat matters is the science. I want to leave the religious implications to theologians and to each person, and let them see how the findings fit into their idea of the universe." John Nobel Wilford, "In the Glow of a Cosmic Discovery, A Physicist Ponders God and Fame," *The New York Times*, 5 May 1992, pp. C1 and C9. See also, John Horgan, "Profile: George F. Smoot," *Scientific American*, Vol. 267, No. 1 (July 1992), pp. 20–21.

137. Gore, *Earth In The Balance, supra*, n. 135, pp. 262–263, quoting Pope John Paul II, "The Ecological Crisis A Common Responsibility," message of His Holiness for the Celebration of the World Day of Peace, 1 January 1990.

138. Ibid., p. 263, quoting Pierre Teilhard de Chardin, *The Phenomenon of Man* (London: Collins, 1959).

139. John Vidal, "A World Shackled By Economic Chains," *Guardian* (London), 8 May 1992.

140. For a good account of the opportunities for a working relationship between industry and the environment, see, Bruce Piasecki and Peter Asmus, *In Search Of Environmental Excellence* (New York: Simon and Schuster, 1990).

141. Gareth Porter and Janet Welsh Brown, *Global Environmental Politics* (Boulder: Westview Press, 1991), p. 65.

142. One promising movement is *Project 88: Harnessing Market Forces to Protect Our Environment*, a project co-sponsored by the late John Heinz, then-Republican Senator of Pennsylvania, along with former Democratic Senator Tim Wirth of Colorado.

143. See, *supra*, Chapter 3, Formation of Regimes, and Maintenance or Development of Regimes.

144. Jan Schneider, *World Public Order of the Environment: Towards an International Ecological Law and Organization* (Toronto: University of Toronto Press, 1979), p. 110.

145. "Developments in the Law," *supra*, n. 15, p. 1494.

CHAPTER 5

Analysis of the Ozone Layer Depletion Regime

One generation goeth, and one generation cometh; but the earth abideth forever.[1]

In order to illustrate the role of regimes within the international legal order, this chapter will analyze the formation, maintenance and compliance mechanisms of the ozone layer depletion regime. The ozone layer depletion regime is a particularly good example of the role of regimes within the international legal order and how they can solidify general obligations into more substantive international law.

INTERNATIONAL ACTION REGARDING OZONE LAYER DEPLETION

International action to regulate the use and production of CFCs and other ozone depleting chemicals[2] resulted in the 1985 Vienna Convention for the Protection of the Ozone Layer (Vienna Ozone Convention). This was followed by the 1987 Montreal Protocol to the Vienna Convention on Substances that Deplete the Ozone Layer (Montreal Protocol) that was subsequently adjusted and amended in 1990 and 1992.[3]

In September 1975, following the publication of research in 1974 linking CFCs with ozone layer depletion,[4] UNEP funded a World Meteorological Organization conference on the implications of US research on the ozone layer depletion.[5] A number of international conferences followed, including the first significant international initiative, a 1977 UNEP sponsored meeting in Washington, DC. At that conference, a "World Plan of Action on the Ozone Layer" was drafted and a Coordinating Committee on the Ozone Layer (CCOL) was created.[6] The Plan called for international cooperation in research concerning ozone layer depletion, with the CCOL to report on that research.

By October 1978, the manufacturing of nonessential uses of CFCs as aerosol propellants was banned in the United States, followed closely by similar action in Canada, Norway and Sweden. The European Community settled on a 30% reduction in CFC aerosol use from 1976, to take effect in 1981.[7]

A UNEP Ad Hoc Working Group of Legal and Technical Experts for the Preparation of a Global Framework Convention for the Protection of the Ozone Layer was established in 1981, meeting seven times over the next three years to negotiate an international convention. From that process evolved the "Toronto Group," a group of states calling for a protocol reducing CFC emissions.[8] The Toronto Group's call for a ban on nonessential uses of CFCs in spray cans faced stiff opposition from the EC, which favored a production capacity cap protocol.[9] Differences could not be overcome, and neither of the proposed protocols was signed. Only the Convention was opened for signature.

The Vienna Ozone Convention was the first formal international agreement concerning the ozone layer.[10] The Convention listed general obligations of the Parties to protect human health and the environment from activities modifying the ozone layer, defined as the "layer of atmospheric ozone above the planetary boundary layer," including the adoption of legal measures to control ozone depletion. Cooperation in research and exchange of legal, scientific and technical information was required, and a Conference of the Parties was established for the review of scientific information and the promotion of appropriate policies.[11] The Convention marks the first time states endeavored to solve an environmental problem before the effects were felt or scientifically proved and set the stage for substantive obligations.[12]

In 1987, building upon the framework laid down by the Vienna Convention and reacting to publication and satellite confirmation of research documenting the "ozone hole,"[13] substantive agreement was reached for reduction of CFCs and halons, resulting in the Montreal Protocol. Under the Protocol, CFC production and consumption was to be frozen at 1986 levels by 1989 (when the Protocol came into force), cut by 20% by 1994, and 50% by 1999. For halons, production and consumption was to be frozen at 1986 levels by 1992 (37 months after the Protocol came into force).[14] Developing ("Art. 5") countries were given a 10 year extension for compliance with these timetables, as well as an additional 10 to 15% allowance for complying with the production deadlines.[15] In addition, the Protocol provided for the calculation of control levels,[16] control of trade with non-parties,[17] assessment of the control measures every 4 years,[18] and reporting of data and exchange of information regarding technology.[19] Non-compliance procedures were as yet not provided for, but left for future development.[20] The Protocol entered into force on January 1, 1989.[21]

The First Meeting of the Parties to the Montreal Protocol[22] took place at Helsinki in 1989, after scientific research revealed that the original phase-out called for by the Montreal Protocol was not adequate to halt the depletion of the ozone layer. This research included the Airborne Antarctic Ozone Experiment in October 1987 proving that chlorine monoxide was the primary source of ozone depletion; NASA's Ozone Trends Panel announcing in March 1988 that the ozone layer had depleted at a rate of 1.7 to 3% over the Northern Hemisphere; and new EPA evidence revealing that ozone layer depletion could cause serious harm to humans.[23]

In Helsinki, the Parties agreed that CFCs should be phased out by 2000, that halons should be phased out as soon as possible, and that other ozone depleting substances should be controlled. Agreement was also reached to develop a funding mechanism to facilitate the transfer of technology to developing countries.[24] The resulting Helsinki Declaration on the Ozone Layer could not legally revise the Montreal Protocol, however, since it requires that any proposed amendments and adjustments of the Protocol be communicated to the Secretariat at least 6 months before a meeting of the Parties at which they are proposed to be adopted.[25]

The following year, the Second Meeting of the Parties to the Montreal Protocol took place in London. Adjustments were made stating that CFCs would be phased out by 2000, with a 50% reduction required by 1995 and an 85% cut by 1997, with again additional time for compliance allowed for developing countries.[26] Halons are to be phased out by 2000, with rates frozen at 1986 levels by 1992, and a 50% cut by 1995.[27] There is a possibility of higher allowances for "essential uses" and if no adequate alternative exists. No definition was given of essential uses.[28] A new Amendment also stated that production and consumption of methyl chloroform was to be phased out by 2005 and carbon tetrachloride by 2000, and additional CFCs were added to the list of controlled substances to be phased out by 2000.[29] No restrictions were imposed on HCFCs, but a resolution was issued outside the Protocol recommending guidelines for their use.[30] Restrictions tightening the prohibition of the trade of ozone depleting substances with non-parties were also included.[31]

An Interim Multilateral Fund was established at the Second Meeting of the Parties for the purposes of providing financial and technical aid, including the transfer of technology, to developing states.[32] The fund was established at US$240 million, although studies revealed that the needs of developing states may reach $500 million over the coming three years.[33] An Executive Committee will monitor the implementation of operational policies, including the disbursement of funds, and will consist of 14 members appointed by the Parties, evenly divided between the developing and industrialized countries.[34] Other issues raised at the meeting included data reporting required under the Protocol, non-compliance procedures, recycling and destruction technologies and assessment panels to review the control mechanisms.[35]

At the Third Meeting of the Parties, held in June 1991, no new adjustments or amendments were adopted. A request was made, however, to the Ad-Hoc Working Group of Legal Experts on the Non-Compliance procedure, to identify possible instances of non-compliance as well as possible measures to be taken against non-compliance.[36]

The adjustments for CFCs and halons came into effect on 7 March 1991, needing no further ratification.[37] The London Amendment to the Protocol, including the requirements regarding methyl chloroform and carbon tetrachloride, the addition of new substances to the list of controlled chemicals, and the creation of the (interim) Multilateral Fund came into effect on 10 August 1992.[38]

The Fourth Meeting of the Parties to the Montreal Protocol convened in Copenhagen in November 1992. Just prior to that meeting, evidence of even greater ozone layer depletion was announced.[39] Once again, the Parties adjusted and amended the Protocol with further restrictions on ozone depleting substances.[40] Adjustments include a 75% reduction of consumption and production of CFCs by 1994, with a total phaseout by 1996. Halons are to be phased out by 1994, and carbon tetrachloride and methyl chloroform by 1996.[41] Developing states are again given leeway to exceed the limits from 10-15%.[42]

The Amendment also dealt with previously unregulated ozone depleting substances and CFC substitutes. The principal CFC substitute at this time, HCFC, is also ozone depleting. Therefore, the Amendment states that consumption of HCFCs is to be capped at 1989 levels in 1996, with a total phase-out by 2030.[43] HBFCs are to be phased out by 1996 (except for essential uses), and methyl bromide is to be frozen by 1995 at 1991 levels.[44] This and future amendments to the Protocol are to apply to Art. 5 developing states after a review in 1995.[45] The Amendment came into force on June 14, 1994.[46]

The Multilateral Fund, or financial arm of the Protocol, was permanently established in Montreal to facilitate compliance. US$ 113.34 million was committed for 1993, at least as much for 1994, and a range of $340-500 million for 1994-96.[47] Terms of reference were adopted for the Fund and its Executive Committee, with the United States to chair the Executive Committee in 1993.[48]

Pursuant to Article 8 of the Montreal Protocol, a non-compliance procedure was formulated. An Implementation Committee is to consider and report on submissions made to the Secretariat regarding possible non-compliance, "with a view to securing an amicable solution of the matter on the basis of respect for the provisions of the Protocol."[49] The Implementation Committee is then to report to the Meeting of the Parties with its recommendations. An indicative list of measures that might be taken for non-compliance by the Parties was also adopted. Included in the list was "appropriate assistance" (such as assistance for data collection and reporting, technology transfer, and financial assistance), the issuing of cautions, and suspension of specific rights and privileges under the Protocol, but possible examples of non-compliance were not adopted as had been hoped for.[50]

The Fifth and Sixth Meetings of the Parties were held in Bangkok (November 1993) and Nairobi (September 1994) respectively, with development issues high on the agenda. At the Bangkok meeting, contentious issues involving developing countries were postponed, while in Nairobi, NGOs including Greenpeace and Friends of the Earth protested what they claimed was the "dumping of obsolete technology" in developing countries.[51]

FORMATION OF THE OZONE LAYER DEPLETION REGIME

Formation of a regime requires the existence of shared expectations regarding future behavior among the relevant states involved.[52] In the case of ozone layer depletion, existence of the regime can be traced to the establishment of the UNEP AD Hoc Working Group of Legal and Technical Experts for the Preparation of a Global Framework Convention for the Protection of the Ozone Layer established in 1981.[53] At that time, there was evidence of expectations concerning protection of the ozone layer through future regulation of the issue-area, if not agreement on what degree of regulation. While unilateral action by some states to regulate CFC use on their own preceded the establishment of the Working Group, there was not yet evidence at that time of the existence of shared values or expectations to regulate the issue-area as a *collective* body. While the unilateral action acted as a *catalyst*[54] in that it "pushed" international action, there was no evidence of an understanding that international action was as yet required. Similarly, the World Plan for Action and the CCOL, while evidence of the need to coordinate research in the issue-area, did not reflect the shared value of the necessity of international action. The legal status of the regime at formation will be discussed below.

MAINTENANCE OF THE OZONE LAYER DEPLETION REGIME

As discussed earlier, the maintenance or development of a regime depends on the extent to which critical issues have been resolved and cognitive expectations have been shaped.[55] The stronger this agreement on cognitive expectations, the stronger the regime obligations or normative (shared) expectations regarding future behavior.[56] In examining the ozone layer depletion regime, the critical issues include the scientific, economic and development aspects of the regime. Without substantial unity on the uncertainty surrounding these issues, the regime would not have evolved substantive regulations.

Scientific Uncertainty

The publication of the Rowland-Molina Hypothesis[57] in 1974 linking CFCs with ozone layer depletion was the beginning of the search for scientific certainty regarding the causes of ozone layer depletion. Additional research followed, including four major reports of the US National Academy of Sciences released between 1976 and 1984. The estimates of depletion varied widely, suggesting uncertainty over the theory linking chlorine monoxide with ozone layer depletion.[58]

Thus, it was not surprising that the 1985 Vienna Ozone Convention did not contain provisions for the international regulation of CFCs when the scientific community was still vacillating on the extent of severity of the depletion.

The discovery of the "ozone hole" in late 1984 contributed to scientific certainty, yet even that did not provide proof that chlorine monoxide was the culprit. This did not occur until late 1987, when an Antarctic scientific expedition and the report of the Ozone Trends Panel in early 1988, confirmed the chlorine monoxide theory.[59] Yet the Montreal Protocol was opened for signature a month before the expedition was completed and six months before the Ozone Trends Panel Report. There was international action, then, notwithstanding the scientific uncertainty.

Haas argues that epistemic communities[60] were influential in overcoming scientific uncertainty in the negotiation of the Montreal Protocol.[61] He states that the epistemic community of atmospheric scientists led the way toward an agreement on ozone by disseminating information suggesting the need for regulation of CFCs, and also was able to pinpoint the objectives of the key country, the United States, which provided the largest market for CFCs and could thus curtail access to other producers.[62] According to Haas, the members of this transnational epistemic community of atmospheric scientists:

> accepted the Rowland-Molina hypothesis [on ozone depletion], developed models to elaborate it and began monitoring for actual ozone depletion, while also publicly supporting policies that would ban CFCs. ...they advocated anticipatory action...this group had members throughout the world.... in frequent contact with one another...[63]

The formation within the United States of an epistemic scientific community as opposed to other states may be partially attributed to the lack of an equivalent (at the time) in Europe to the NASA research and satellite-monitoring initiatives concerning the ozone layer, which helped to unify US scientific opinion. In May 1988, 20 leading European scientists addressed a statement to the EC Community noting that the gap between the United States and Europe in stratospheric sciences was widening.[64] In countries other than the United States, then, the influence of the epistemic community came later, after the Montreal Protocol.[65]

Regardless of how long the international epistemic community took to develop, however, it was important for the creation of stronger obligations within the regime. This can be seen from the twice-amended Protocol, which expanded greatly on the obligations required of parties. This could not have been accomplished if only the United States were justifying the measures.[66] Further evidence that the ozone layer was depleting rapidly[67] no doubt helped make the task of the epistemic community easier in Copenhagen. Cognitive expectations or knowledge concerning scientific uncertainty concerning ozone layer depletion has coalesced, leading to the creation of shared or normative expectations.

Economic Uncertainty

The uncertainty associated with the economic cost of CFC replacement is another critical issue in the ozone layer depletion regime. If replacements or alternative technologies had proved too costly or even impossible, the agreement at Copenhagen would never have occurred.

The Toronto Group[68] noted that American industry had demonstrated that alternatives to CFC propellants were technically and economically feasible.[69] By 1986, an official of the largest US CFC producer, DuPont, stated that CFC substitutes could be available by 1991.[70] Prior to that time, there had been little motivation for industry to maintain this position,[71] and most CFC producers had argued that scientific evidence was too inconclusive to warrant regulation.[72] But, in 1987, the Montreal Protocol provided the necessary incentive for industry to develop alternatives to ozone depleting substances.[73] With CFCs now being phased-out, replacement technology was necessary.

The outlook for replacements changed dramatically in 1988 when DuPont, the largest producer of CFCs, announced that it would begin to phase out its production.[74] The 1990 London Revisions[75] requiring CFCs, halons and carbon tetrachloride to be phased out by 2000 and methylchloroform by 2005 brought on a new sense of urgency for replacements.

In 1991, the Technology and Assessment Panel established under the Montreal Protocol[76] stated that it was technically feasible to phaseout CFCs and halons by 1995-1997 and that "innovation to replace CFCs has been rapid, effective and economical," and that the "most important barriers to the successful transfer of ... replacing technologies are more likely to be informational, organizational and financial rather than political, technical or economic."[77]

The Fourth Meeting of the Parties[78] reported that elimination costs had become much lower than had been predicted in 1989 and it was technically and economically feasible to phase out CFCs, methyl chloroform and carbon tetrachloride between 1995 and 1997, and halons by 1995.[79]

More importantly, industry has demonstrated that it can substitute replacements or alternative technologies for ozone depleting substances. Recently, Hewlett-Packard, an international manufacturer of measurement and computation products and systems used in industry, science, medicine and education, announced that it had *eliminated* use of CFCs in its manufacturing processes worldwide.[80] It also announced it had eliminated all uses of methyl chloroform. Compaq Computer Corporation, a world leader in the manufacture of personal computers, also announced that it had *eliminated* CFCs from its manufacturing processes.[81] In addition, the German Company DKK recently announced that it had developed a refrigerator using propane and butane, instead of ozone depleting CFCs and HCFCs.[82]

Thus, cognitive expectations or knowledge concerning economic uncertainty regarding CFC replacement costs have coalesced and contributed to the acceleration of the phase-out of ozone depleting substances.[83] The progression from Vienna to Montreal to London to Copenhagen has resulted in the phase-out of CFCs from a general intention to undertake a phase-out, to an actual phase-out by 1996.[84] In addition, other substances have been added to the controlled list,[85] including HCFCs, the principle substitute for CFCs.[86] As more replacements become available and economically feasible, more substances will also be phased out.[87]

Development Uncertainty

Developing states, concerned that a ban on ozone depleting substances would threaten their economic development, have become a force to be reckoned with in the ozone layer depletion regime. During the negotiations for strengthening the Montreal Protocol, "most observers were... unprepared for the intensity of concerns subsequently expressed by many developing countries despite [the earlier] concession [of the 10 year transitional period for CFC use accorded under the Protocol]."[88] The industrialized countries' push for a total phase-out of CFCs convinced the developing states that they would have to acquire new technology as soon as possible and to ensure that the industrialized world would help them in doing so.[89]

Although delegates from industrialized states alluded to "environmental blackmail,"[90] a stalemate was avoided with the agreement that parties will "take every practicable step" to transfer technology to developing states "under fair and most favorable conditions."[91] In addition, concessions were made to give developing states more time to switch from CFC use to substitutes and a fund was set up to make the transition less economically painful.[92] These incentives were seen as necessary to entice countries such as China and India to accede to the Protocol.[93] Without ratification and implementation by developing states, the Montreal Protocol will be of little value and its provisions rendered relatively useless.[94] Thus, recognition that the Multilateral Fund was vital for the elimination of controlled substances in developing states was stressed again at the Fourth Meeting of the Parties in Copenhagen, as well as subsequent meetings at Bangkok and Nairobi.[95] It should be pointed out, however, that China and India have not yet signed the Copenhagen amendment.[96] Nevertheless, cognitive expectations regarding development have evolved within the ozone layer depletion regime, leading to normative or shared expectations facilitating the inclusion of developing states.

CATALYSTS IN THE OZONE LAYER DEPLETION REGIME

The catalysts of leadership, international non-state actors, crisis and domestic regulations all contributed to the formation and/or the maintenance of the ozone layer regime.[97]

Leadership

The United States played a leadership role in the formation and maintenance of the ozone layer depletion regime. While Europe debated the wisdom of regulating ozone depleting CFCs, it is generally undisputed that the United States was a leader on the issue.[98] This was due in part to the domestic regulations that the United States was required to enact under the US Clean Air Act,[99] but the United States was nonetheless taking the lead for international regulations. One observer notes, however, that even the United States' leadership "was highly uneven,"since US support was threatened at various stages of the regime development. This included "the last-minute attempt by State Department officials to reject the 1985 Convention; the counterattack through the (US) Domestic Policy Council in spring 1987 (to attempt to reconsider the US negotiating position calling for international regulation of CFCs); and the Spring 1990 attempt, originating in the office of White House Chief of Staff John Sununu, to scuttle the delicate negotiations on a financial agreement (the Multilateral Fund)."[100] Nevertheless, the overall US commitment has contributed to the formation and the development of the regime. The recent change to the perceived "environmentally friendly" US Clinton Administration may help perpetuate this leadership.

Eventually the developing states, particularly China and India, created their own leadership role regarding funding and technology transfer in the negotiations for adjustments and amendments to the Protocol.[101] At Copenhagen, developing states, heavily dependent on the use methyl bromide, kept the substance from being phased-out.[102]

International Non-state Actors

The role of UNEP as a catalyst in the formation and maintenance of the ozone layer depletion regime is significant. UNEP's Governing Council selected ozone layer depletion as one of five priority areas in 1976, and in 1977 adopted the World Plan of Action on the Ozone Layer.[103] The chief US diplomat to the treaty negotiations stated that: "UNEP was indispensable in mobilizing data and informing world public opinion...the strong personality of its executive director, Mostafa Tolba...was a driving force in achieving the eventual consensus (for international regulation)."[104]

The World Bank is also a catalyst for further development of the ozone layer depletion regime. Although the policies of the Bank are often criticized,[105] it still plays a major role in environmental lending. In the fiscal year 1991, the annual volume of World Bank lending for environmental projects had increased to $1.6 billion, or approximately 7% of total Bank funding.[106] In addition, the Bank is one of the primary operators of the Montreal Protocol Multilateral Fund,[107] as well as the Global Environmental Facility (GEF).[108] Notwithstanding developing states' opposition, the status of the Bank as a financially healthy and stable lending institution, in addition to its tangible role in the Multilateral Fund and the GEF, makes it a catalyst in the development of the ozone layer depletion regime.

Non-governmental organizations have also played a role in the formation and maintenance of the ozone layer depletion regime.

One such organization, the Natural Resources Defense Council, lobbied successfully in the United States for the banning of CFCs from aerosols in 1978, and later brought legal action against the US EPA that forced the EPA to implement CFC regulations under provisions of the Clean Air Act.[109] Following the Montreal Protocol, Friends of the Earth International (FOEI) made ozone layer depletion its number one priority, and their national affiliates played a large role in lobbying governments and industries to support the banning of CFCs and thus strengthened the regime.[110]

Transnational corporations can also act as catalysts. The announcements of Hewlett-Packard and Compaq discussed above[111] played such a role in the development of the ozone layer depletion regime. The creation of global business organizations such as the Industry Cooperative for Ozone Layer Protection, which provides information for the facilitation of CFC alternatives by electronic firms, is another example of industry enhancing the development of the regime.[112]

Domestic Regulations

In 1986, the CFC industry in the United States began to lobby for an international agreement, as it expected the forthcoming Protocol to the Vienna Convention to be weaker than the expected US rules brought under the Clean Air Act.[113] On the other hand, a too-weak international agreement might have forced the EPA to regulate unilaterally, again mandated by the Clean Air Act.[114] American industry feared US unilateral controls would undercut their competitiveness,[115] although it would be fair to say unilateral regulations were a concern of all industry. The result was an international Protocol that prevented the US from having to act unilaterally under the Clean Air Act. In addition, many states have adopted regulations that are more stringent than the Montreal Protocol.[116] Thus, these domestic regulations are catalyzing the regime development.

Crisis

The threat to human health arising from ozone depletion was a definite catalyst for the formation and the maintenance of the ozone layer depletion regime.[117] Rowland and Molina's 1974 paper linking CFCs with ozone layer depletion brought the problem to light, pointing out the link between increased UV light and possible skin cancer.[118] Less than 10 years later, the Vienna Convention was signed. The "ozone hole" presented tangible evidence of a crisis and was followed two years later by the Montreal Protocol.[119] The Antarctic Expedition and the Ozone Trends Panel confirming the link between chlorine monoxide and ozone layer depletion preceded the amending of the Protocol in 1990.[120] By April 1991, the ozone depletion over the US was found to have amounted to 4.5 to 5% in the last decade, prompting the US EPA chief William Reilly to state: "it is unexpected, it is disturbing and it possesses implications we have not yet had time to fully explore."[121] The headlines ran "Bad News From Above,"and "A Bigger Hole In The Ozone: EPA Predicts 200,000 More Skin-Cancer Deaths."[122] A year later, NASA detected levels of chlorine monoxide (endproducts of CFCs which destroy ozone) over the Arctic 50% higher than that previously seen in Antarctica, creating a radiation risk for populated areas of the Northern Hemisphere.[123] The Protocol was again amended shortly after.[124] Evidence in early 1993 of an even greater amount of ozone layer depletion points towards even further adjusting and amending of the Protocol. The sense of crisis, then, has preceded the formation as well as each stage of further development of the regime.

COMPLIANCE IN THE OZONE LAYER DEPLETION REGIME

The ozone regime is a good example of how compliance can be brought about through regimes, through the process of norm and rule evolution, dispute settlement procedure, accountability and transparency, and conditional cooperation and exclusion.

The evolution of norms and rules is demonstrated by the latest commitment to eliminating CFCs, the Copenhagen Revisions.[125] Tracing the development of the regime from the Ad Hoc Meeting of Experts attempting to bring about a framework convention, to the Convention, to the addition of the Protocol and its subsequent amendments, illustrates the process of rule evolution, or the shaping of cognitive expectations leading to shared or normative expectations regarding future behavior.[126]

In addition to dispute settlement procedures included in the Vienna Ozone Convention, non-compliance procedures are provided for within the Montreal Protocol through an Implementation Committee to resolve disputes.[127] The Implementation Committee had tested the draft non-compliance procedure over a period of two years and found it to be "both efficient and appropriate for supporting its work."[128]

Accountability and transparency is maintained within the ozone regime by reporting requirements and set targets.[129] While some developing states still appear to have serious problems in fulfilling data-reporting requirements, the Ad Hoc Group of Experts on the Reporting of Data had identified several technical and administrative problems and possible solutions.[130] In addition, the parties noted in a decision that all the states that did report data either met or exceeded their obligations for control measures.[131]

The regime also excludes non-parties through trade bans,[132] although non-parties complying with the relevant provisions of the Protocol are exempt from trade bans on an interim basis, with a final decision to be made at the Fifth Meeting of the Parties.[133] The adjusted Protocol sets trade barriers for controlled substances, products containing controlled substances and products made with controlled substances.[134] Imports and exports of controlled substances and imports of products containing controlled substances will all eventually be banned, but products produced with, but not containing, controlled substances, will only be subject to an import ban should the Parties consider it "feasible."[135]

THE LEGAL STATUS OF THE OZONE LAYER DEPLETION REGIME

The present legal status of the ozone layer depletion regime is not in dispute. The Vienna Convention and amended Montreal Protocol, as international treaties, qualify as binding international law.

Formation of the regime and creation of a legal obligation, however, can be traced to an earlier stage in the regime, where shared expectations are perceived as authoritative and effective, thus creating a legal obligation so far as the policy-oriented school of international law is concerned.[136] In the ozone layer depletion regime, these shared expectations can be said to have existed from the time of the negotiations for international regulations, or, more precisely, at the creation of the Ad Hoc Meeting of Experts for the preparation of a convention, from which evolved the Vienna Ozone Convention. At that point in time, shared expectations existed regarding states' obligation to protect the ozone layer, with the expectation also of future regulatory measures of an undetermined degree.

The legal obligation attested to above can be illustrated through the policy-oriented approach to lawmaking; or the prescribing of policy as a process of communication. This was described earlier as requiring an examination of the: participants, subjectivities and objectives, situations or arenas, resources, strategies, and outcome in terms of shared expectations.[137]

Participants

The participants in the formation of the ozone layer depletion regime included the major CFC producers and users, as well as international organizations (UNEP), NGOs (Greenpeace, Friends of the Earth).[138] These participants, acting in their official capacity, were all involved in the prescriptive process, described above.[139]

The extent to which the state participants represented the target audience is also important in adding to the participants' authority, as it is the expectations of the target audience that are crucial in lawmaking.[140] As outlined above regarding international action on ozone layer depletion, the target audience of the leading CFC producers and consumers, namely the United States and the European Community, were participants in the process of prescription. This can be traced at least as far back as the first significant international initiative on ozone layer depletion, the 1977 UNEP Meeting of Experts in Washington DC, where the World Plan of Action on the Ozone Layer was drafted.[141] Unilateral action to ban CFC use in aerosol propellants was taken by the United States, the EC and others, between 1978 and 1981.[142] These states also partook in the Ad Hoc Working Group for the Protection of the Ozone Layer.[143]

In addition to states, UNEP also played a large role in the

formation of the regime and the prescriptive process. The Meeting of Experts, as well as the Ad Hoc Working Group, were both coordinated by UNEP.[144] NGO's such as Friends of the Earth and the Natural Resources Defense Council also contributed as participants.[145]

Since the creation of shared expectations regarding the obligation to protect the ozone layer, developing states have begun to play a large role as participants in the regime.[146] In addition, other organizations have begun to take on the role of participants, particularly the World Bank and transnational corporations.[147]

Subjectivities

As discussed above,[148] the subjectivities or perceptions of participants regarding the content of their communications, cannot be directly examined but only analyzed on the basis of past behavior. With regard to the state participants, the most important observations can be made with regard to their domestic activities. Thus, the fact that the United States banned CFC use in nonessential aerosol propellants by 1978, followed by Canada, Norway and Sweden, is a telling sign of these states subjectivities towards protection of the ozone layer.[149] The EC, while not establishing an outright ban, did implement a 30% reduction in CFC aerosol use which took effect in 1981.[150]

The actions outlined above take on even greater significance, since CFC production is concentrated in a few states. In the 1970s, the United States accounted for about half of the world total, with most of the remaining production taking place in the EC.[151] These states also took part in the Ad Hoc Working Group for the Preparation of a Global Framework Convention for the Protection of the Ozone Layer,[152] implying perceptions or expectations that the ozone layer be protected, and the expectations of an unknown degree of regulation of ozone depleting substances.

It is not difficult to ascertain the subjectivities of UNEP. Their sponsorship of the 1977 Experts Meeting, which drafted the World Plan of Action on the Ozone Layer, illustrates UNEP's perception or expectation that the ozone layer should be protected and further destruction be prevented. Their sponsorship of the Ad Hoc Working Group to prepare a convention underscores this expectation.

From the above, the subjectivities of the participants clearly point to expectations that the ozone layer be protected and that there be future regulation of ozone layer depleting substances. Varied demands as to the extent of future regulation does not detract from the general expectation that the ozone layer be protected.

Situations

The situations where the above subjectivities were played out were formal, institutionalized and organized international conferences. Thus, the UNEP Experts Meeting, the CCOL and the Ad Hoc Working Group were all organized (under the rubric of UNEP) situations or participants to play out their attitudes or subjectivities. Thus, the situation was not limited to a geographical region, but was held in a global forum. Neither was the situation a one-off gathering, but was of extended and frequent duration.

Resources or Bases of Power

The most important resources used by participants in the ozone layer depletion prescriptive process included scientific knowledge and skill. Thus, the Rowland-Molina hypothesis, as well as other major scientific findings contributed to scientific knowledge used by the participants.[153] UNEP attempted to utilize scientific skill through the workings of the CCOL, which coordinated scientific research on the ozone layer undertaken by national and international agencies. The chemical industry also contributed their resources, through sponsoring ozone research worth several million US dollars per year.[154]

Eventually, economic and development knowledge would play a larger role in the prescriptive process, as more substantive regulation was advocated by participants. Thus, this knowledge later contributed to the lawmaking process by raising the level of shared expectations and therefore, the level of regulation.[155] At the beginning of the prescription process, however, the scientific resources available were more influential as bases of power.

Strategies

The strategies used to generate the flow of words and behavior by the main participants concerning ozone layer depletion were explicit: domestic regulations and international declarations. Thus, diplomatic strategies on the international level were used in pursuit of the participants objectives to shape expectations for prescriptions.

In this respect, the flow of communication between participants was formally incorporated in such documents as the World Plan of Action on the Ozone Layer and draft control articles such as those put forth by the Toronto Group and the EC.[156] All of these exhibited attitudes towards regulation. The World Plan in particular reveals this attitude, as the measures adopted in the Vienna Ozone Convention were all contained in the Plan.[157]

As with, resources, economic strategies in terms of replacement technology were used later in the prescriptive process, once the basic obligation was in place. From that point, economic strategies were utilized to further more substantive regulations.[158]

Outcome

The outcome of the above ongoing process of interaction is a prescription entailing a legal obligation (under the policy-oriented approach) to protect the ozone layer, with additional expectations of future regulations of an unknown degree. While admittedly, the obligation identified is vague, it must be remembered that many rules and principles of international law are vague, such as the general principle to prevent harm to the environment described earlier. The important point to remember is that these vague rules may develop into more substantive regulations, depending on the intensity of shared expectations regarding future behavior.

Until the Vienna Ozone Convention came into force, the prescription could not be said to qualify as a treaty. Thus, the prescription must have qualified as a customary rule of international law. This entails determining what shared expectations of future behavior have been created through an ongoing process of interaction involving policy, authority and control.

The critical test regarding legal obligation under the policy-oriented approach is the existence and content of the shared expectations of politically relevant groups, that are maintained by the continuation of communication regarding the authority and control intentions of those whose support is essential for the norms' efficacy. If the target audience will perceive behavior as authoritative state practice and likely to be complied with, then it can be characterized as practice accepted as law.[159] The test in brief is one of shared expectations regarding authority (legitimacy) and control (effectiveness) as perceived by the relevant target audience, which in this case as stated above, are the state participants.

From the prescriptive process above, a policy to protect the ozone layer can be identified. This is clear from both individual states' efforts to regulate CFC use, as well as the group participant effort to agree to negotiate a Convention. While the degree of intensity of the policy was not yet clear at the formation of the regime, it is difficult to dispute that the actions taken did not reflect a policy to protect the ozone layer.

The expectation that the ozone layer was to be protected needed to be (and continues to need to be) sustained through an ongoing authority signal and control intention.

The prescriber participants qualify as legitimate in the sense that they are authoritative. It is difficult to dispute the authority present in the formation of the ozone layer depletion regime. The individuals involved acted in an official capacity for the states they represented, as did the individuals associated with international and non-governmental organizations. Of course, states play the most authoritative role and so their actions are the most important. Indeed, it is states who played the largest role, imposing domestic regulations regarding CFC production and agreeing to negotiate a Convention to protect the ozone layer. The fact that these states represent the principal participants among the target audience is important, since it is the expectations of the target audience that are critical to policy-oriented lawmaking.

Finally, a control or effectiveness intention can be ascertained from the willingness of the prescriber participants to make the prescription effective. Control does not require unanimity or even wide consensus, but does require enough interest and willingness on the part of some participants to make it effective. Clearly, in the case of ozone layer depletion there was interest on the part of the major CFC producing states to make a regulatory policy effective. This can be seen through the intent of the Ad Hoc Committee, composed of those states, to negotiate a convention to protect the ozone layer.

Thus, the behavior or practice of the participants was perceived by the participants as both authoritative (legitimate) and as controlling (effective) or likely to be complied with. While admittedly the authority signal and control intention were both weak at formation, they were present at a degree sufficient for the policy content entailing a general obligation to protect the ozone layer. The legal obligation to protect the ozone layer can be characterized as practice accepted as law, thus fulfilling the requirements of the formation of customary law,[160] at least from the policy-oriented perspective of lawmaking.

It is important to remember that while "it is often difficult to determine whether or not a new custom has crystallized into international law,"[161] it is equally important to try. If one views law as a policy process based on shared expectations, then the point at which these shared expectations can be identified is critical. While the approach here may not be accepted by those not aligned with the policy-oriented school, it is difficult to ignore that the shared expectations to protect the ozone layer necessarily had to be in place for the Vienna Ozone Convention and the ensuing Montreal Protocol to evolve. Combined with authority and control, the existence of this policy equates with lawmaking under the policy-oriented approach.

While admittedly it is easier to make the argument that the formation of the regime coincided with the creation of the Vienna Ozone Convention, making the more difficult argument that the regime was formed prior to that Convention allows for a broader understanding of the legal order. Such an argument does not ignore the legitimate process of lawmaking, but it does necessitate taking the perspective of the policy-oriented approach. Without this perspective, regime theory is still useful to the legal scholar, but unnecessarily restricts the study of law by excluding part of the lawmaking process.

AN EVALUATION OF THE OZONE LAYER DEPLETION REGIME

A positive evaluation of the ozone layer depletion regime is not difficult to make. The policy content, authority signal and control intention at the time the ozone layer depletion regime came into existence was admittedly weak. All of these aspects have strengthened, however, since the formation of the regime, making the law more substantive. Thus, the general obligation to protect the ozone layer created by the negotiating process was "firmed up" with the signing of the Vienna Convention, and more substantive obligations followed with the Montreal Protocol.

The development of this regime has been strengthened by the evolution of cognitive expectations on certain critical issues, which allowed for the evolution of normative or shared expectations regarding future behavior. In addition, catalysts have aided this formation and development. Thus, shared expectations have risen regarding regulation, and authority and control have continued to be present. The compliance mechanisms are also in place. While the legal status of the regime is not in dispute, the regime created legal obligations before a formal Convention had evolved.

The regime is, therefore, a good example of the role of regimes within the international legal order, as well as proof of the evolutionary aspects of regimes. The lawmaking process continues as the regime evolves. As a result, the regime can include at any one time, regulations that are not binding under international law as shared expectations may not yet be present. It is important to remember that :

> states have the will to protect the environment on their own terms and by the methods preferred by them, under which they have some control over the pace of regime change.[162]

Thus, while the present legal status of the ozone layer depletion regime has evolved to a stage of treaty law, its legal status in the early stages of the regime should not be overlooked or denied. Indeed, it is that stage of the regime that presents evidence of the important role of regimes within the international legal order, revealing the presence of the legal order long before it is usually recognized as existing with regard to a specific issue-area.

An analysis of the climate change regime will now be undertaken for comparison.

NOTES

1. *Ecclesiastes* 1:4.

2. Including halons, HCFCs, carbon tetrachloride, methyl chloroform, methyl bromide, and HBFCs. See, *supra*, Chapter 1, for a description of their uses in industry.

3. The Vienna Ozone Convention was adopted in March 1985 and the Protocol in September 1987, *International Legal Materials* Vol. 26, No. 6 (1987), pp. 1516–1540 and pp. 1541–1561 respectively. The 1990 London Revisions (amendment and adjustments) to the Protocol are reprinted in *International Legal Materials* Vol. 30, No. 2 (1991), pp. 537–554. The 1992 Copenhagen Revisions (amendment and adjustments) can be found in the *Report of the Fourth Meeting of the Parties to the Montreal Protocol on Substances That Deplete the Ozone Layer*, UNEP/Oz.L.Pro.4/15, 25 November 1992.

4. See *supra*, Chapter 1.

5. Richard Elliot Benedick, *Ozone Diplomacy: New Directions in Safeguarding the Planet* (Cambridge: Harvard University Press, 1991), p. 40.

6. See Edward A. Parson, "Protecting the Ozone Layer," *Institutions For The Earth* (Cambridge: MIT Press, 1993), p. 35 and Benedick, *Ozone Diplomacy*, *supra*, n. 5, p. 40.

7. See Benedick, *Ozone Diplomacy*, *supra*, n. 5, p. 24, Parson, "Protecting the Ozone Layer," *supra*, n. 6, pp. 36–38, and Sharon Roan, *Ozone Crisis* (NY: John Wiley & Sons, Inc, 1989) p. 84.

8. See, Parson, "Protecting The Ozone Layer," *supra*, n. 6, pp. 37–38. The Toronto Group consisted of Canada, Finland, Norway, Sweden and the United States, with supporters including Australia, Austria, Denmark and Switzerland. See also, Roan, *Ozone Crisis*, *supra*, n. 7, pp. 114–117.

9. Benedick quotes Patrick Szell, a British official involved in the negotiations as stating: "not all countries... were prepared to be so sweeping or quick [as the Toronto Group] to condemn such useful chemical substances,"concluding that "their hesitance was vindicated" when newer estimates showed reduced predictions of future ozone depletion and noted that if the Toronto Group had insisted on their protocol, "a sizeable proportion of the world's CFC-producing countries would simply have refused to have anything to do with it." Benedick, *Ozone Diplomacy*,

supra, n. 5, p. 44.

10. The Convention entered into force on September 22, 1988. As of May 1995, 151 states have ratified. Source: Treaty Section, UN Legal Office, New York.

11. Vienna Ozone Convention, Arts. 4 & 6, *supra*, n. 3. See also, Dale S. Bryk, "The Montreal Protocol and Recent Developments To Protect The Ozone Layer," *Harvard Environmental Law Review* Vol. 15, No. 1 (1991), p. 280.

12. See, UNEP, *Action On Ozone* (Nairobi: UNEP, 1989), p. 8.

13. See, *supra*, Chapter 1.

14. Montreal Protocol, *supra*, n. 3, Art. 2. CFCs 11, 12, 113, 114 and 115 were regulated, along with halons 1301, 1211 and 2402. CFC-11 and CFC-12, used in refrigeration, air-conditioning and aerosols, have the greatest ozone depletion potential.

15. Ibid., Arts. 2 and 5. For the purpose of the Protocol, the developing countries are identified in "Decision of the First Meeting of the Parties to the Montreal Protocol on Substances that Deplete the Ozone Layer,"Art. 12E, UNEP/Ozl.Pro.1/5, reprinted in UNEP, *Handbook for the Montreal Protocol On Substances That Deplete The Ozone Layer*, (Nairobi: UNEP Ozone Secretariat, May 1991), pp. 57–58. In order to qualify for the 10 year extension, developing countries must have an annual calculated level of consumption of the controlled substances of less than 0.3 kilograms per capita. See, *infra*, n. 26, for extensions relating to new substances controlled by the London Revisions.

16. Montreal Protocol, *supra*, n. 3, Art. 3, where formulas were laid out for determining production, imports and exports, and consumption.

17. Ibid., Art. 4, outlining the restrictions regulating the import and export of controlled substances with non-parties, as well as the technologies for producing controlled substances.

18. Ibid., Art. 6, to be done on the basis of available scientific, environmental, technical and economic information.

19. Ibid., Art. 7, mandating annual reports on production, imports, and exports.

20. Ibid., Art. 8.

21. As of May 1995, there are 149 ratifications under the Protocol, Source: Treaty Office, UN Legal Office, NY.

22. The purpose of the meetings of the Parties is outlined in the Protocol and include taking any action necessary to achieve the purposes of the Protocol. Montreal Protocol, *supra*, n. 3, Art. 11(4).

23. See *supra*, Chapter 1.

24. Helsinki Declaration on the Protection of the Ozone Layer, *International Legal Materials* Vol. 28, No. 5 (1989) pp. 1335–1336.

25. Amendments to the Protocol require a 2/3 majority vote (if consensus fails). They enter into force after at least 2/3 of the Protocol Parties have ratified it(unless the Protocol provides otherwise), and are binding only on those Parties that ratified, Vienna Convention, Art. 9(4),(5) *supra*, n. 3.

Adjustments, changes in stringency and timing of already controlled substances, required a 2/3 majority vote (if consensus fails) of Parties present and voting representing at least 50% of the total consumption of the controlled substances of the Parties, and is binding on all Parties, Montreal Protocol, Art. 2(9), *supra*, n. 3. This requirement for adjustments was amended in London to require separate majorities of Art. 5 countries present and voting, as well as non-Art. 5 states present and voting. London Revisions, *supra*, n. 3, Art. 2(9)C. This represents a major shift of power towards developing countries, Winfried Lang, "Ozone Layer," *Yearbook of International Environmental Law* Vol. 3 (1992), p. 225.

26. London Revisions, *supra*, n. 3, Arts. 2A & 5. For Parties operating under Article 5, in addition to not exceeding an annual calculated level of consumption of 0.3 kilograms per capita of substances already controlled under the Montreal Protocol, *supra*, n. 3, these Parties must not exceed an annual calculated level of consumption of 0.2 kilograms per capita of new substances added in London. Art. 5(2). See also, United Nations, *Report of the 2d Meeting for the Parties to the Montreal Protocol on Substances that Deplete the Ozone Layer*, UNEP/Oz.L.Pro.2/3, 29 June 1990.

27. London Revisions, *supra*, n. 3, Art. 2B.

28. Ibid. But see *infra*, n. 41.

29. Ibid., Art. 2E, D & C respectively.

30. Ibid., Annex VII. See also, Bryk, "Montreal Protocol," *supra*, n. 11, p. 286.

31. London Revisions, *supra*, n. 3, Art. 4. In addition, Parties may be allowed to import and export controlled substances to a non-parties deemed to be in conformity with the Protocol. Art. 4(8).

32. Ibid., Art. 10.

33. American Society of International Law, "Ozone," *International Environmental Law Interest Group Newsletter* Vol. 3, No. 1 (September 1992), p. 6. See also, "Green Aid," *Our Planet: Magazine of the UNEP*, Vol. 2, No. 4 (1990), p. 9.

34. London Revisions, Art. 10 & Annex IV, Appendix IV, *supra*, n. 3. See also, Daniel Goldberg, *The Montreal Protocol Multilateral Fund: A Model for the Framework Convention on Climate Change*, (Washington, DC: Center for International Environmental Law, 1992), and Bryk, "Montreal Protocol," *supra*, n. 11, p. 287.

35. Bryk, "Montreal Protocol," *supra*, n. 11, pp. 288–290. See also, Benedick, *Ozone Diplomacy*, *supra*, n. 5, esp. Chapter 13.

36. "Montreal Protocol: Third Meeting of the Parties," *Environmental Policy and Law*, Vol. 21, No. 5/6 (1991), pp. 251–252. See also, American Society of International Law, "Ozone Depletion," *International Environmental Law Interest Group Newsletter* Vol. 2, No. 2 (November 1991), p. 6.

37. American Society International Law, "Montreal Protocol," *International Environmental Law Interest Group Newsletter* (May 1991), pp. 5–6.

38. American Society of International Law, "Ozone," *supra*, n. 33, p. 6. As of May 1985, there are 103 ratifications. Source: Treaty Section, UN Legal Office, NY.

39. See *supra*, Chapter 1.

40. See, *Fourth Meeting of the Parties*, *supra*, n. 3.

41. Ibid., Annex I, p. 32. The phase-out will not apply if the Parties agree to permit the level of production or consumption that is necessary for "essential" uses. The Parties adopted a procedure for the approval of "essential" uses, defined as necessary for health or safety, or critical to the functioning of society, and there are no available alternatives or existing stocks of banked or recycled material. Ibid., Decision IV/25, pp. 24–26.

42. Ibid. The 10 year deferral still applies as well, Art. 5, see, *supra*, n. 15. The Parties decided that individual cases should be considered for the classification of "developing countries,"and that no formal definition be given. Decision IV/7, pp. 14–15.

43. See, Ian Rowlands, "Copenhagen Meeting on the Montreal Protocol on the Ozone Layer," *LSE Center for the Study of Global Governance Newsletter* Vol. 2, No. 1 (Spring 1993), pp. 2–3.

44. *Report of the Fourth Meeting*, *supra*, n. 3, Annex III, pp. 36–42. Developing states were given leave to exceed the freeze on methyl bromide by 10%. The United States, facing a phase-out of methyl bromide by 2000 under its Clean Air Act, had introduced an amendment to the Protocol calling for a phase-out by 2000 for all Parties, but was met by opposition from developing states, where the use of the substance as a soil and crop fumigant is increasing. A resolution was adopted stating that the methyl bromide should become subject to controls for developed states. Annex XV.

45. *Report of the Fourth Meeting*, *supra*, n. 3, Decision IV/4, p. 29. Art. 5. Lang, "Ozone Layer," *supra*, n. 25, p. 226.

46. As of May 1995, 45 Parties have ratified the Amendment. Source: Treaty Section, UN Legal Office, NY.

47. Ibid., Decision IV/18, pp. 19–21.

48. Ibid., Annexes IX–XIV, pp. 53–70, Decision IV, p. 21.

49. Ibid., Annex IV, pp. 46–47.

50. Ibid., Annex V, p. 48. See, "Third Meeting of the Parties," *supra*, n. 36, p. 251, Decision III/2. This was due mostly to the US view that non-payment of contributions to the Multilateral Fund did not qualify as non-compliance, since those contributions were non-compulsory. Thus, consensus on examples of non-compliance was absent. See, Winfried Lang, "Ozone Layer," *Yearbook of International Environmental Law* Vol. 2 (1991), p. 109. See, also, *American Society of International Law*, "Ozone Depletion," *International Environmental Law Interest Group Newsletter* Vol. 2, No. 2 (November 1991), p. 6.

51. Ozone Depletion Network Online Today, 13 September 1994 and 11 October 1994. The Seventh Meeting of the Parties is scheduled for the fall of 1995 in Vienna.

52. See, *supra,* Chapter 3, Regime Formation.

53. See, *supra*, n. 8.

54. See, *infra*, Chapter 5, Domestic Regulations.

55. See, *supra*, Chapter 3, Maintenance or Development of a Regime.

56. Ibid.

57. See, *supra*, Chapter 1.

58. In 1976, the estimate was for 2-20% depletion; in 1979, 16.5%; in 1982, 5-9% depletion; and in 1984, 2-4%. See Roan, *Ozone Crisis*, *supra*, n. 7, p. 112.

59. See, *supra*, Chapter 1.

60. See, *supra*, Chapter 4, Overcoming Scientific Uncertainty.

61. Peter M. Haas, "Do Regimes Matter? Epistemic Communities and Mediterranean Pollution Control," *International Organization*, Vol. 43, No. 3 (Summer 1989), pp. 402–403. Haas states that epistemic communities were influential as well in the Mediterranean Action Plans and the European acid rain policies. See also Haas, *Saving the Mediterranean: The Politics of International Environmental Cooperation* (NY: Columbia University Press, 1990) and Haas, "Obtaining International Environmental Protection Through Epistemic Consensus," *Millennium: Journal of International Studies*, Vol. 19, No. 3, pp. 347–363.

62. Haas, "Epistemic Consensus," *supra*, n. 61, p. 354.

63. Ibid., p. 356.

64. Benedick, *Ozone Diplomacy*, *supra,* n. 5, p. 29.

65. For example, Benedick states that in the UK, support did not develop until September 1988 , when then-Prime Minister Thatcher spoke to the Royal Society calling for immediate action regarding ozone depletion. Ibid., p. 114.

66. See, *infra*, Chapter 5, Development Uncertainty, for the role of developing states at the London Meeting.

67. See, *supra*, Chapter 1.

68. See, *supra*, n. 8.

69. See Benedick, *Ozone Diplomacy*, *supra*, n. 5, p. 42.

70. See Parson, "Protecting the Ozone Layer," *supra*, n. 6, p. 41.

71. In 1986, DuPont had stated that it had ceased research into alternatives for nonaerosol CFC uses 5 years earlier. See, Benedick, *Ozone Diplomacy*, *supra*, n. 5, p. 33.

72. See, Arjun Makihijani, Amanda Bickel and Annie Makihijani, "Still Working on the Ozone Hole: Beyond the Montreal Protocol," *Technology Review* Vol. 93, No. 4 (May-June 1990), pp. 52–59.

73. See, Peter Morrisette, "The Evolution of Policy Responses to Stratospheric Ozone Depletion," *Natural Resources Journal* Vol. 29, No. 3 (Winter 1989), p. 818.

74. Makihijani et al, "Ozone Hole," *supra*, n. 72, p. 55.

75. See, *supra*, n. 3.

76. Art. 6, *supra*, n. 3.

77. *Montreal Protocol 1991 Assessment: Report of the Technology and Economic Assessment Panel*, 1991 Assessment (Nairobi: UNEP, December 1991), pp. 12(1), ES-4.

78. See, *supra*, n. 3.

79. *Fourth Meeting of the Parties*, *supra*, n. 3, Synthesis Report of the Assessment Panel, p. 6.

80. See, "Hewlett-Packard Eliminates CFCs," Business Wire, 20 May 1993, Compuserve 1455. The alternatives include water-based cleaners and a "no-clean" process using non-corrosive materials that do not have to be cleaned off. Hewlett-Packard spent four years and over $60 million developing its ozone-friendly substitutes.

81. See, "Compaq Computer Eliminates CFCs," Business Wire, 18 May 1993, 1231 Compuserve. Compaq is using "no clean" alternatives as well, see, *supra*, n. 80.

82. See, Greenpeace Press Release, "Ozone-Friendly Fridge Breakthrough As Antarctic Ozone Hole Worsens," Compuserve, 30 September 1992. However, the international regulatory effort has created a black market in CFCs which slows efforts to reduce their use and seek alternatives such as the CFC-free refrigerator. See, Julie Edelson Halpert, "Freon Smugglers Find Big Market," *The New York Times*, 30 April 1995., p. 1.

83. In addition, the amended Protocol allows for the transfer of production allowances to another party, in effect, allowing for tradeable permits, providing for greater economic efficiency. London Revisions,

supra, n. 3, Art. 2(5).

84. See, *supra*, Chapter 5, International Action Regarding Ozone Layer Depletion.

85. Ibid.

86. See, Friends of the Earth, *Funding Change: Developing Countries and the Montreal Protocol* (London: FOE, 1990). See, also, Greenpeace International, "HCFCs: An Unacceptable Solution," Compuserve, December 1992.

87. Particularly when industry sees economic benefits in doing so. As evidence of this, market investment in a US chemical manufacturing firm has risen since the company, American Pacific Corp., acquired the option to buy the global rights to "Halotran,"a fire-extinguishing chemical designed to replace the ozone-depleting halons. See, Diana B. Henriques, "They Hope To Cash In By Fixing the Ozone Hole," *International Herald Tribune*, 15 June 1992, p. 11. The list of alternatives and possible alternatives for all ozone depleting substances is too long to be described here. For a general overview, see, K.M. Sarma, "Protection of the Ozone Layer: Technology Development and Transfer," (Nairobi: UNEP Ozone Secretariat, May 1993), where the latest status of alternative chemicals and processes is indicated. CFC alternatives for aerosols are for the most part available, as are alternatives for CFCs used in foams and where CFCs and methyl chloroform are used as solvent cleaning agents. See, also, Greenpeace, *Climbing Out of the Ozone Hole: A Preliminary Survey of Alternatives to Ozone Depleting Substances* (October 1992) and *Making the Right Choice For the Ozone Layer* (September 1992), as well as the *Report of the Technology and Economic Assessment Panel*, *supra*, n. 77.

88. Benedick, *Ozone Diplomacy*, *supra*, n. 5, p. 148.

89. Ibid.

90. Ibid., p. 189.

91. London Revisions, Article 10A, *supra*, n. 3.

92. Ibid., Art. 5 and see, *supra*, Chapter 5, International Action Regarding Ozone Layer Depletion.

93. See, Benedick, *Ozone Diplomacy*, *supra*, n. 5, especially Chapter 12, "The South Claims A Role."

94. Thus, at the Copenhagen meeting, Lang notes that the extension of control had to be balanced by new concessions in favor of developing states. "Ozone Layer," *supra*, n. 25, p. 226. Both China and India are now Parties to the Protocol as well as the London Amendment. In addition, Mexico has stated that it would phase out CFCs by 2000, ahead of the schedule required for developing countries, utilizing the Multilateral Fund for its transition. American Society of International Law, "CFCs," *International Environmental Law Interest Group News-*

letter, Vol. 2, No. 1 (August 1991), p. 3. It was agreed at the time of the implementation of the Multilateral Fund that the dollar amount would be increased by $40 million when China ratified and $40 million when India did so. But see Anil Markandya, "Economics and the Ozone Layer," in David Pearce, et al, *Blueprint 2* (London: Earthscan Publications Ltd, 1991), pp. 72–23. In addition, eventual non-compliance is an "economic proposition only in a country with a large internal or external non-Party market for CFC consumption." See, Alice Enders and Amelia Porges, "Successful Conventions and Conventional Success: Saving The Ozone Layer," in *The Greening of World Trade Issues*, ed. Kym Anderson and Richard Blackhurst (London: Harvester Wheatsheaf, 1992), p. 140.

95. *Fourth Meeting of the Parties*, *supra*, n. 3, Report of the Chairman of the Executive Committee of the Interim Multilateral Fund, p. 6. There was also concern expressed by parties not operating under article 5 status as developing states, that they were encountering serious, but hopefully transitory economic difficulties due to their economies being in transition. These particular states regretted that the Parties "appeared unwilling to recognize the existence of a third group of countries— those with economies in transition—as well as the two established groups of developed and developing countries." Statements, p. 11. The regime will need to take account of these states for successful implementation. See, also, *Report of the Technology and Economic Assessment Panel*, *supra*, n. 77, and Ozone Depletion Network Online Today, *supra*, n. 51.

96. Treaty Section, UN Legal Office, 9 May 1995.

97. See, *supra*, Chapter 4, for a general discussion of regime catalysts.

98. See, Benedick, *Ozone Diplomacy*, esp. Chapter 3, *supra*, n. 5, and Roan, *Ozone Crisis*, *supra*, esp. Chapter 7, n. 7.

99. US Clean Air Act, 42 USC 7457(b). See Benedick, *Ozone Diplomacy*, *supra*, n. 5, pp. 23–24. See. also, *infra*, Chapter 5, Domestic Regulations. This type of leadership, then, evolved more from what Young refers to as "skilful negotiation" than from the type based on "intellectual contributions." See, *supra*, Chapter 4, Leadership.

100. Parson, "Protecting the Ozone Layer," *supra*, n. 6, p. 70.

101. See, Benedick, *Ozone Diplomacy*, *supra*, n. 5, pp. 188–189, 196, in particular, quoting India's environment minister at the London meetings to revise the Protocol, Maneka Gandhi, as demanding of the developed world: "Either you [sell us] the technology or you change your laws or you change your patent rights... Start working on it." Ibid., p. 189.

102. See, Rowlands, "Copenhagen Meeting," *supra*, n. 43, pp. 2–3. A resolution calling for its eventual phaseout was adopted, although a phaseout is not expected of Art. 5 Parties.

103. Gareth Porter and Janet Welsh Brown, *Global Environmental Politics* (Boulder, CO: Westview Press, 1991), p. 48,

104. Benedick, *Ozone Diplomacy*, *supra*, n. 5, p. 6.

105. See, *supra*, Chapter 4, International/Intergovernmental Organizations.

106. Kenneth Piddington, "The Role of the World Bank," in *The International Politics of the Environment*, ed. Andrew Hurrell and Benedict Kingsbury (Oxford: Clarendon Press, 1992), p. 225.

107. See, *supra,* Chapter 5, International Action Regarding Ozone Layer Depletion.

108. See, *supra*, Chapter 4, International/Intergovernmental Organizations and *infra*, Chapter 6, International Action Regarding Climate Change.

109. Porter and Brown, *Global Environmental Politics*, *supra*, n. 103, p. 60. See also, Benedick, *Ozone Diplomacy*, *supra*, n. 5, p. 28, and Roan, *Ozone Crisis*, *supra*, n. 7, p. 113.

110. Porter and Brown, *supra*, n. 103, pp. 60–61. During the second meeting of the parties to the Protocol in 1990, FOE, along with Greenpeace, advised Australia and Norway, who were pressing for a 1997 phase-out date of CFCs, pp. 61–62.

111. See, *supra*, Chapter 5, Economic Uncertainty.

112. The ICOLP was formed by two commercial rivals, AT&T and Northern Telecom (Canada), and a government agency, the US EPA, which is often in an adversarial position with private business. The organization's membership includes the Japan Electrical Manufacturers Association, the State Institute of Applied Industry (from the former USSR) and the US Air Force. Braden Allenby, "Achieving Sustainable Development Through Industrial Ecology," *International Environmental Affairs* Vol. 4, No. 1 (Winter 1992), p. 68, fn 23.

113. Porter and Brown, *Global Environmental Politics*, *supra*, n. 103, p. 66. The Clean Air Act authorized the EPA administrator to regulate "any substance... which in his judgment may reasonably be anticipated to affect the stratosphere, especially ozone in the stratosphere, if such effect may reasonably be anticipated to endanger public health or welfare."

114. Benedick, *Ozone Diplomacy*, *supra*, n. 5, p. 66.

115. Ibid., p. 64.

116. See, *Report of the Technical and Economic Assessment Panel*, *supra*, n. 77, Annex D.

117. See, for instance, Benedick, *Ozone Diplomacy*, *supra*, n. 5, esp. Chapter 9, and Roan, *Ozone Crisis*, *supra*, n. 7.

118. See, *supra*, Chapter 1. Ozone Layer Depletion.

119. See, *supra*, Chapter 5, International Action Regarding Ozone Layer Depletion and *supra*, Chapter 1, Ozone Layer Depletion.

120. See, *supra*, Chapter 5, International Action Regarding Ozone Layer Depletion, and *supra*, Chapter 1, Ozone Layer Depletion.

121. William K. Stevens, "Ozone Loss Over US Is Found To Be Twice As Bad As Predicted," *The New York Times*, 5 April 1991, pp. A1 and D18.

122. See, Tom Wicker, "Bad News From Above," *The New York Times*, 10 April 1991, p. A25, and "A Bigger Hole In the Ozone: EPA Predicts 200,000 More Skin-Cancer Deaths," *Newsweek*, 15 April 1991, p. 64.

123. See, *supra*, Chapter 1, Ozone Layer Depletion, and *supra*, Chapter 5, International Action Regarding Ozone Layer Depletion.

124. See, *supra*, Chapter 5, International Action Regarding Ozone Layer Depletion.

125. Ibid.

126. See, *supra*, Chapter 3, Maintenance or Development of Regimes.

127. See, *supra*, Chapter 5, International Action Regarding Ozone Layer Depletion.

128. See, *Fourth Meeting of the Parties*, *supra*, n. 3, Report of the Implementation Committee, p. 7. See, also, Martti Koskenniemi, "Breach of Treaty or Non-Compliance? Reflections on the Enforcement of the Montreal Protocol," *Yearbook of International Environmental Law* Vol. 3 (1992), pp. 123–162.

129. Montreal Protocol, *supra*, n. 3, Arts. 2, 7.

130. *Fourth Meeting of the Parties*, *supra*, n. 3, p. 8.

131. Ibid., Decision IV/9, p. 15. But see Lang, "Ozone Layer," *supra*, n. 25, who states that "among developing countries, CFC use presents a rather mixed picture."

132. Montreal Protocol, Art. 4, *supra*, n. 3.

133. See, *Fourth Meeting of the Parties*, *supra*, n. 3, Decision IV/17 C, p. 19.

134. Ibid. The Protocol provides for trade bans, not sanctions, since they are not "penalties or restrictions on products other than ozone-depleting chemicals or products containing CFCs." See, Enders and Porges, "Successful Conventions," *supra*, n. 94, p. 140. See also, *supra*, Chapter 3, Conditional Cooperation and Exclusion.

135. *Fourth Meeting of the Parties*, *supra*, n. 3, Article 4(4). Lang, "Ozone Layer," *supra*, n. 25, p. 226.

136. See, *supra*, Chapter 3, Formation of Regimes.

137. See, *supra*, Chapter 2, Policy-Oriented Lawmaking.

138. See, *supra*, Chapter 5, International Action Regarding Ozone Layer Depletion.

139. See, *supra*, Chapter 2, Policy-Oriented Lawmaking,

140. Ibid.

141. See, *supra*, Chapter 5, International Action Regarding Ozone Layer Depletion.

142. Ibid.

143. Ibid.

144. Ibid., see also, *supra*, Chapter 5, International Non-state Actors.

145. See, *supra*, Chapter 5, International Non-state Actors.

146. See, *supra*, Chapter 5, Development Uncertainty.

147. Ibid.

148. See, *supra*, Chapter 2, Policy-Oriented Lawmaking.

149. See, *supra*, Chapter 5, International Action Regarding Ozone Layer Depletion.

150. Ibid.

151. Parson, "Protecting the Ozone Layer," *supra*, n. 6, p. 29.

152. *Supra*, Chapter 5, International Action Regarding Ozone Layer Depletion.

153. See, *supra*, Chapter 1, Ozone Layer Depletion, and Chapter 5, Scientific Uncertainty.

154. Parson, "Protecting the Ozone Layer," *supra,* n. 6, pp. 35–36.

155. See, *supra*, Chapter 5, Maintenance of the Ozone Layer Depletion Regime.

156. See, *supra*, Chapter 5, International Action Regarding Ozone Layer Depletion.

157. Except for the dispute resolution process, and the voting status and competency of the EC. See, Parson, "Protecting the Ozone Layer," *supra*, n. 6, p. 39.

158. See, *supra*, Chapter 5, Economic Uncertainty.

159. See, *supra*, Chapter 2, Policy-Oriented Lawmaking.

160. See, *supra*, Chapter 2, Customary Law.

161. Patricia W. Birnie & Alan E. Boyle, *International Law & the Environment* (Oxford: Clarendon Press, 1993), p. 15.

162. Patricia Birnie, "International Environmental Law: Its Adequacy For Present and Future Needs," in *The International Politics of the Environment*, ed. Andrew Hurrell and Benedict Kingsbury (Oxford: Clarendon Press, 1992), p. 84.

CHAPTER 6

Analysis of the Climate Change Regime

For... ourselves and our Posterity[1]

In analyzing the climate change regime, parallels between it and the ozone layer depletion regime will become apparent, but so also will differences, because of the greater degree of scientific, economic and development uncertainty in the climate change regime. This has prevented the development of more substantive obligations. In that respect, however, the role of regimes in the international legal order will be underscored, since the present status of the present climate change regime highlights the value of regimes often overlooked in a more traditional view of international law.

INTERNATIONAL ACTION REGARDING CLIMATE CHANGE

The UN Framework Convention on Climate Change (FCCC) was opened for signature at the UN Conference on Environment and Development in Rio de Janeiro, June 1992.[2] 155 states signed the FCCC, which came into force in March 1994.[3]

This Convention was negotiated in a relatively short period of time; it took less than two years from the date the UN General Assembly Resolution 45/212 of December 1990[4] established the Intergovernmental Negotiating Committee (INC) to produce a framework convention on climate change, until the Convention was opened for signature in June 1992.

The Convention followed on from the findings of key scientific and policy-oriented conferences, the first occurring in 1985. At that time, the United Nations Environment Programme (UNEP), together with the World Meteorological Organization (WMO), and the International Council of Scientific Unions (ICSU), a non-governmental organization, sponsored an international scientific conference in Villach, Austria to examine climate change.[5] The conference recommended that task forces be formed to examine policy options concerning climate change, as some warming appeared inevitable, the rate of which "could be profoundly affected by government policies on energy conservation, on the use of fossil fuels, and emission of some greenhouse gases."[6] This conference was followed-up by two workshops in 1987, a science-oriented gathering held in Villach and the other focusing on policy, held in Bellagio, Italy.[7] The joint report recommended the development of a "costing framework" for comparison of the costs of differing policy strategies and also suggested the setting of a maximum temperature increase from global warming per decade.[8]

The following year, more than 300 scientists and policymakers from 46 countries, UN and other international bodies, and non-governmental organizations gathered in Toronto in June 1988, at the World Conference on the Changing Atmosphere, sponsored by the government of Canada.[9] The Conference Statement warned that "humanity is conducting an unintended, uncontrolled, globally pervasive experiment whose ultimate consequences could be second only to a global nuclear war."[10] An "Action Plan for the Protection of the Atmosphere" was called for, as well as a World Atmosphere Fund to provide the financial resources to implement the Action Plan.[11] More specifically, the Action Plan called for an international framework convention, national legislation to protect the atmosphere as well as national action plans to address climate change problems "at their roots."[12] Reference was also made to differentiated responsibility, whereby developed states, being the main source of greenhouse gas emissions, accordingly bear the main responsibility for addressing climate change.[13]

The Legal Working Group of the Toronto Conference recognized that, while there was an existing body of international environmental law, it was relatively fragmented and incomplete, thus possibly requiring the creation of "new principles, rules and institutional frameworks."[14]

Concerns over recognition of the atmosphere as a global commons were raised by the Geopolitical Working Group, which stressed that "sovereignty is not 'ceded', but 'pooled'" within a commons; there are "rights of use", not property rights; all have an equal responsibility to care for the commons; and that "individual use is subject in principle to common consent and decisions are by consensus."[15]

Following the Toronto Conference, in February 1989, Canada again convened a Legal and Policy Experts Meeting in Ottawa on the atmosphere, focusing on the legal and institutional framework concerning the atmosphere and climate change.[16] The statement outlined elements for both a broad treaty on the atmosphere and a narrower convention on climate change, with accompanying protocols as appropriate. Concerning the elements for inclusion in a convention on protection of the atmosphere, the experts concluded that the atmosphere "constitutes a common resource of vital interest to mankind,"[17] and that all states had an obligation to co-operate to protect the atmosphere.[18]

A month after the Ottawa Meeting, the government of the Netherlands hosted, in March 1989, a ministerial meeting at the Hague to discuss the obligation of states regarding atmospheric changes. Proposing an alternative approach to the convention outlined in Toronto, the participants agreed to encourage the development of a new institutional authority within the UN to cope with global warming, whether it be via an enhancement of existing institutions or through the creation of a new organization.[19] The Declaration envisaged the International Court of Justice implementing these standards, a shift from their traditional role of determining liability.[20] It should be pointed out that the conference participants did not include the United States, which had not been issued an invitation, nor the United Kingdom, which had declined to attend. Thus, it cannot be assumed that complete consensus exists as this time regarding the use of an international mechanism to enforce international environmental obligations.[21]

Another Ministerial Meeting was convened in Noordwijk, the

Netherlands, in November 1989. This time, 67 countries participated, as well as the EC Commission and 11 international organizations.[22] While limits on emission levels of greenhouse gases were not set, agreement that a climate change convention be drafted as soon as possible signalled that the prospect of international cooperation for action existed in this area.[23] The Declaration also reaffirmed that climate change is a common concern of mankind, while stressing the differentiated responsibility of states.[24]

In May 1990, at the Bergen Conference on Sustainable Development states agreed that the industrialized world was primarily responsible for greenhouse gas emissions and therefore assumed the greater responsibility for dealing with the problem. The Bergen Declaration advocated this principle of common but differentiated responsibility, along with the precautionary principle, whereby potentially harmful activities should be restricted or prohibited before serious damage results.[25]

Meanwhile, UNEP and the WMO had again joined forces concerning climate change through the establishment of the Intergovernmental Panel on Climate Change (IPCC) in November 1988, subsequently endorsed by the General Assembly.[26] The General Assembly requested UNEP and WMO, through the implementation of the IPCC, to take action and make recommendations about climate change regarding the state of scientific knowledge, the socio-economic impact and the formulation of possible response strategies.[27] Accordingly, three IPCC Working Groups were created, operating in coordination under the IPCC: scientific analysis (Working Group I)[28], impacts (Working Group II)[29] and response strategies (Working Group III).[30] The coordinators' report on prospective legal measures regarding climate change suggested that a convention on climate change should resemble in format the Vienna Ozone Convention.[31] That is to say, the convention should provide for general principles and obligations, while providing for separate protocols to delineate specific obligations. However, the report was careful to point out that "views differ substantially on the role and powers of the institutions to be created by the Convention, particularly in exercising supervision and control over the obligations undertaken."[32]

The final report of the IPCC, based on the findings of its three Working Groups, was drawn up in August 1990, at Sundsvall,

Sweden. Significantly, agreement was reached that scientific evidence concerning global warming signalled a real threat to the Earth.[33] As scientific uncertainty[34] poses one of the greatest challenges to the development of a regime for climate change, the agreement at Sundsvall was laudatory. The agreement came at an opportune time, as the Second World Climate Conference in Geneva was due to take place, where the IPCC report was to be formally presented.

Eleven years after the first gathering was held, the WMO, UNEP and the ICSU jointly sponsored the Second World Climate Conference in November 1990.[35] The Conference was visualized as the "official unveiling" of the IPCC report on climate change.[36] The UNEP Executive Director opened the conference by declaring that climate change has created "a threat potentially more catastrophic than any other threat in human history" and that "nothing less than a complete change in attitudes and lifestyles will succeed" in stopping the warming,"while recognizing that there was differentiated responsibility for climate change."[37] The declaration of the Conference called for states to develop programs to reduce greenhouse gas emissions, but no targets were set.[38]

The following month, the UN General Assembly created by resolution the Intergovernmental Negotiating Committee, whose task was to prepare a framework convention on climate change.[39]

The first negotiating session for a climate treaty was held in Washington, D.C., in February 1991.[40] Hopes that the Chantilly Conference[41] might result in a "Bretton Woods," in that rules of a new order might evolve,[42] were not fulfilled. Nevertheless, an agreement was reached establishing the guidelines for negotiating a final treaty on climate change.[43] The guidelines set up two working groups: Working Group I to examine "appropriate commitments"[44] for the reduction of greenhouse gases, the protection of forests, and compensation and technical assistance for developing countries, and Working Group II to draft the treaty.[45]

The second session of the INC took place in Geneva, June 1991, where co-chairs were selected for the two working groups established at Chantilly; Working Group I was to be chaired by Mexico and Japan, while Canada and Vanuatu were selected to head Working Group II.[46] Discussions centered on whether specific commitments to reduce greenhouse gas emissions should be included in the convention, with the United States and the then-

USSR opposing such binding commitments and the European Community seeking specific commitments to reduce CO_2. A compromise "pledge and review" concept was put forward by which states would pledge specific action to slow emissions, and would also be subject to a review of the action taken.[47]

Disagreements also arose concerning a financial mechanism. Most industrialized states supported the use of existing mechanisms like the Global Environmental Facility (GEF), while many developing countries pushed for a new fund outright.[48]

Nairobi was the site of the third session of the INC, held in September 1991. Disagreements still remained over the use of specific targets and timetables in a convention, particularly for the United States, which regarded such targets as premature. The United States also argued for a comprehensive approach, rather than focusing on CO_2 alone. The pledge and review concept did not receive great support, as some states still held out hope for specific commitments.[49]

The fourth and fifth sessions of the INC, held in Geneva, December 1991, and New York, February 1992 respectively, did not produce much progress. Disagreements still remained as to specific commitments for slowing greenhouse gas emissions, as well as the issue of financial aid to developing states and the financial mechanism to implement the aid. Legal requirements, such as entry into force and dispute settlement techniques, also remained unresolved, as did the issue of a comprehensive approach versus focusing solely on CO_2.[50]

The final session of the INC prior to the UN Conference on Environment and Development was held in New York in early May 1992. Despite the previous disagreement at prior negotiating sessions, agreement was finally achieved at the final INC session and the UN FCCC was adopted. However, the FCCC did not include any specific caps on timetable and emissions of greenhouse gases.[51]

The FCCC was signed in Rio de Janeiro in June 1992. Substantively, the Convention adopts a comprehensive approach to the problem of climate change by including all known sources and sinks of greenhouse gases (other than those controlled under the Montreal Protocol).

Specifically, the Convention requires all parties to "develop, periodically update, publish and make available... national inventories" of the sources and sinks of its greenhouse gases, as well as to formulate and implement national measures to mitigate climate change.[52]

For developed states, this information, along with information on their policies to mitigate climate change and the projected effect of such policies, must be provided within six months after the Convention enters into force, and will be reviewed periodically by the Conference of the Parties.[53] These policies are to be created "with the aim of returning individually or jointly to their 1990 levels" of greenhouse gas emissions.[54] For developing states, their required reports of inventories and national measures must be submitted within three years after the Convention enters into force or after receiving financial assistance.[55] Least developed states may make the reports at their discretion.[56]

The Convention also requires developed states to provide the financial resources for the developing states to comply with their obligations,[57] and to "promote, facilitate and finance...the transfer of, or access to, environmentally sound technologies and know-how."[58]

In addition to the less stringent reporting requirements for developing states, the Convention also allows "a certain amount of flexibility" regarding commitments for states moving towards market economies, as well as for those states who have special needs such as low-lying countries, or those states highly dependent on the income generated from the production and/or consumption of fossil fuels.[59]

In order to implement the Convention, a Conference of the Parties is established to review the Convention and to assess the measures taken by the Parties, as well as to facilitate the exchange of information between the Parties.[60] In addition, the Subsidiary Body for Science and Technological Advice was established under the Convention to provide advice on science and technology issues to the Conference of the Parties.[61]

A financial mechanism is also provided by the Convention,[62] and has been entrusted to the Global Environmental Facility (GEF), established under the control of the World Bank, UNEP and the UN Development Programme (UNDP).[63] The GEF was established as a US$1 billion fund to aid projects designed to reduce ozone depletion, global warming, marine pollution and loss of biodiversity.[64] At a meeting of the GEF Participants, it was agreed, among other things, that the GEF would continue to finance the same focal areas and that a Participants' Assembly would be formed for decision-making.[65] Decisions are normally to be made by consensus, except that when that is not possible, a voting system would be substituted to "guarantee both a balanced and equitable representation of the interests of developing countries, as well as give due weight to the funding efforts of donor countries."[66] The exact details of such a system remain to be worked out, along with other crucial issues such as the amount of total funding for the implementation of the climate change agreement. A further meeting was held in December 1992 to attempt to further the process of restructuring the GEF, concentrating on the legal framework and the decision-making aspects of the GEF.[67] In May 1993, Beijing was the site for the next meeting of the Participants. Although it was confirmed that consensus would be the primary instrument for decision-making, with voting used only as a last resort, decisions regarding funding and governance were put off until further meetings.[68]

A Subsidiary Body for Implementation has also been established under the Convention, to assist the Conference of the Parties in assessing and reviewing implementation of the Convention.[69] When disputes arise, the Convention provides that the parties "shall seek a settlement of the dispute through negotiation or any other peaceful means..."[70] While parties may agree to submit a dispute to the International Court of Justice or to arbitration, if the disputing parties are unable to agree on a dispute settlement mechanism, the matter shall be submitted to conciliation. A conciliation commission, composed of members appointed by each party concerned and a jointly appointed chairman will deliver a "recommendatory award, which the parties shall consider in good faith."[71] The Convention requires additional conciliation procedures to be adopted as soon as practicable, perhaps following along the lines of the non-compliance procedure of the Montreal Protocol.[72]

In order to ensure that the Convention undergoes a smooth transition into force after ratification, the International Negotiating Committee met in December 1992 to prepare for the first meeting of the Conference of the Parties.[73] At that meeting, the INC defined the tasks to be undertaken by the Conference of the Parties and for which the INC should prepare. They include the formulation of methods to calculate emissions and removals of greenhouse gases, communication of national plans,[74] implementation of the financial mechanisms and other matters relating to the implementation of the Convention.[75] The INC met again for its seventh session in New York, March 1993, calling for a report on the functioning of operational linkages between the Conference of the Parties and the financial mechanism. The INC also proposed to explore the feasibility of a joint project with UNEP to establish and operate an information exchange system to support the reporting requirements and response measures of developing states called for in the Convention.[76] The eighth and ninth sessions of the INC, held in August 1993 and February 1994 respectively, addressed the concept of joint implementation and the adequacy of the commitments included in the FCCC.[77] The tenth session of the INC in August 1994 discussed the need for greater industry participation in the evolution of the FCCC.[78] Following the eleventh session of the INC in February 1995, the First Meeting of the Conference of the Parties was held in Berlin during late March and early April 1995. At that meeting, government representatives agreed to undertake negotiations by 1997 to make specific reductions on emissions.[79]

FORMATION OF THE CLIMATE CHANGE REGIME

The existence of shared expectations regarding future state behavior in the area of climate change,[80] can be said to have formed by the time the UN General Assembly resolved in 1990 to create the International Negotiating Committee to prepare a Framework Convention on Climate Change.[81] At that point, shared expectations regarding the need to combat climate change existed. Therefore, the establishment of the INC can be said to represent the formation of the climate change regime.

The creation of the Intergovernmental Panel on Climate Change (IPCC) in 1989 can not be said to have been the point of formation of the climate change regime, since its purpose was to investigate the impacts and possible responses to potential climate change. At that point there was not yet evidence of expectations of a need to regulate climate change. Similarly, the findings of the

IPCC in 1990, before the INC came into existence, is also not the point of formation of the climate change regime but rather, an expression of the opinion of that panel.[82] Although those findings gave a sense of urgency to the need for action, they did not reveal shared expectations among states to regulate climate change. This was shown, however, by the establishment of the INC with the purpose of negotiating the FCCC. The legal status of the regime at formation will be discussed below.

MAINTENANCE OF THE CLIMATE CHANGE REGIME

As with ozone layer depletion, the critical issues to the climate change regime include science, economics and development. The maintenance or development of the regime depends on the extent to which the uncertainty surrounding these critical issues has been resolved and cognitive expectations have been shaped leading to normative or shared expectations regarding future behavior.[83]

Scientific Uncertainty

While man has rapidly acquired new scientific knowledge concerning the phenomena of global warming leading to climate change, there is still uncertainty as to the potential effects.[84] This has had an obvious effect on the climate change regime, which lacks detailed regulations.[85]

The fact remains, then, that there is still debate as to the potential impact. For example, in the United States the Marshall Institute has produced studies which question the impact of climate change, and recent evidence reveals that the impact to date has been relatively benign.[86] Similar views have been voiced in the United Kingdom.[87] Views such as these have prevented a coherent epistemic community forming for the climate change regime.

At the time of this writing, it must be concluded that the scientific uncertainty surrounding climate change has contributed to the lack of substantive legal obligations within the regime. The basis of the normative behavior expected of states has been laid out within the regime, however, and the regime can be expected to evolve from that point. This was the case with ozone layer depletion — as the science became more certain and as the danger became more evident, the regime evolved into the Montreal Protocol, which itself has evolved twice trough adjustments and amendments.[88]

Economic Uncertainty

Since the scientific effects of global warming are still uncertain, the economic ramifications are also difficult to determine.[89] Indeed, there are two opposing economic responses to global warming: prevention at any cost in order to avoid possible catastrophic damage or a "no regrets" approach.[90] Until the effects, and therefore the economic costs, are better known, then both economic viewpoints will have validity, and will prevent strong international agreement on economic grounds.

Compared to ozone depletion, overcoming economic uncertainty for climate change is much more difficult. The economic costs will undoubtedly prove much higher, as ozone depletion is limited to the replacement of CFCs and other ozone-depleting substances, while climate change involves many greenhouse gases. Because of the near-impossibility of greenhouse gas replacement, at least in the foreseeable future, an economic system to regulate greenhouse gases will need to be implemented. As already indicated in Chapter 4, the difficulties of implementing, let alone choosing between, an emission permit or tax on greenhouse gases are great. Even before that point, agreement has to be reached on what level of greenhouse gases, national and international, is acceptable in order that a permit or tax system could be implemented.[91] Thus, economic incentives must be relied upon to legitimize any substantive prohibitions in the climate change regime. In other words, states must be convinced of the economic viability of any long-range undertakings. To accomplish this, business concerns must be met, since the initial burden to reduce pollution will fall on corporations.[92] Industry has begun to play a role in the climate change issue, partly as some firms have realized a profit-motive in the venture, partly as a public-relations venture.[93] Profit-motive schemes can be helped along through such devices as environmental tax breaks or similar incentives, so long as the incentives are perceived as fair and not draconian.[94]

But convincing firms, let alone states, of long term economic gains in the face of short term losses is not an easy task. The importance of this was reflected by the establishment of the Business Council For Sustainable Development, headed by Stephan Schmidheiny who served as principal adviser for business and industry to the Secretary-General of UNCED. The Council endeavored to analyze how the international business community can adapt and contribute to the achievement of the goal of sustainable development.[95]

In addition, while including environmental costs in pricing has long been called for by environmentalists, industry leaders now appear to be warming to that view. The chairman of Dow Chemical has called for full-cost pricing to reflect the environmental and social costs of goods and services.[96] By so doing, firms would realize the differing environmental costs of their products, with a corresponding effect on technology choice and product design.[97] However, this view has not yet been internalized by industry as a whole.

Economic uncertainty has prevented strict emission targets from being implemented in the climate change regime to date, aside from a general "aim" (for developed states) to return to 1990 levels of greenhouse gas emissions.[98] Nevertheless, with that provision, the regime has set the base behavior from which more restrictive rules can evolve. The ozone layer depletion regime evolved in that manner. However, the phase-out in that regime is being introduced gradually, in order to avoid economic hardships and to allow time for substitutes to be introduced.[99] This legitimized the phase-out from an economic point of view. A similar arrangement will no doubt need to be made in the climate change regime.

Development Uncertainty

The unknown extent to which developing states will contribute to climate change as they attempt to attain a greater standard of living and the unknown amount of financial support these states will require in combatting climate change is a critical issue within the climate change regime.[100] This uncertainty is closely tied to the economics of global warming; uncertainty in that area necessarily affects development issues. So long as the overall cost remains uncertain, then so does the cost of subsidizing developing states in terms of financial aid and technology transfer.

The majority of greenhouse gas emissions are at the present time attributed to the industrialized world. However, the less-developed states are poised to take the lead in overall emissions upon attaining a certain level of development. Once again, the uncertainty of this issue is greater for climate change than it was for ozone depletion.

To accommodate the financial needs of developing states, the ozone layer depletion regime provides for financial and technical assistance under the Multilateral Fund.[101] The GEF is the operational facility for the FCCC financial mechanism.[102]

In order to accommodate the technological needs of developing states, the FCCC states that exchange of technology should be promoted,[103] but only requires the adoption of national policies to limit emissions of greenhouse gases (aiming to return to 1990 levels) from developed states and those states with economies in transition.[104] The developing world is only required to publish national inventories of emissions as well as programs outlining measures to mitigate climate change.[105] While the purpose of the provision on adoption of national policies by developed states was to demonstrate the difference in economic and equitable starting points between themselves and the less-developed world, and to illustrate that developed states were "taking the lead in modifying... emissions,"[106] it can only be hoped that the provision will be extended to the developing world as soon as possible. Without policies to facilitate a cut in future emissions from that sector of the global population, the convention will be of little use.

The developing states are in a position to wield a great deal of influence in the financial arrangements as well. If these states do not feel that the ensuing financial arrangements are legitimate, then their degree of involvement is likely to be low. Similarly, the developed states must also be satisfied with the ultimate financial arrangement, since they will be providing the necessary financial aid. Thus, the uncertainty surrounding this issue remains significant in the climate change regime.

Nevertheless, while difficulties still remain as to the actual transfer of financial and technology aid, the inclusion of developing states and their special interests has been made in the climate change regime.

CATALYSTS IN THE CLIMATE CHANGE REGIME

The catalysts to be examined here include leadership, international non-state actors, crisis and domestic regulations. Each of these factors played a role in catalyzing the ozone layer depletion regime[107] and thus could be expected to play a large part in the regime of a similar global environmental problem, climate change.[108]

Leadership

To date, no state has assumed a major leadership role in the climate change regime. The United States hosted the first meeting of the INC February 1991[109], but despite this, was not supportive of the EC position advocating binding regulations for the reduction of CO_2.[110] This stance, kept up throughout the next three meetings of the INC, was largely attributed to the influence of John Sununu, the Chief of Staff to President Bush.[111] His resignation led some to believe that the United States would be more amenable to targets for CO_2 emissions.[112] The United States, however, was steadfast in its refusal to submit to CO_2 targets, declaring a "comprehensive approach" of all greenhouse sources and sinks was mandated, and was supported on that front by other states.[113] Nevertheless, the decision of President Bush to attend was given great attention by the press, perhaps underlying the need for a leader state in the climate change regime.[114]

Once at UNCED, however, the leadership on climate change became more-or-less up for grabs. The EC attempted to acquire the role, drafting a document calling for firmer commitments on the reduction of greenhouse gases than those present in the climate change convention.[115] Japan pledged to increase foreign environmental aid.[116] The United States called on other states to come up with specific plans for combatting greenhouse gases by 1 January 1993.[117] Germany pledged to increase development aid to 0.7% of its gross national product, although did not offer a timetable for doing so, pointing to the financial burden of reunification.[118] No one state, then, could be said to have emerged as a leader at UNCED.

Regarding future leadership, the European Community might be expected to assume such a role; the European Commission has proposed to introduce carbon taxes.[119] Japan, while pledging international aid, has not taken much more initiative,[120] and Germany has been preoccupied with the economic aspects of reunification. In addition, the recent US National Academy of Sciences report which states that adaptation to global warming is possible for the United States and similarly situated industrialized states,[121] does not exactly propel states into adopting a leadership role.

While no state can as yet claim a clear leadership role in the climate change regime comparable to that of the United States in the ozone negotiations,[122] it does not necessarily mean that one state will not emerge eventually.[123] The issue is so much more complex in terms of economics, science and development, that it is difficult for a state to take a lead when so much remains uncertain.[124] Indeed, the environment is only one of several important policy areas where the world's leaders are unable to reach accord.[125]

Although any state can strive for a leadership position, as the then Senator Al Gore pointed out:

> It is safe to say that if...[the US] do[es] not lead the world on this issue [of global warming], the chances of accomplishing the massive changes necessary to save the global environment will be negligible. If the United States does choose to lead, however, the possibility of success becomes much greater.[126]

While this may be a result of fact that the United States is presently the largest contributor of greenhouse gas emissions[127] rather than possessing any unique leadership attributes, US leadership would surely act as a catalyst for further negotiations.[128] The United States was the first state to have produced the action plan required under the Climate Change Convention,[129] meeting the US proposal for states to do so before 1 January 1993.[130] It could very well be that the US may eventually emerge as a leader on this issue,[131] particularly as the US Vice President has championed the environment as part of his political career.[132]

International Non-state Actors

International non-state actors have taken a great interest in the climate change issue, both governmental and nongovernmental, as well as transnational corporations. These organizations can often prod individual states into action, when initiative within state governments is lacking.

UNEP acted as a catalyst in the formation of the climate change regime by co-sponsoring the Villach and Bellagio workshops on global warming, as well as the IPCC, which undertook scientific and policy studies in preparation for a climate change convention. However, primary responsibility for the negotiating of a climate change convention was effectively stripped from UNEP, and given to the ad-hoc UN body, the International Negotiating Committee, which reported directly to the UN General Assembly.[133] This move, along with the name given to the Rio Conference as the UN Conference on Environment and Development, was intended to afford greater influence to the developing world.[134] Nevertheless, UNEP helped place environment near the top of the world agenda, with the help of the media.[135] Thus it appears that the role of UNEP has been a catalyzing factor, and will continue to be, in the climate change area.

The World Bank's role as administrator of the GEF, which is serving as the operator of the financial mechanism of the FCCC, was discussed above.[136] Its role as a catalyst in the development of the regime should remain, barring some unexpected development regarding the GEF. Commenting several weeks after the conclusion of UNCED, the International Institute for Economics stated: "Of the international organizations, the World Bank emerged as a clear winner... Despite objections from the G77 about the Bank's lack of democratic accountability, there is essentially no other financial mechanism available that inspires the confidence of donors."[137]

NGOs have also played a catalytic role in both the creation and the development of the climate change regime.[138] One commentator described their role at UNCED as more active and more influential within intergovernmental negotiations than ever before.[139] ICSU played a catalytic role in its sponsorship of the Villach Conference.[140] Greenpeace and Friends of the Earth are positioning to continue their role as advocates of a safer climate, particularly in influencing public opinion.[141] At UNCED, although "some governments could be heard to grumble about the 'privileges' granted to the NGOs," their inclusion was guaranteed by the Conference Secretary General,[142] thus ensuring the voice of NGOs in the process and contributing to public opinion.

Public opinion, as every politician realizes, can be an important motivational tool. Should the public decide that climate change is a concern that they would prefer their respective governments to take a more active role in, then it is highly probable that governments will sit up and take notice. Business is also not immune to public opinion: "the pressures to perform environmentally are not just to meet the law but to meet public expectations, which goes beyond what is required by law."[143] The potential catalytic role of transnational corporations and industry in the role of the regime was acknowledged when the Secretary-General of UNCED requested an adviser for business and industry.[144] The central message of this adviser was that "what was good for the environment was (probably) good for the business as well."[145]

More and more, corporations are realizing the importance of reconciling business goals with environmental goals,[146] or what Schmidheiny referred to as "eco-efficiency."[147] While these environmental concerns of businesses to date may not be specific to climate change, they reflect a shift in attitude which may eventually incorporate climate change concerns more specifically.

Domestic Regulations

Domestic environmental regulations have the potential to foster international regulations in the same area and remain a potential catalytic tool in the climate change regime, at least in those states where strict domestic regulations are enforced by a stringent legal system. However, at this point in the climate change regime, domestic regulations have not proven catalytic, since substantive legislative proposals from major greenhouse gas contributors have either not materialized or are conditional on similar action from other states.[148]

Crisis

The climate change regime has failed to acquire the same

sense of urgency as the ozone layer depletion regime. Although certain low-lying states feel quite differently about the matter, the effects are still perceived as too remote, at least among the western industrialized states whose participation is critical, to evoke the sense of crisis necessary to stimulate action. While scientists are sure of a warming trend, they are still unsure as to the cause possible ramifications.[149] Thus, the Villach Conference, the Toronto Conference, the UNCED negotiations, as well as the overall regime, lacked the same urgency of action. Until that time, the view of climate change may very well be "apocalypse tomorrow-but there is plenty of jam today."[150]

COMPLIANCE IN THE CLIMATE CHANGE REGIME

Compared to the ozone layer depletion regime, compliance mechanisms are not in place to the same degree. However, while the ozone layer depletion regime may be more straight forward on this point, this is not to say that the climate change regime does not provide for compliance at all. Even without mechanisms fully in place (and thus the greater emphasis in this chapter than in the last on the evolving aspects of compliance within the regime) the climate change regime has begun to provide for compliance.

Evolution of Norms and Rules

Within international law, compliance is expected when there are legal rules laid out for state behavior. Regimes provide an extremely conducive atmosphere for the evolution of normative behavior into legal rules, as cognitive expectations lead to normative or shared expectations regarding future behavior.[151]

The FCCC itself is the tangible result of the evolution of cognitive expectations into rules, albeit weak rules at this stage in the development of the regime. The Villach, Toronto and World Climate Conferences, the INC negotiating sessions, and the many meetings leading up to UNCED all aided this evolution for expected state behavior.[152] The expectation that developed states must at least "aim" to control greenhouse gas emissions at 1990 levels is now codified in the FCCC, and developed states have pledged to conclude a protocol setting specific limits and goals for further reductions.[153] From this Convention, protocols can be added as normative or shared expectations develop, thus providing a mode of evolution for new regulations. Richard Benedick, who, as chief US negotiator for the ozone treaty has first-hand experience of environmental negotiation, stated that the Rio Conference on climate change "should not be judged by immediate results, but by the process it sets in motion," namely the evolution of normative expectations.[154]

Thus, as cognitive expectations emerge regarding the critical issues of the regime, then normative expectations or obligations will ensue. While these obligations will eventually harden into formal law, at certain times the obligation will not rise to that level if the degree of consensus cannot yet support more, as is the case with the climate change regime.

Dispute Settlement Mechanisms

Dispute settlement is obviously important to the climate change regime, and is probably the most difficult aspect of the regime to administer. There are provisions in the regime convention for the reporting of information regarding implementation to the Conference of the Parties.[155]

As of now, settlement of disputes between any 2 or more parties regarding the interpretation or application of the Convention is to be resolved through negotiation or any other peaceful means of their choice.[156] States may agree to submit disputes to the International Court of Justice or to arbitration in accordance with procedures to be adopted by the Conference of the Parties as soon as possible.[157] Submission to the ICJ does not seem likely, given the past practice of states and is present in the Convention more as legal "boilerplate," just as it is similarly present in the Vienna Ozone Convention.[158] The agreement, following the Vienna Ozone Convention, goes on to say that if states have not been able to settle a dispute within 12 months, then any of the disputing parties may request conciliation. A conciliation commission shall then be created chosen by the parties concerned, which shall give a recommendation to be considered in good faith.[159] The Convention requires additional procedures relating to conciliation to be adopted.[160]

The Convention may follow the example of the non-compliance procedure agreed upon in the Copenhagen Adjustments to the Montreal Protocol, although this cannot be assumed.[161] Regulations arrived at and adjusted by agreement of the parties tend to limit the "sphere of autointerpretation by the states of their obligations."[162] Although compliance can never be guaranteed, it stands to reason that where states have worked out the rules of the game for themselves which they believe are legitimate, non-compliance will probably be less than if states were not involved in the rulemaking process. At this time, however, such a mechanism does not yet exist within the climate change regime.

Accountability and Transparency

Because rule-making and dispute settlement are internal to a regime, accountability and transparency are very important considerations. The climate change regime to date has begun to deal with accountability through reporting[163] and targets,[164] albeit very loosely, as well as provisions for further negotiation.[165]

Internal accountability is very important since compliance with international law is ultimately based on cooperation and good will, particularly when the issue at hand, namely greenhouse gas emission reduction, is still very contentious. As the regime gains strength and overcomes uncertainty, so will the reporting requirements, thus assuring greater accountability and transparency as to non-conformance.

Exclusion and Conditional Cooperation

Exclusion, in the form of trade bans, from the climate change regime is most likely not possible at this time, since the sources of greenhouse warming are too many to allow for feasible trade bans. If trade restrictions did manage to evolve, trade with non-parties "would have a major impact on the principles of the multilateral trading system," due to the vast requirements that would be necessary to regulate the trade.[166] Concerned by this, GATT has adopted a programme on the follow-up of UNCED regarding trade results.[167]

It will be difficult, therefore, to sanction free-riders to the regime,[168] which makes cooperation all the more important. But states can hedge their bets by making their cooperation conditional on other states' acquiescence to the regime's regulations. Thus, conditional cooperation can play a large factor in the regime since parties are likely to base compliance on the mutual compliance of other party members.[169]

THE LEGAL STATUS OF THE CLIMATE CHANGE REGIME

With the adoption of the FCCC, the climate change regime undoubtedly entered into the realm of binding international law. But as with ozone layer depletion, formation of the regime came before a treaty was negotiated. Instead, this author argues that formation of the climate change regime came about with the creation of the International Negotiating Committee (INC).[170]

In keeping with the requirements of regime formation laid out in this work and following the policy-oriented approach to international law, formation and legal obligations ensue from the creation of shared expectations regarding future behavior.[171] The formation of the climate change regime created an obligation among its members to combat climate change, with the accompanying expectation of future commitments in order to fulfil that obligation. In order to illustrate this, it is necessary to once again identify the various phases of the lawmaking process as adhered to by the policy-oriented school. These are the participants, their subjectivities, the situations where subjectivities are mediated and expectations about authority and control are shaped, the resources available to the participants, the strategies of communication used, and the outcomes in shared expectations.[172]

Participants

As described above regarding international action on climate change,[173] a number of significant international initiatives took place leading to the establishment of the INC. The most important of these were the Villach Conference, the World Conference on the Changing Atmosphere, the Ottawa Meeting, the Hague and Noordwijk conferences, as well as the World Climate Conferences. The IPCC also contributed to the prescriptive process. In addition, UNGA Resolutions contributed to the creation of the climate change regime and the ensuing legal obligations.[174]

The principal participants in these initiatives included states. The fact that these state participants also represent the principal participants among the target audience is also important, since it is the expectations of the target audience that are critical to law-making.[175] International organizations, both governmental and non-governmental, particularly UNEP, WMO and ICSU also played a large role.[176]

Subjectivities

An analysis of the subjectivities of the participants, or perceptions about the content of their communications reveal attitudes indicating an intent to combat climate change. Since the subjectivities of one participant are not open for direct examination by another, they can only be ascertained from a contextual analysis of past behavior.[177] From the international action concerning climate change, the pattern of behavior is that of states seeking international regulation of greenhouse gases. At Toronto, an Action Plan for the Protection of the Atmosphere was called for, in Ottawa the legal and policy experts called for the development of the legal and institutional framework for a climate change convention. At Noordwijk, the Declaration acknowledged in principle the need to control greenhouse gas emissions with a climate change convention. At Bergen, ministers pledged support for a climate change convention and to establish national strategies and/or targets to reduce greenhouse gas emissions.

While the demands regarding degree of regulation varied considerably[178], the underlying expectation that states had a duty to combat climate change was present throughout the international activity described above. The UNGA Resolution creating the INC provides evidence of this, and thus capped a long display of behavior by states towards the combatting of climate change, through some as yet unknown degree of regulation of greenhouse gas emissions.

Situations

The arenas or situations where the above subjectivities were played out were formal and organized conferences, as well as meetings of the General Assembly. The extent of international activity reveals that the interaction was not infrequent or merely regional, thus indicating a general and sustained pattern of behavior that showed general support for the asserted claim of combatting climate change through future regulation of greenhouse gas emissions.

Resources or Bases of Power

Regarding resources, or knowledge and skill, scientific knowledge was the most important resource in the hands of the participants, since climate change is ultimately a scientific problem.[179] As such, the science was subject to manipulation by the participants, both for and against regulation.[180] The IPCC played a large role with respect to use of science as a resource, in effect raising the profile of climate change with its warnings of dire consequences should the problem go unheeded.[181]

Economic and development knowledge have played a role in the negotiation of the FCCC, and will continue to play a role in the further development of the regime,[182] particularly as monetary costs become more clear. Those resources, however, were not utilized to a significant degree in the formation of the climate change regime, as they were not that necessary since the general obligation to combat climate change was weak and did not yet require any specific commitments.

Strategies

The strategies used in generating the flow of words and behavior in the prescription process were relatively explicit; declarations and UNGA resolutions.[183] Thus, diplomatic strategies on the international level were used. Economic strategies were later utilized in the FCCC, with regard to prospective aid for developing states in the implementation of the regime.[184]

Outcome

The outcome of the above ongoing process of interaction is a prescription entailing a general obligation to combat climate change, through the future regulation of greenhouse gas emissions. As with the formation of the ozone layer depletion regime, while the obligation is vague, it lays the groundwork for more substantive obligations, as shared expectations evolve.

As outlined in Chapter 2,[185] the critical test for determining legal obligation under the policy-oriented approach is the existence and content of shared expectations of politically relevant groups and individuals, that are maintained by the continuation or abatement of communication regarding the authority and control intentions of those whose support is essential for the norms' efficacy.[186] If the practice of states is perceived by the target audience as having been carried out by appropriate entities and in an appropriate manner, and is perceived as likely to be complied with, then it can be characterized as "practice accepted by law."[187] The test in brief is one of authority (legitimacy) and control (effectiveness). The content of the norm giving rise to the climate change regime had been (and continues to be) constant: a general obligation to combat climate change through the future control or regulation of greenhouse gas emissions. While this is certainly far short of specific targets and timetables, this policy content that consistently comes through in the relevant international activity taking place prior to and including the creation of the INC.[188] As one observer of the climate change regime process noted, the lack of firm commitments does not prevent the implicit message that more stringent measures may be on the way and that it is not business as usual. As such, "a cautious government or business should already be thinking about how to limit or switch away from its use of fossil fuels."[189]

The expectation that climate change is to be combatted with the as-yet-undetermined degree of control of greenhouse gas emissions needed to be (and must continue to be) sustained through an ongoing authority signal and control intention.

As authority is necessary in order to distinguish a prescription from demands backed up only by credible threats. It is difficult to dispute the authority present in the creation of the climate change regime - the individuals involved acted in an official capacity for the states they represented, as did those individuals associated with international organizations, such as the United Nations and its various bodies. In addition, the fact that these states represented the principal participants among the target audience is important, since it is the expectations of the target audience that are critical to policy-oriented lawmaking.[190]

The capacity and willingness to make the prescription of regulating greenhouse gas emissions effective was also present at the formation of the climate change regime. While all the international action concerning climate change was important,[191] the formation of the INC was the most meaningful, as it best demonstrates the participants' willingness to make the policy of controlling greenhouse gas emissions meaningful. Control does not require unanimity or even wide consensus, but requires enough interest and willingness on the part of participants to make it effective. The creation of the INC appears to meet this requirement, as its sole purpose was to negotiate a framework convention on climate change.[192]

While the authority signal and control intention were weak at the formation of the climate change regime, they were present at a degree sufficient for the policy content entailing a general obligation to combat climate change. As such, it can be characterized as practice accepted as law, as required for the formation of customary law,[193] at least under the policy-oriented approach. While "it is often difficult to determine whether or not a new custom has crystallized into international law, and, if so, at what point,"[194] the attempt must be made. This is particularly true in the policy-oriented approach, which emphasizes the creation of shared expectations regarding future behavior.

While it is easier to make the argument that the formation of the climate change regime coincided with the FCCC, a formal treaty undisputed as a source of international law, making the more difficult argument that the regime was formed prior to the FCCC allows for a greater view of the scope of the legal order.

In so doing, "the what of inquiry is necessarily broader than the what of conventional analysis."[195] This is not to say that the legitimate process of lawmaking is ignored. It is, however, a view of lawmaking that requires an acceptance of the policy-oriented approach. Without this viewpoint, regime study is still useful to legal scholars, but unnecessarily restricts the study of law by excluding communications conveying authoritative information about community policies that can be designated as law, so long as it is both consistent with the expectations of legitimacy by the target audience (authoritative decisions) and effective (controlling).

EVALUATION OF THE CLIMATE CHANGE REGIME

The above discussion illustrates that the climate change regime, even with the FCCC, does not yet have substantive obligations. General reporting requirements and an "aim" to return to 1990 emission levels are certainly not very substantive, although developed states have pledged to negotiate specific reductions. This is because uncertainty surrounding critical issues has not yet been overcome to a degree sufficient to shape cognitive expectations, which in turn shape normative or shared expectations regarding future behavior. In addition, while transnational organizations are starting to catalyze the regime development, the catalysts of leadership, domestic regulations and a sense of crisis are missing.

An analysis of the compliance mechanisms reveals that while there are mechanisms for accountability, the evolution of rules and dispute settlement mechanisms are weak, and exclusion mechanisms are not yet in place.

An objective, overall assessment of the climate change regime, then, reveals that it is regulatory-weak. This does not, however, mean that there are no prospects for improvement. The regime is in place, and will evolve should shared expectations evolve as well.[196] How the regime evolves (in a progressive or a regressive manner) depends on the expectations involved. If expectations do not evolve, then neither will the regime.

The recent Meeting of the Conference of the Parties, however, offers some optimism, as the developed parties agreed to negotiate fixed emission limits on greenhouse gases.

While the climate change regime may not appear to be of much value in terms of substantive regulations at this point in its development, the regime in its present (and past) state highlights part of the international legal order often overlooked. By revealing the presence of the regime, the presence of the legal order is also revealed and thereby strengthened.

While realist skeptics may disparage this "legal presence" as little more than an academic exercise in a futile search for evidence of an international legal order, it is difficult to ignore that the shared expectations of combatting climate change necessarily had to be in place for the FCCC to come into existence and for its future evolution. The important point is that there is a path or a process (regime formation and maintenance) to substantive legal regulations — a path that if overlooked, may prevent the reaching of one's destination.

NOTES

1. Preamble, *The Constitution of the United States of America.*

2. *International Legal Materials* Vol.31, No. 4 (1992), pp. 849–873.

3. As of May 1995, 129 states had deposited instruments of ratification. Source, Treaty Section, UN Legal Office, New York.

4. UN General Assembly Resolution 45/212, *Resolutions and Decisions adopted by the General Assembly during the First Part of its 45th Session*, UN Press Release GA/8165, p. 263.

5. See *World Climate Programme Impact Studies, Developing Policies for Responding to Climate Change* (WMP/TD-No. 225), April 1988.

6. Environmental Law Institute, "Introduction by the Environmental Law Institute," in *Addressing Global Climate Change: the Emergence of a New World Order?*, principal authors, Alexandre Timoshenko and Nicholas Robinson (Washington, DC: Environmental Law Institute, 1989), pp. 3–4.

7. See, *Developing Policies for Responding to Climate Change, supra*, n. 5, , p. i.

8. Environmental Law Institute, "Introduction," *supra*, n. 6 p. 4. The suggested target rate of temperature increase was 0.1 degree Celsius.

9. See, "Conference Statement" in *Conference Proceedings, The Changing Atmosphere: Implications for Global Security*, (WMO/OMM-No. 710), p. 292.

10. Ibid.

11. Ibid. The Conference Statement also called for a 20% reduction of 1988 level of carbon dioxide emissions by 2005. Ibid., pp. 296–297.

12. Ibid., pp. 296–299.

13. Ibid.

14. "Working Group Reports", *Conference Proceedings, supra*, n. 9, p. 346. The Working Group advocated a framework convention with additional protocols creating standards for the protection of the atmosphere.

15. Ibid., p. 334.

16. Protection of the Atmosphere: Statement of the Meeting of Legal and Policy Experts, Ottawa, Canada, February 22, 1989, reprinted in "Selected Legal Materials," *American University Journal of International Law and Policy* Vol. 5, No. 2 (Winter 1990), pp. 529–542.

17. Ibid., p. 531. The meeting decided that the atmosphere represented a "common resource" as opposed to a "shared resource". Sylvia Maureen Williams, "The Protection of the Ozone Layer in Contemporary International Law," *International Relations* Vol. X, No. 2 (1990), p. 175.

18. Ibid., p. 533.

19. Hague Declaration on the Environment, *International Legal Materials* Vol. 28, No. 5 (1989), pp. 1308–1310.

20. Ibid. See also, Glen Plant, "Institutional and Legal Responses to Global Warming," in *International Law and Global Climate Change*, ed. Robin Churchill and David Freestone (London: Graham & Trotman, 1991), p. 166.

21. See Plant, "Institutional and Legal Responses," *supra*, n. 20.

22. Noordwijk Declaration on Climate Change, *Environmental Policy and Law* Vol. 19, No. 6 (1989), pp. 229–231. See also, IUCC, Fact Sheet 218, "The Noordwijk Ministerial Declaration on Climate Change," *Climate Change Dossier* (Geneva: IUCC, 1992).

23. The Declaration recognized that "global environmental problems have to be approached through international co-operation," notwithstanding "the principle of the sovereign right of States to manage their natural resources independently." Noordwijk Declaration, *supra*, n. 22.

24. Ibid., reaffirming GA Res. 43/53, *infra*, n. 26, and *supra*, Chapter 2, Common Heritage, Shared Resources and Common Concern.

25. Bergen Conference on Sustainable Development, UN Doc. A/CONF.151/PC/10, and *supra*, Chapter 2, Precautionary Principle.

26. UN Resolution on the Protection of the Global Climate, GA Res. 43/53, A/RES/43/53 (6 December 1988), *UN General Assembly Official Records of the General Assembly*, 43rd Session, Supplement No. 49 (A/43/49), p. 133.

27. Ibid.

28. The stated purpose of Working Group I was to "provide a scientific assessment of: the factors which may affect climate change..., the responses of the atmosphere-ocean-land-ice system, current capabilities of modelling...climate changes and their predictability, [and] the past climate record and...anomalies." *IPCC Policymakers Summary of the Scientific Assessment of Climate Change*, Report Prepared for IPCC by Working Group I, June 1990, p. 3 (NY: WMO and UNEP,

1990).

29. "The responsibility of Working Group II is to describe the environmental and socio-economic changes over the next decades caused by increasing concentrations of greenhouse gases." *IPCC Policymakers Summary of the Potential Impacts of Climate Change*, report from Working Group II to IPCC, June 1990, p. 1 (NY: WMO and UNEP, 1990).

30. Working Group III's primary task "was, in the broad sense, technical, not political [and] to lay out as fully and fairly as possible a set of response policy options and the factual basis for those options." *IPCC Policymakers Summary of the Formulation of Response Strategies*, Report Prepared for IPCC by Working Group III, June 1990, p. 1 (NY: WMO and UNEP, 1990).

31. IPCC Response Strategies Working Group, *Legal Measures: Report of Topic Coordinators* (Canada, Malta and the United Kingdom) (NY: WMO and UNEP, 1990), p. 1.

32. Ibid., Executive Summary, p. iii.

33. "Talks Next Month on Global Warming Pact," *Times* (London), 31 August 1990, p. 8.

34. See, *supra*, Chapter 4, Critical Issue of Science.

35. The WMO had earlier hosted the first World Climate Conference in 1979 at Geneva. That Conference Report warned of climate trends that could result in "disastrous effects on the biosphere and on humanity." Environmental Law Institute, "Introduction," *supra*, n. 6, p. 3.

36. Ibid., p. 7. An evaluation of the World Climate Programme was also to be undertaken.

37. "Global Warming Conference Begins," *International Herald Tribune*, 30 October 1990, p. 2. The 10-day conference was attended by 500 international scientists and ended in 2-day meeting of 80 ministers, including then Prime Minister Margaret Thatcher of Britain. Mrs. Thatcher stated that a "clear case for precautionary action" concerning climate change existed at the present time, although she cautioned that more scientific research was needed. "Thatcher Exhorts Action on Climate," *International Herald Tribune*, 7 November 1990, p. 2.

38. "US Resists Greenhouse Gas Accord," *International Herald Tribune*, 8 November 1991, p. 2. The head of the US delegation stated that the US would implement initiatives concerning energy efficiency, but no commitments to percentage reductions would be made, as "...we do not know how to guarantee [them]". This contrasted with the position taken by the environmental ministers of 18 European nations, including the 12 EC states and the 6 members of the European Free Trade Association (EFTA), to freeze emission levels of carbon dioxide by the year

2000. "Europeans Will Freeze Emissions of Gases Triggering Global Warming," *International Herald Tribune*, 6 November 1990, p. 2.

39. UN Resolution 45/212, *supra*, n. 4.

40. This conformed with GA Res. 45/212, Ibid., declaring that the negotiating sessions should be held at Washington, D.C., February 1991, and subsequently at Geneva and Nairobi, in May/June 1991, September and November/December 1991, and as appropriate between January and June 1992.

41. The conference was held outside of Washington, D.C., in Chantilly, Virginia.

42. Jessica Mathews, "Brave New World Order," *Guardian* (London), 15 February 1991, p. 27.

43. See, American Society of International Law, "Climate Change," *International Environmental Law Interest Group Newsletter* Vol. 1 (May 1991), p. 3.

44. "Talks on Warming: A Slight US Shift," *International Herald Tribune*, 16-17 February 1991, p. 2. Critics of US policy stated that the use of the term "appropriate", reportedly inserted by White House insistence, was too broad and would prevent absolute requirements of emission reductions. Ibid.

45. American Society of International Law, "Climate Change," *supra*, n. 43, See also, "INC Climate Change Convention: First Discussions," *Environmental Policy and Law* Vol. 21, No. 2 (1991), pp. 50–52. Jean Ripert of France was elected Chair of the INC.

46. Sebastian Oberthur, "Climate Negotiations: Progress Slow," *Environmental Policy and Law* Vol. 21, No. 5/6 (1991), pp. 193–195. See also, American Society of International Law, "Climate Change," *International Environmental Law Interest Group Newsletter* Vol. 2 No. 1 (August 1991, p. 3).

47. See, Michael Grubb and Nicola Steen, *Pledge and Review Processes: Possible Components of a Climate Convention*, Report of a Workshop (London: Royal Institute of International Affairs, 1991). where recommendations as to the meaning and strengthening of the concept were put forth, as well as a survey of precedents. See, Glen Plant, "'Pledge and Review': A Survey of Precedents," *Pledge and Review Processes: Possible Components of a Climate Convention* (London: Royal Institute of International Affairs, 1991), pp. V–XIV.

48. See, American Society of International Law, "Climate Change," *supra*, n. 46, Oberthur, "Climate Negotiations," *supra*, n. 46 and *infra*, Chapter 6, Development Uncertainty.

49. American Society of International Law, "Climate Change," *International Environmental Law Interest Group Newsletter* Vol. 2, No. 2 (November 1991), p. 3. See also, Dan Bodansky, "INC 3 & 4: Draft

Convention on Climate Change," *Environmental Policy and Law* Vol. 22 No. 1 (1992), pp. 5–15.

50. American Society of International Law, "Climate Change," *International Environmental Law Interest Group Newsletter* Vol. 2, No. 3 (March 1992), p. 2. See also, "INC: Fifth Session," *Environmental Policy and Law* Vol. 22, No. 2 (1992), p. 80.

51. This was largely attributed to "the sense that in order to satisfy US objections the obligations in the Convention had been unreasonably diluted." See, *The Earth Summit: The United Nations Conference on Environment and Development*, introduction and commentary by Stanley P. Johnson (London: Graham & Trotman, 1993), p. 78. The United States claimed that energy-efficient actions to which it had already committed would bring it close to limiting emissions in 2000 to 1990 levels, but that strict adherence to timetables might harm its economy. See, William K. Stevens, "143 Lands Adopt Treaty To Cut Emission of Gases," *The New York Times*, 10 May 1992, Section 1, p. 14, "Global Warming Pact Without Targets Gets US Approval," *International Herald Tribune*, 11 May 1992, p. 2.

Disagreement concerning critical issues, then, remained. See, *infra*, Chapter 6, Maintenance of the Climate Change Regime.

52. FCCC, *supra*, n. 2, Art. 4(1)a, b.

53. Ibid., Art. 4(2)b, Art. 12(5).

54. Ibid., Art. 4(2)b, no timetable for doing so was given.

55. Ibid., Art. 12(5).

56. Ibid. Requirements of future communications for all Parties shall be determined by the Conference of the Parties.

57. Ibid., Art. 4(3).

58. Ibid., Art. 4(5).

59. Ibid., Art. 4(6), (8). Annex I highlights those countries that qualify.

60. Ibid., Art. 7.

61. Ibid., Art. 9.

62. Ibid., Art. 11.

63. Ibid., Art. 21(3).

64. "Green Aid," *Our Planet: The Magazine of the UNEP*, Vol. 2, No. 4 (1990), p. 9.

65. See, GEF Administrator, *Global Environment Facility: The Pilot Phase and Beyond*, Working Paper Series Number 1 (Washington, DC: May 1992).

66. Ibid., p. 7.

67. See, Chairman's Summary, Global Environment Facility, Participant's Meeting, Abidjan, Cote d'Ivoire, 3-5 December 1992 (Washington, DC: GEF Administrator, 1992).

68. Ibid.

69. FCCC, *supra*, n. 2, Art. 10.

70. Ibid., Art. 14(1).

71. Ibid., Art. 14(5), (6).

72. Ibid., Art. 15(7). Also adopted at the UN Conference on Environment and Development were the Rio Declaration and Agenda 21, an action plan for the environment and development. The Rio Declaration on Environment and Development encompasses 27 principles reflecting a compromise between developed and developing states, and between environment and development goals. While not specifically related to climate change, both the Declaration and Agenda 21 are of importance to the issue of climate change. *International Legal Materials* Vol. 31, No. 4 (1992), pp. 874–880. See also, American Society of International Law, "UNCED," *International Environmental Law Interest Group Newsletter* Vol. 3, No. 1 (September 1992), pp. 6–7. While they may eventually become part of formal international law through custom or treaty, the documents stand their best chance of early inclusion into the legal order through a regime, just as the FCCC has evolved. Indeed, a regime encompassing environment and development may be evolving. A "complex regime," see *supra*, Chapter 3, Definition of Regimes, might include both the climate change issue and the broader issues encompassed by Agenda 21.

73. *Alliance for Sound Atmospheric Policy Newsletter,* Arlington, Virginia, Newsletter of 14 December 1992. See also, American Society of International Law, "Climate Change," *International Environmental Law Interest Group Newsletter* Vol. 3, No. 1 (September 1992), p. 3.

74. The US presented at the meeting its National Action Plan for Global Climate Change, pursuant to Articles 4 and 12 of the Convention which calls for parties to publish national inventories of greenhouse gas emissions by sources, removals by sinks, mitigation measures, and policies to implement the Convention. In June 1992, US President George Bush proposed that parties to the Convention present and review their national action plans. See, *National Action Plan for Global Climate Change*, US Department of State Publication, December 1992.

75. See, FCCC, Art. 7, *supra*, n. 2, for the full list of duties of the Conference of the Parties.

76. Report of the Intergovernmental Negotiating Committee for a Framework Convention on Climate Change, seventh session, NY, 15-20 March 1993, A/AC.237/31, 27 April 1993. In accordance with FCCC Art. 12(7).

77. See, American Society of International Law, "Climate Change," *International Environmental Law Interest Group Newsletter* Vol. 5, No. 1, (March 1994), p. 3

78. See, "Adequacy Debate: II Precautionary Approach Also Applies to Economy," *UN Climate Change Bulletin*, Issue 6, 1st Quarter 1995, pp. 7–8.

79. See, Stephen Kinzer, "UN Parley Delegates Back Talks on Global Warming," *The New York Times*, 8 April 1995, p. 4.

80. See, *supra*, Chapter 3, Formation of Regimes.

81. See, *supra*, Chapter 6, International Action Regarding Climate Change.

82. Working Group III, concerned with laying out a set of possible response policy actions, stressed that it was not its purpose to "recommend political actions, much less to carry out a negotiation on the many difficult policy questions...". *IPCC Policymakers Summary of the Formulation of Response Strategies*, *supra*, n. 30, p. 1.

83. See, *supra*, Chapter 3, Maintenance or Development of Regimes.

84. See, *supra*, Chapter 1, Climate Change, and Chapter 4, Critical Issue of Science.

85. See, *supra*, Chapter 6, International Action Regarding Climate Change.

86. See, *supra*, Chapter 1, Climate Change. See also, F. Seitz, K. Bendetsen, R. Jastrow and WA Nierenberg, *Scientific Perspectives on the Greenhouse Problem* (George C. Marshall Institute: Washington, DC, 1989). Other skeptics include R. Lindzen, "Some Coolness Concerning Global Warming," *Bulletin American Meteorological Society*, Vol. 71 (1990), pp. 288–299, HW Elisaesser, "A Different View of the Climatic Effect of Carbon Dioxide-Updated," *Atmosphera*, Vol. 3 (1990), pp. 3–29, and WE Reifsnyder, "A Tale of Ten Fallacies: The Skeptical Enquirer's View of the Carbon Dioxide Climate Controversy," *Agriculture and Forest Meteorology*, Vol. 47 (1989), pp. 349–371.

87. See, for instance, Wilfred Beckerman, "Global Warming and International Action: An Economic Perspective," in *The International Politics of the Environment*, ed. Andrew Hurrell and Benedict Kingsbury (Oxford: Clarendon Press, 1992), pp. 253–289.

88. The end of the Cold War may inadvertently propel more scientists towards the environment as they search for areas in which to concentrate their research. This may help advance scientific certainty. See, William K. Stevens, "With Cold War Over, Scientists Are Turning To 'Greener' Pastures," *New York Times*, 27 October 1992, p. C4.

89. See, *supra*, Chapter 4, Critical Issue of Economics.

90. Ibid.

91. There is the additional problem of verification of targets. In this regard, it is uncertain whether individual greenhouse gases or sectors (energy, forestry, agriculture) contributing to emissions will be targeted. See, Julian E. Salt and Owen Greene, "Climate Convention-Verification or Not?" *Peace Studies Briefings*, Dept. of Peace Studies, University of Bradford, released 10 June 1992, Rio de Janeiro.

92. See, Jessica Mathews, "When Environmentalism Jibes With Economics," *International Herald Tribune*, 11 November 1992, p. 5. Annual costs of environmental compliance with US domestic laws alone is estimated to reach $198 billion by 2000, from $125 billion in 1992. See, Diedre Carmody, "'Greening' of the Business Magazine," *The New York Times*, 16 November 1992, p. D6.

93. See, Matthew L. Wald, "How A Big Oil Company Took the Green Pledge," *International Herald Tribune*, 13-14 February 1993, p. 9. See, also, *infra*, Chapter 6, International Non-state Actors.

94. In this vein, a new magazine, Eco, has been launched in the United States. It is aimed at government officials, chief executives and top financial officers at large and midsize corporations. Its purpose is to fill the gap between environmental advocacy magazines and business trade books. ECO's advisory board includes US Vice-President Gore and Russell E. Train, chairman of the National Commission on the Environment and a former administrator of the EPA. See, Carmody, "'Greening'," *supra*, n. 92, p. D6.

95. Stephan Schmidheiny with the Business Council For Sustainable Development, *Changing Course: A Global Business Perspective On Development and the Environment* (Cambridge, Mass, MIT Press, 1992). See, also, Donella H. Meadows, Dennis L. Meadows, and Jorgen Randers, *Beyond The Limits* (London: Earthscan Publications Ltd., 1992), the sequel to *The Limits To Growth*, published by the Club of Rome 20 years earlier.

See, also, "Business Charter for Sustainable Development Principles for Environmental Management," adopted at the Second World Industry Conference on Environmental Management, reprinted in *Issues in Science and Technology* Vol. 8, No. 2 (Spring 1992), pp. 30–31.

96. Mathews, quoting Frank Popoff, "Environmentalism," *supra*, n. 92, p. 5.

97. See, Peter F. Drucker, *The New Realities* (NY: Harper & Row Publishers, 1989), pp. 135–136.

98. FCCC, *supra*, n. 2, Art.4(2)b.

99. See, *supra*, Chapter 5, International Action Regarding Ozone Layer Depletion.

100. See, *supra*, Chapter 4, Critical Issue of Development.

101. See, *supra*, Chapter 5, Development Uncertainty.

102. See, GEF Administrator, *Global Environmental Facility: The Pilot Phase and Beyond*, *supra*, n. 65.

103. FCCC, *supra*, n. 2, Art. 4(1)h.

104. Ibid., 4(2)a, b and c. Those states with economies in transition to free market economies are allowed some flexibility in the implementation of national plans to mitigate and adapt to climate change. Such states are identified in Annex 1 of the Convention.

105. Ibid., Art. 4(1)a.

106. Ibid., Art 4(2)a.

107. See, *supra*, Chapter 5, Catalysts in the Ozone Layer Depletion Regime.

108. In their role in the formation and maintenance of the regime, these catalysts may contribute to raising the acceptable level of compliance, see, *infra*, Chapter 6, Compliance in the Climate Change Regime.

109. See, *supra*, n. 40.

110. "INC Climate Change Convention: First Discussions," *supra*, n. 45, p. 52.

111. "Where Sununu Stands," *The New York Times*, 10 September 1991, p. C9.

112. William K. Stevens, "Washington Odd Man Out, May Shift On Climate," *The New York Times*, 18 February 1992, p. C1.

113. Notably, Norway. See, Bodansky, "INC 3 & 4: Draft Convention on Climate Change," *supra*, n. 49, p. 10.

114. Bush's decision was "announced" in the British press 5 days before President Bush released a statement in Washington, DC to that effect, perhaps revealing more of an international concern than a (US) domestic concern regarding his presence in Rio. See, Martin Walker, "Bush To Attend Rio On Global Warming," *Guardian* (London), 8 May 1992, and Keith Schneider, "Bush Plans To Join Other Leaders At Earth Summit in Brazil in June," *The New York Times*, 13 May 1992, p. A8.

115. "US Lashes Back at Summit," *International Herald Tribune*, 10 June 1992, p. 1. The EC also pledged to increase aid for environmental projects by $4 billion, but offered no timetable. See, "Bush Takes The Offensive at Rio Summit," *International Herald Tribune*, 13-14 June 1992, p. 1.

116. Japan pledged to increase its foreign environmental aid by an average of $1.45 billion per year, as well as try to reduce its carbon dioxide emissions to 1990 levels by 2000. See, Paul Lewis, "Negotiators In Rio Agree To Increase Aid to Third World," *The New York Times*, 14 June 1992, Section 1, pp. 1 and 10, and "Japan Pledges $7 Billion Toward Earth Summit Goals," *Asbury Park Press* (NJ), 14 June 1992, p.

A7. The Japanese government has also begun an inquiry into the environmental policies of Japanese firms abroad. See, "Japan Investigates 'Pollution Exports'," *International Herald Tribune* 14 July 1992, p. 15. However, the Japanese Prime Minster did not attend UNCED, because of internal disputes relating to how much Japan could afford to spend to finance environmental protection abroad, as well as a split within the Japanese business community between those seeking regulations and those wishing to avoid restrictions. There was also a parliamentary distraction relating to the deployment of troops abroad. See T.R. Reid, "Japan Hasn't Found Act It Needs To Star In Rio," *International Herald Tribune*, 3 June 1992, p. 2.

117. "Bush Takes The Offensive At Rio Summit," *International Herald Tribune*, 13-14 June 1992, p. 1. The US pledged an additional $150 million, for a total of $270 million annually, for other nations' forestry programs. See, Michael Wines, "Bush Offers Plan To Save Forests," *The New York Times*, 2 June 1992, p. A1. But see also, *The Earth Summit, supra*, n. 51, p. 448, pointing out that the United States argued that since it had never agreed to the overall UN Official Development Assistance target of 0.7% GNP, then it could not re-affirm a commitment it had never made.

118. Paul Lewis, "Negotiators In Rio Agree To Increase Aid To Third World," *The New York Times*, 14 June 1992, section 1, pp. 1 and 10. The UK and Japan also agreed to move towards the target, but also did not commit to a timetable. The US did not accept the commitment. See *supra*, n. 117.

119. See, Draft Directive, *Official Journal* 1992 No. C 196/1, submitted 2 June 1992.

120. See, Andrew Pollack, "Ecological Savior Abroad, Japan Lags at Home," *International Herald Tribune*, 1-2 August 1992, pp. 1–2, where the author quotes Naomi Kamei, Japanese coordinator for Friends of the Earth, as stating: "we don't quote our membership, it's so low."

121. See, William R. Cline, *Global Warming: The Economic Stakes* (Washington, DC: Institute for International Economics, 1992), pp. 49–50, and National Academy of Sciences, *Policy Implications of Greenhouse Warming* (Washington, DC: National Academy Press), p. 68.

122. See, *supra*, Chapter 5, Leadership.

123. State leadership and international organizations are separate catalysts in a regime. While individuals may also assume a leadership role, he or she ultimately needs the backing of either a state or an international organization in order to bring legitimacy to the issue-area. For example, Mostapha Tolba, head of the UN Environment Programme, was credited with an instrumental role in the ozone negotiations. Richard Elliot Benedick, *Ozone Diplomacy* (Cambridge: Harvard University

Press, 1991), p. 6. Some individuals at the Rio Summit garnered laurels: India's Minster of Environment, Kamal Nath; Singapore Ambassador-at-Large Tommy Koh; and the Malaysian chief negotiator, Wen Lian Ting, nicknamed the "Dragon Lady" for her notorious negotiating skills. See, James Brooke, "Delegates From 4 Nations Warm to a High-Profile Role: Global Powerbroker," *The New York Times*, 12 June 1992, p. A10. In addition, the Administrator of the US Environmental Protection Agency, William Kane Reilly, was highly regarded as having represented environmental interests within a perceived anti-environmental Bush Administration. See, Keith Schneider, "US Chief at Summit Walks a Tightrope," *International Herald Tribune*, 3 June 1992, p. 2.

124. Interestingly, environmental leadership might evolve from national security concerns. See, for example, former US President Jimmy Carter, "Redefining Security For The 90's," *International Herald Tribune*, 9 July 1991, p. 6, Michael Oppenheimer, "Don't Miss the Green Bandwagon," *International Herald Tribune*, 30 March 1990, and Philip Shabecoff, quoting US Senator Sam Nunn calling environmental destruction "a growing national security threat," in "Security Shift To Ecology Seen," *International Herald Tribune*, 30 June-1 July, 1990, p. 4.

125. See, Tom Redburn, "Unpopular G-7 Leaders Keep Bickering on Issues," *International Herald Tribune* , 6 July 1992, pp. 1 and 9, where the author points out some of the issues where the G-7 states are at odds: world trade, aid to former Soviet republics, global economy, national security and relations with other states, and the environment.

126. Al Gore, Jr., *Earth In The Balance* (London: Earthscan, 1992), pp. 176–177.

127. National Academy of Sciences, *Policy Implications of Global Warming*, *supra*, n. 121, p. 7. On a per capita emissions basis, however, the US falls to 9th overall, behind Canada and Brazil, among others. See, Robin Churchill, "Controlling Emissions of Greenhouse Gases," in *International Law and Climate Change*, ed. Robin Churchill and David Freestone (London: Graham & Trotman, 1991), p. 150.

128. The perceived need for an active US role in climate change negotiations is further evidenced by action taken by UN officials during the UNCED conference, fearing demonstrations against President Bush, to close the Rio conference center to representatives of private environmental groups and to sharply reduce the number of accredited delegations. An EC spokesman cautioned: "We don't want a slugging match of everybody against the US." See, James Brooke, "To Protect Bush, UN Will Limit Access To Talks," *The New York Times*, 8 June 1992, p. A5. See, also, *Earth Summit*, *supra*, n. 51, p. 79, where the commentator, alluding to the undermining of the environmental credibility of the

United States at UNCED, noted that while "dumping on the US always makes good copy," "the isolation of the US was one of the least satisfactory aspects of the Rio Conference and one where the world as a whole may pay the price for a long time to come."

129. US Department of State, *National Action Plan for Global Climate Change* (Washington, DC: Dept. of State, 1992), presented at the 6th session of the INC, Geneva, December 1992. See also, Andrew Warren, "Lesson From America," *Guardian* (London), 19 June 1992, p. 27, which notes that the US has already adopted the world's most stringent clean air legislation and has set out a range of federal energy saving programs, projected to save between 125 and 200 million tons of greenhouse gas emissions by the year 2000.

130. See, Statement of President Bush, "International Cooperation on Environment and Development," address to UNCED, Rio de Janeiro, 12 June 1992 proposing the completion of national action plans by 1 January 1993. See, also, "Bush Takes The Offensive At Rio Summit," *International Herald Tribune*, 13-14 June 1992, p. 1. The US also pledged an additional $150 million, for a total of $270 million annually, for other nations' forestry programs. See, Michael Wines, "Bush Offers Plan To Save Forests," *The New York Times*, 2 June 1992, p. A1.

131. See, ABC News This Week with David Brinkley, Transcript #553, 31 May 1992, statement of William Reilly, US EPA Administrator, where Mr. Reilly stated that "there's no question that we have made a commitment in the climate convention... to move toward stabilization of greenhouse gases.... We are now going to undertake the efforts. We've already begun them." See, also, William K. Reilly, "Aiming Before We Shoot: The Quiet Revolution in Environmental Policy,"speech delivered at the National Press Club, Washington, DC, 26 September 1990.

132. See, Gore, *Earth In The Balance*, *supra*, n. 126. As a self-proclaimed environmentalist, Vice-President Gore may be in a strong position to broaden the influence of science, thus strengthening that critical issue within the climate change regime. Yet it is important to remember that he is not a scientist and thus not a member of that epistemic community as such. Rather, he is a politician whose ambitions differ from those of the scientific epistemic community. See, *supra*, Chapter 4, Overcoming Scientific Uncertainty.

133. See, *supra*, n. 4.

134. See, Gareth Porter and Janet Welsh Brown, *Global Environmental Politics* (Boulder, CO: Westview Press, 1991), pp. 50–51.

135. See, William K. Stevens, "Rio Raises Environment Issue To Lasting World-Class Status," *International Herald Tribune*, 15 June 1992, p. 2.

136. See, *supra*, Chapter 6, International Action Regarding Climate Change, and Chapter 4, International Non-state Actors.

137. Perspectives, No. 9 (1992), quoted in *The Earth Summit*, *supra*, n. 51, p. 487.

138. See, for instance, David Tolbert, "Climate Change and the Role of International Non-Governmental Organizations," in *International Law and Global Climate Change*, ed. Robin Churchill and David Freestone (London: Graham & Trotman, 1991), pp. 95–108.

139. See, Richard E. Benedick, "Behind the Diplomatic Curtain: Inner Workings of the New Global Negotiations," *Columbia Journal of World Business* Vol. 27, No. 3,4 (Fall/Winter 1992), pp. 52–61. Two NGOs, Kyote Forum and EcoFund '92, published on a daily basis *Earth Summit Times*, the official newspaper of UNCED.

140. See, *supra*, Chapter 6, International Action Regarding Climate Change, and *supra*, Chapter 4, Non-governmental Organizations.

141. See, *supra*, Chapter 4, Non-governmental Organizations. One commentator warns, however, that consumer pressure is a fragile force, see Frances Cairncross, "UNCED, Environmentalism and Beyond," *Columbia Journal of World Business* Vol. 27, No. 3,4 (Fall/Winter 1992), pp. 12–17. Nevertheless, in response to public pressure, the US EPA has created an Office of Environmental Equity an Environmental Justice Bill has been introduced in the US Congress in response to growing awareness of environmental risks. Source, The District of Columbia (US) Bar, Environment, Energy and Natural Resources Section. Interestingly, a study released in October 1992 by the Environmental Research Associates, Princeton, NJ, revealed the role of children in influencing their parents' attitude towards the environment. See, Ruth M. Bono, "In the Ozone, A Child Shall Lead Them," *The New York Times*, 10 January 1993, section 4A, p. 7.

142. *The Earth Summit*, *supra*, n. 51, pp. 9–10.

143. See, Carmody, quoting Don Verrico, manager of environmental communications at the DuPont Company,"'Greening'," *supra*, n. 92, p. D6.

144. See, Schmidheiny, *Changing Course*, *supra*, n. 95.

145. *The Earth Summit*, *supra*, n. 51, p. 10.

146. See, for example, the special issue of *Columbia Journal of World Business* Vol. 47, No. 3/4 (Fall/Winter 1992) concentrating on "corporate environmentalism,"particularly Richard Poduska et al, "The Challenge of Sustainable Development: Kodak's Response," pp. 286–291. See, also, AT&T, *An Investment In Our Future,* An AT&T Environment & Safety Report, November 1991, outlining its pollution prevention program utilizing benchmarking processes. Benchmarking in research and development, whereby goals and improvement opportunities

are outlined, is becoming an increasingly important management tool and can be adapted to environmental concerns as AT&T has shown. See, Thomas J. Bean and Jacques G. Gros, "R&D Benchmarking at AT&T," *Research-Technology Management* Vol. 35, No. 4 (July-August 1992). See, also, "Management Brief: Food For Thought," *Economist*, 29 August 1992, pp. 62–64, a case study examining the way McDonald's coped with protests about environmental damage caused by the fast-food industry.

147. See, *The Earth Summit*, *supra*, n. 51, p. 10.

148. For example, an EC proposal to introduce carbon taxes, is conditional on the United States and Japan doing the same. The United States has shown no signs of doing so and Japan has decided against a tax for the time being: "In the event that such an initiative lacks international conformity, it would invite the international migration of industry."See, Robert Thomson, "Japan Hedges on Carbon Tax," *Financial Times* (London), 9 December 1992, p. 14.

149. See, Chapter 1, *supra*, Climate Change.

150. Peter Wilby, "Apocalypse Tomorrow—But There Is Plenty Of Jam Today," *Independent on Sunday* (London), 11 November 1990, p. 20.

151. See, *supra*, Chapter 3, Maintenance or Development of Regimes.

152. See, *supra*, Chapter 6, International Action Regarding Climate Change.

153. See, *supra*, FCCC, Art. 4(2)b, n. 2, and Stephen Kinzer, "UN Parley Delegates Back Talks on Global Warming," *The New York Times*, 8 April 1995, p. 4.

154. Stevens, "Rio Raises Environment Issue To Lasting World-Class Status," *supra*, n. 135, p. 2.

155. See, *supra*, FCCC, Art. 12, n. 2.

156. Ibid., Art. 14(1).

157. Ibid., Art. 14(2).

158. Vienna Convention on the Protection of the Ozone Layer, *International Legal Materials*, Vol.26, No. 6 (1987), pp. 1516–1540, Art. 11.

159. See, FCCC, *supra*, n. 2, Art. 14(5), (6).

160. Ibid., Art. 15(7).

161. See, *supra*, Chapter 5, International Action Regarding Ozone Layer Depletion. See, also, Daniel Bodansky, "The United Nations Framework Convention on Climate Change: A Commentary," *The Yale Journal of International Law* Vol. 18, No. 2 (Summer 1993), p. 548 where the author states a significant degree of consensus has emerged on

creating such a mechanism.

162. Oscar Schachter, *International Law In Theory and Practice* (Dordrecht: Martinus Nijhoff Publishers, 1991), p. 75.

163. See, *supra*, FCCC, Art. 12, n. 2.

164. Ibid., Art. 4(2)b.

165. The convention allows for review of the provisions. Art. 4(2)d, Art. 15. The dates for the reviews were chosen to correspond to the anticipated dates for completion of the next IPCC assessments, late 1994 to mid-1955 for the 2nd full assessment and 1998 for the third. See, R.A. Reinstein,"Climate Negotiations," *The Washington Quarterly* Vol. 16, No. 1 (Winter 1993), pp. 92–93.

166. See, Alice Enders and Amelia Porges, "Successful Conventions," in *The Greening of World Trade Issues* (London: Harvester Wheatsheaf, 1992) pp. 141–142.

167. These include the GATT Committee on Trade and Development to promote sustainable development through trade liberalization and the GATT Group on Environmental Measures and International Trade to be involved with making trade and environmental policies mutually supportive. See, "GATT to Play an Active Role in UNCED Follow-up," *Focus: GATT Newsletter* No. 96 (January-February 1993), p. 5. GATT, however, while allowing trade restriction on products whose use or presence causes pollution, views the setting of production and process standards as being done through international bodies possessing competence on environmental matters, and not through GATT. There is nothing in the GATT or in the draft Uruguay Round text permitting trade restrictions based on production methods. See, "Trade and the Environment," excerpts from an address by GATT Deputy Director-General Charles R. Carlisle, *Focus: GATT Newsletter* No. 97 (March 1993), p. 4.

168. Abram Chayes and Antonia Chayes argue that "the free-rider problem has been overestimated," since (citing Mancur Olson) "if the benefits of the collective good to one or a group of parties outweigh the costs to them of providing the good, they will continue to bear the costs regardless of the defections of others." *On Compliance* Vol. 47, No. 2 (Spring 1993), p. 201.

169. See, *supra*, Chapter 3, Conditional Cooperation and Exclusion.

170. *Supra*, Chapter 6, Formation of the Climate Change Regime.

171. See, *supra*, Chapter 3, Formation of Regimes.

172. See, *supra*, Chapter 2, Policy-Oriented Lawmaking.

173. See, *supra*, Chapter 6, International Action Regarding Climate Change.

174. Ibid.

175. See, *supra*, Chapter 2, Policy-Oriented School.

176. Ibid.

177. See, *supra*, Chapter 2, Policy-Oriented Lawmaking.

178. The report of the IPCC Response Strategies Working Group, *Legal Measures: Report of Topic Coordinators*, emphasized this, stating: "views differ substantially on the role and powers of the institutions to be created" by a regulatory process. See, *supra*, n. 31.

179. See, *supra*, Chapter 1, Climate Change.

180. See, *supra*, Chapter 6, Scientific Uncertainty.

181. See, *supra*, Chapter 6, International Action Regarding Climate Change.

182. See, *supra*, Chapter 6, Economic Uncertainty and Development Uncertainty.

183. See, *supra*, Chapter 6, International Action Regarding Climate Change.

184. Namely, the finance mechanism of the FCCC. See, *supra*, Chapter 6, International Action Regarding Climate Change.

185. *Supra*, Chapter 2, Policy-Oriented School.

186. W. Michael Reisman, "International Lawmaking: A Process of Communication," *Proceedings of the American Society of International Law*, April 1981, p. 113.

187. See, *supra*, Chapter 2, Policy-Oriented Lawmaking.

188. *Supra*, Chapter 6, International Action Regarding Climate Change.

189. Bodansky, "Framework Convention on Climate Change," *supra*, n. 161, p. 558. Professor Bodansky is in a good position to evaluate the expectations of the participants in the climate change regime, as this work is the culmination of extensive research observing the INC process.

190. See, *supra*, Chapter 2, Policy-Oriented Lawmaking.

191. *Supra*, Chapter 6, International Action Regarding Climate Change.

192. Ibid.

193. See, *supra*, Chapter 2, Customary Law.

194. Birnie & Boyle, *International Law & the Environment* (Oxford: Clarendon Press, 1993), p. 15.

195. W. Michael Reisman, "The View From the New Haven School," in *American Society of International Law: Proceedings of the 86th Annual Meeting*, by the American Society of International Law, Washington, DC (1992), p. 121. Professor Reisman's comment on the New Haven School underscores the compatibility of the policy-oriented approach and regime theory, as both seek a wider explanation of why

states cooperate than traditional theories do.

196. While the media coverage of the UNCED conference portrayed a sense of failure; see, for example, Nicholas Schoon, "Fog of Self-Interest Blocks Views From Rio," *Independent on Sunday* (London), 14 June 1992, p. 12, Barbara Crossette, "A Rio Lesson: Nations and Grass Roots Are Often Poles Apart," *International Herald Tribune*, 16 June 1992, p. 4., and Harvey Morris, "Pessimists Fear That History May Well Repeat Itself," *Independent* (London), 3 June 1992, p. 10, it is the view of this book that successful groundwork has been laid for the development of a climate change regime.

CHAPTER 7

The Future of Regimes in the International Legal Order

International relations and foreign policy, then, depend on a legal order, operate in a legal framework, assume a host of legal principles and concepts which shape the policies of nations and limit national behavior.[1]

While the detailed study of regimes within the international legal order may be relatively new,[2] regimes themselves are not a new phenomena. Indeed, regimes are present wherever states share expectations regarding their future behavior concerning the regulation of an issue-area. These shared expectations, in the sense that the policy-oriented school interprets that phrase,[3] create legal obligations. As a result, regimes provide a rich source of material for the study of the international legal order, as they allow for the analysis of how and why states undertake lawmaking. It is appropriate, then, for international law to take account of this concept.

THE LIMITATIONS OF TRADITIONAL INTERNATIONAL LEGAL THEORY

The classic international legal paradigm whereby binding rules are derived from the sources of treaties, customary law, or general principles of law is not wrong, but is incomplete. In an attempt to rectify this, the policy-oriented approach to international law takes full account of all aspects of the decision-making process within the international legal order. This is particularly important in the light of such present day scenarios as implicit understandings between states, social revolutions overturning traditional orders, the interdependence of states, the permeability between the domestic and international affairs of a state, and the expansion of science and technology which has given way to informal standard setting.[4]

The policy-oriented view of international law as an ongoing process where policy content, an authority signal and a control intention are necessarily present, attempts to explain how law is made. This is important to the legal scholar, since, "if we fail to learn *how* to prescribe, the individual and collective consequences may be grave."[5] However, the school is "concerned not only with the processes in which certain policies that self-describe as law are made, but with the aggregate of processes in a community by which political perspectives at varying levels of consciousness are shaped and changed."[6] It is this concern that makes the school amenable to the use of regime theory;[7] indeed, the school's definition of what it calls an arena[8] (or a social situation specialized to the shaping and sharing of power outcomes) is strikingly similar to that which international relations specialists have labelled regimes.[9] Within that arena, there is a decision-making process in which lawmaking occurs, a process of great importance to legal scholars.

THE CONCEPT OF REGIMES AS PART OF THE INTERNATIONAL LEGAL ORDER

The concept of regimes was discussed above as the process of development of legal regulations by both state and non-state actors through collective decision-making, governing a specific issue-area and creating legal obligations among the actors.[10]

Regimes are formed when shared expectations exist regarding future behavior.[11] As a result, regimes fit within the policy-oriented approach to international law, which views the legal order as a process of decision-making and not just as a set of rules.[12] Although these shared expectations are difficult at times for states to achieve, (as well as for scholars to identify) it is a critical aspect, since "the strongest circumstantial evidence for the sense of an obligation...is the care that states take in negotiating[13] [these shared expectations]."

As cognitive expectations evolve with respect to critical issues, then normative or shared expectations governing state behavior regarding the issue-area are shaped and the regime is further developed,[14] so long as the elements of authority and control remain present.

How uncertainty regarding critical issues is overcome is specific to the regime and the nature of the critical issues. In general, however, the flexibility of the regime in adapting to changing knowledge is important, particularly when knowledge is rapidly acquired. Catalysts can aid in the formation and maintenance of the regime, helping to overcome uncertainty, but are not critical to the regime itself.[15]

Compliance with international law cannot be enforced in the same manner as domestic law. Thus, other methods must be utilized in international law, and in regimes as well. These include the evolution of rules harmonious with the regime's objective, dispute settlement procedures, accountability and transparency, and exclusion and conditional cooperation.[16] Dispute settlement procedures allow for the dispute to be settled by the members of the regime on the basis of the regime norms and rules, thus reducing ambiguity. Accountability is obtained through procedures such as reporting and monitoring. Exclusion from the regime can be forced upon recalcitrant members, and members can also rely on conditional cooperation.[17]

These elements for compliance may take time to evolve within a regime. As seen from the description of the ozone layer depletion regime, these methods utilized in compliance are present to a much greater degree than in the climate change regime.[18] Whether or not such methods will evolve within the climate change regime will depend on the extent to which the shared expectations of the members evolve. However, the climate change regime has begun to address accountability and dispute-settlement. There are reporting requirements in place in the FCCC, and it does provide for a dispute settlement mechanism.[19] During the INC process, "delegations generally agreed that the mechanism should be forward rather than backward-looking," and so "would be similar to the non-compliance procedure established under the Montreal Protocol."[20] It appears, then, that the climate change regime is slowly evolving to include these compliance measures.

CLIMATE CHANGE AND OZONE LAYER DEPLETION REGIMES

Analyses of the climate change and ozone layer depletion regimes were made above.[21] The regimes can be compared on the basis of the similarity of the issue-area underlying each regime. Both climate change and ozone layer depletion are global environmental problems based on scientific theory that require international cooperation if the problems are to be successfully dealt with.

The analysis of the ozone layer depletion regime reveals a regime that has overcome uncertainty regarding critical issues and has been developed to include substantive regulations, with substantial success.[22] The climate change regime has not yet developed to that stage, because of remaining uncertainty concerning critical issues. Cognitive expectations, then, have not yet been shaped to the degree where substantive normative or shared expectations have evolved regarding future behavior. However, developed members of the regime have pledged to set emission caps on greenhouse gases. Thus, the regime does contain obligations for its members and so plays a vital role in the legal order. As Abram and Antonia Chayes note:

> It is a mistake to call these... merely 'aspirational' or 'hortatory.' To be sure, they embody 'ideals' of the international system, but...they were designed to initiate a process that over time, perhaps a long time, would bring behavior into greater congruence with those ideals. These expectations have not been wholly disappointed. The vast amount of public and private effort devoted to enforcing these agreements — not always in vain — evinces their obligational content.[23]

PROSPECTS FOR PROGRESS IN THE LEGAL ORDER

International law must take account of the success of regimes in implementing regulations in such contentious and global areas as the environment. Regimes are found not only in the realm of environmental protection, but throughout international law. There is nothing in the definition, formation or maintenance of a regime that limits its application to the regimes employed in this book.[24] Rather, regimes can be found throughout the international legal order, in various stages of development. For example, the regime regulating international air traffic is much more established than the regime regulating human rights, where there is greater uncertainty regarding critical issues. While a detailed study of other regimes cannot be undertaken here, a brief sketch of the nuclear nonproliferation regime can be undertaken to show that regimes exist in other areas of the international legal order.

Research into the nuclear nonproliferation regime has been plentiful.[25] This regime includes two major treaties, the Nonproliferation Treaty and the Latin American Nuclear Weapons Free Zone Treaty; an international organization, the International Atomic Energy Association which accounts for nuclear materials; a treaty and other measures dealing with the issue of protection of nuclear materials;[26] nontreaty agreements on export controls; informal understandings that certain technologies will not be exported; intelligence sharing; and a very active diplomacy carried out regarding the regime.[27]

This regime was not always in place. Rather, it has evolved as shared expectations regarding future behavior concerning nuclear nonproliferation have evolved.

Regimes, then, are not new phenomena within the international legal order. They have just not been the subject of much serious study by international lawyers. The examination in this book of the climate change and ozone layer depletion regimes reveals that there are great prospects for progress in the international legal order. From previously unregulated areas, legal obligations have evolved regarding areas of great environmental significance.

But the climate change and ozone layer depletion regimes have also shown that merely studying the resulting obligations is not the best method for examining the legal order. Rather, observing the regime process whereby cognitive expectations form, normative or shared expectations regarding behavior follow, and obligations ensue, is very significant. Not to do so is to ignore the fact that international law does not exist in a vacuum. By understanding observing how and why states willingly regulate an issue area, through a policy-oriented approach to international law, the prospects for strengthening the legal order are enhanced.

Examining the regime process strengthens the argument that the international legal order exists and that it has a large role to play in the affairs of states. While the idea that the legal order is a process is not a new idea, the exploration of that process in a discussion of institutional arrangements or governance systems has not been undertaken in great detail within international law.

Because laws heighten public expectations, it is important that policy makers ask whether prospective laws are consistent with a government's ability to achieve the goals established by those laws.[28] Because regimes take account of the underlying critical issues, they are adept at realizing regulations that the regime states can implement and, in the process, are able to strengthen the overall legal order.

Thus, "the value of regimes for the development of international environmental law should be self-evident."[29] Regimes help to "explain the different levels of normativity within a treaty," they highlight the "latent conflicts of interest (economic, political, North-South) that determine regime building and regime-maintenance," and they "allow ambitious actors to accept meager initial results... while maintaining expectations of more decisive action during the later evolution of the regime..."[30]

It may be true that for international law to change or evolve, "it will be ... pressure that makes that change."[31] Knowledge of how that occurs is of great importance in bringing change about. Regimes, then, are worthy of study by international lawyers, not least because they are already part of the legal order, in which they play a vital role.

Regimes are valuable for study even for those legal scholars who do not subscribe to the policy-oriented school. While such non-policy-oriented scholars may not agree on the timing of formation of a regime, because of theoretical differences as to what is "law," this does not mean that regimes are of no value to them. Regime study can still allow for analysis of extra-legal factors that may influence lawmaking, and so can provide empirical evidence for comparative study of different areas of lawmaking.

INCORPORATING REGIMES INTO INTERNATIONAL LEGAL STUDIES

If regime theory is to take hold within international law, and the above studies of the climate change and ozone layer depletion regimes are testimony that they should, then international legal scholars will have to become more involved in interdisciplinary research, to a greater extent than mere collaboration on joint projects. As Oran Young has put it, there is between disciplines "a deeper division concerning not only what we know but also what there is to know and how we come to know what we know."[32]

Such a pessimistic view does not mean, however, that the methodological difficulties that may arise from the attempt to bring international law and regime theory together are so large as to prevent meaningful interdisciplinary work.[33] The relative ease with which the policy-oriented school can absorb regimes into its framework of law, as well as the similarities between the two with regard to basic definitions,[34] point more towards a meeting of the two mindsets than to the opposite. This, of course, may well depend on the perspective that this author has taken, namely that of international law from a policy-oriented approach. But it is difficult for the international relations scholar to ignore similarities as well.[35]

However, the picture is not completely perfect. Within regime theory itself, different perspectives are taken. This was outlined in Chapter 3 with regard to regime definition and formation. Thus, there are divisions within the regime literature in international relations between those who view cooperation in rationalist, game theoretic terms, and those who view cooperation with greater regard for questions of normativity and obligation.[36]

Such differences are important and should not be overlooked. This is true not only for those studying regime theory from the perspective of international relations, but also for those coming from a legal perspective, since both disciplines are eventually working towards the same goal of identifying why states cooperate, although legal scholars may view it in more prescriptive terms than international relations specialists. If differences are too great within a single discipline, then it complicates interdisciplinary work as well.

But while these underlying divisions may appear to pose problems for unity regarding regime theory, it has not served to impede progress towards understanding regimes. Indeed, it appears to have served to propel more research in the area, with scholars suggesting a closer look at the domestic policy level with regard to regimes and cooperation in an attempt to overcome divergent theoretical perspectives.[37]

Thus, divisions between regime theorists are not necessarily irreconcilable, nor does it suggest irreconcilable differences between international law and international relations with regard to regime theory. The closeness of the policy-oriented school and regime theory in general attest to that.[38]

While international law is not politics or economics or sociology, it is surely shaped by these areas, and understanding not only that but the manner in which those disciplines go about their scholarly pursuits is essential. The use of regime theory within international law requires that this interdisciplinary linkage be observed and incorporated as part of international legal studies. It may not be an exaggeration to say: "The stakes here are very high; the consequences, very significant."[39]

NOTES

1. Louis Henkin, *How Nations Behave*, 2d ed. (NY: Columbia University Press, 1979), p. 22.

2. As mentioned in Chapter 3, Introduction to International Regimes, *supra*, the study of regimes in the context of international law with regard to the conceptual and theoretical issues of regime theory, until quite recently, was virtually non-existent.

3. See, *supra*, Chapter 2, Policy-Oriented School and Policy-Oriented Lawmaking.

4. Chapter 2, *supra*, n. 62.

5. W. Michael Reisman, "International Lawmaking: A Process of Communication," *Proceedings of the American Society of International Law*, April 1981, p. 103.

6. Ibid.

7. See, Michael G. Schechter, "The New Haven School of International Law, Regime Theorists, Their Critics and Beyond," paper given at the annual meeting of the International Studies Association, 26 March 1993.

8. "The identifying characteristic of an arena is a structure of expectations shard among the members of a community." Myres S. McDougal and Harold Lasswell, "The Identification and Appraisal of Diverse Systems of Public Order," *American Journal of International Law* Vol. 53, No. 1 (January 1959), p. 8.

9. Regimes are "principles, norms, rules and decision-making procedures around which actor expectations converge in a given issue-area." Stephen Krasner, "Structural Causes and Regime Consequences: Regimes as Intervening Variables," in *International Regimes* ed. Stephen D. Krasner (Ithaca: Cornell University Press 1983), p. 1.

10. See *supra*, Chapter 3, Definition of Regimes.

11. *Supra*, Chapter 3, Formation of Regimes.

12. See *supra*, Chapter 3, Legal Status of Regimes.

13. Abram Chayes and Antonia Chayes, "On Compliance," *International Organization* Vol. 47, No. 2 (Spring 1993), p. 186. While the authors were speaking of treaties, they were alluding to very weak treaty obligations. In that respect, their comments are applicable to regime formation.

14. See, *supra*, Chapter 2, Policy-Oriented School, Policy-Oriented Lawmaking, Chapter 3, Definition, Formation, and Maintenance of Regimes, and Chapter 4 with regard to critical issues concerning development. See, also, Stephan Haggard and Beth A. Simmons, "Theories of International Regimes," *International Organization*, Vol. 41, No. 3 (Summer 1987), pp. 491–513, regarding cognitive theories of regimes.

15. See *supra*, Chapter 4, Catalysts.

16. See, *supra*, Chapter 3, Effectiveness of Regimes.

17. Ibid.

18. See, *supra*, Chapters 5 and 6.

19. See, *supra*, Chapter 6, International Action Regarding Climate Change.

20. Daniel Bodanksy, "The United Nations Framework Convention on Climate Change: A Commentary," *The Yale Journal of International Law* Vol. 18, no. 2 (Summer 1993), p. 548.

21. See *supra*, Chapters 5 and 6.

22. Scientists are now predicting that the increase in the build-up of ozone depleting chemicals in the atmosphere should halt before the end of the century. See, *supra*, Chapter 1, Ozone Layer Depletion.

23. Chayes and Chayes, "On Compliance," *supra*, n. 13, p. 197.

24. See, Winfried Lang, "Diplomacy and International Environmental Law-Making: Some Observations," *Yearbook of International Environmental Law* Vol. 3 (1992), who states "the concept of regime and the idea of an evolutionary or step-by-step approach, are not, of course, restricted to international environmental regulations," p. 122.

25. See, for example, Joseph Nye, Jr., "Maintaining a Nonproliferation Regime," in *Nuclear Proliferation; Breaking the Chain* ed. George Quester, pp. 15–38 (Madison: University of Wisconsin Press, 1981) and Lawrence Scheinman, "Nonproliferation Regime: Safeguards, Controls and Sanctions," in *The Nuclear Connection* ed. A. Weinburg et al, pp. 177–210 (NY: Paragon Press, 1985).

26. Convention on the Physical Protection of Nuclear Material, *International Legal Materials* Vol. 18, No. 6 pp. 1419–1433 (1979).

27. See, Richard Williamson, "Building the International Environmental Regime: A Status Report," *Inter-American Law Review* Vol. 21, no. 3 (Summer 1990), pp. 741–743.

28. See, Gary C. Bryner, *Blue Skies, Green Politics: The Clean Air Act of 1990* (Washington, DC: CQ Press, 1993), p. 34.

29. See Lang, "Diplomacy and International Environmental Law-Making," *supra*, n. 24, p. 121. While Lang maintains that regimes "are initially established through framework conventions or protocols," thus differing from the requirements for formation put forth in this regime, his observations with regard to the value of regimes are applicable here.

30. Ibid.

31. Anthony Day, quoting David Scheffer, senior associate at the Carnegie Endowment for International Peace, "Morality Versus International Law," *International Herald Tribune*, 15 February 1993, p. 6.

32. Oran A. Young, "Understanding International Regimes: Contributions From Law and the Social Sciences," paper given at the annual meeting of the American Society of International Law, Washington, DC, 1-3 April 1992, p. 39. One promising project is a three year study of the effectiveness of national fulfillment of international environmental commitments, sponsored by the International Institute for Applied Systems Analysis (Austria). The interdisciplinary and international team selected is composed of scholars from political science, law and economics.

33. See, for example, Oran Young's comments regarding the "two-cultures problem" between international law and international relations. While he admitted that it would not be easy to join the two "cultures,"

there was some opportunity for collaboration. "Remarks," *American Society of International Law: Proceedings of the 86th Meeting*, Washington, DC (1992), pp. 174–175.

34. The policy-oriented definition of arena and the regime theorists' definition of regime, see, *supra*, n. 8 and 9.

35. See Schechter, "New Haven School," *supra*, n. 7, Although there are still international relations specialists disregarding the linkage, see *supra*, Chapter 3, Introduction to International Regimes.

36. See, Haggard and Simmons, "Theories of International Regimes," *supra*, n. 14, pp. 491–517, and Helen Milner, "International Theories of Cooperation Among Nations," *World Politics* Vol. 44, No. 3.(April 1992), pp. 466–496.

37. Haggard and Simmons, "International Regimes," *supra*, n. 14 and Milner, "Theories of Cooperation," *supra*, n. 36.

38. See also, Young, "Remarks," *supra*, n. 33.

39. George Bush, "US Committed to Safe Environment," an address to the IPCC, Washington, DC, 5 February 1990. President Bush was referring to the crucial [interdisciplinary] components to global resolution of the climate change problem: science, social and economic impacts, and appropriate [legal] strategies.

SELECT BIBLIOGRAPHY

Abbott, Kenneth W. "Modern International Relations Theory: A Prospectus for International Lawyers." *Yale Journal of International Law* Vol. 14 (1989), pp. 335–411.

Barratt-Brown, Elizabeth P. "Building a Monitoring and Compliance Regime Under the Montreal Protocol." *Yale Journal of International Law* Vol. 16, No. 2 (Summer 1991), pp. 520–570.

Bean, Thomas J. and Jacques G. Gros. "R&D Benchmarking at AT&T." In *Research Technology Management* Vol. 35, No. 4 (July-August 1992), pp. 32–37.

Benedick, Richard Elliot. *Ozone Diplomacy: New Directions In Safeguarding The Planet*. Cambridge: Harvard University Press, 1991.

Birnie, Patricia W. and Alan E. Boyle. *International Law and the Environment*. Oxford: Clarendon Press, 1992.

Bodansky, Daniel. "The United Nations Framework Convention on Climate Change: A Commentary." *Yale Journal of International Law* Vol. 18, No. 2 (Summer 1993), pp. 451–558.

Brownlie, Ian. *Principles of Public International Law*. 4th ed. Oxford: Clarendon Press, 1990.

Burley, Anne-Marie Slaughter. "International Law and International Relations Theory."*American Journal of International Law* Vol. 87, No. 2 (April 1993), pp. 205–239.

Caldwell, Lynton K. *International Environmental Policy: Emergence and Dimensions*. 2d ed. Durham: Duke University Press, 1990.

Caron, David D. "Protection of the Stratospheric Ozone Layer and the Structure of International Environmental Lawmaking." *Hastings International and Comparative Law Review* Vol. 14, No. 4 (Symposium Issue 1991), pp. 755–780.

Charlesworth, H.C.M. "Customary International Law and the Nicaragua Case."*Australian Yearbook of International Law* Vol. 11 (1983-87), pp. 1–31.

Chayes, Abram and Antonia Chayes. "On Compliance." *International Organization*. Vol. 47, No. 2 (Spring 1993), pp. 175–205.

Chinkin, C.M. "The Challenge of Soft Law: Development and Change in International Law." *International and Comparative Law Quarterly* Vol. 38, Part IV (October 1989), pp. 850–866.

Churchill, Robin and David Freestone, ed. *International Law and Global Climate Change*. London: Graham & Trotman, 1991.

Cline, William R. *The Economics of Global Warming*. Washington, DC: Institute for International Economics, 1992.

________. *Global Warming: The Economic Stakes*. Washington, DC: Institute For International Economics, 1992.

D'Amato, Anthony. *The Concept of Custom in International Law*. London: Cornell University Press, 1971.

________. "Trashing Customary International Law." *American Journal of International Law* Vol. 81, No. 1 (January 1989), pp. 101–105.

Donoghue, Joan E. *Legal Dimensions of Compliance and Dispute Resolution in a Global Climate Regime*. Paper given at the annual conference of the International Studies Association, Atlanta, Georgia, April 1992.

Dupuy, Pierre. "Soft Law and the International Law of the Environment." *Michigan Journal of International Law* Vol. 12, No. 2 (Winter 1991), pp. 420–435.

Evans, Tony and Peter Wilson. "Regime Theory and the English School of International Relations: A Comparison." *Millennium: Journal of International Studies* Vol. 21, No. 3 (Winter 1992), pp. 329–351.

Franck, Thomas M. *The Power of Legitimacy Among Nations* (NY: Oxford University Press, 1990).

Goldie, L.F.E. "Special Regimes and Pre-emptive Activities in International Law." *International Comparative and Legal Quarterly* Vol. 11, Part 3 (July 1962), pp. 670–700.

Grubb, Michael. *The Greenhouse Effect: Negotiating Targets*. London: Royal Institute of International Affairs, 1989.

Gruchalla-Wesierski, Taduesz. "A Framework for Understanding 'Soft Law.'" *Revue De Droit De McGill* Vol. 30 (1984), pp. 37–88.

Haas, Peter M. *Saving the Mediterranean: The Politics of International Environmental Cooperation*. NY: Columbia University Press, 1990.

Haas, Peter M., Robert O. Keohane and Marc A. Levy ed. *Institutions for the Earth*. Cambridge, MA: MIT Press, 1993.

Haggard, Stephan and Beth A. Simmons. "Theories of International Regimes." *International Organization* Vol. 41, No. 3 (Summer 1987) pp. 491–517.

Handl, Gunther. "Environmental Security and Global Change: The Challenge to International Law." In *Environmental Protection and International Law*, ed. Winfried Lang, Hanspeter Neuhold and Karl Zemanek, pp. 59–87. London: Graham & Trotman, 1991.

Higgins, Rosalyn. "International Law and the Avoidance, Containment and Resolution of Disputes." In *Recueil des Cours* 1991-V. Dordrecht: Martinus Nijhoff Publishers, 1993.

Hurrell, Andrew and Benedict Kingsbury. *The International Politics of the Environment*. Oxford: Clarendon Press, 1992.

Jurgielewicz, Lynne M. "Long Lines At Disney World Reduced By Sunstroke! Or Can International Law Control Climate Change?" *Revue Generale de Droit* Vol. 22, No. 2, 1990, pp. 459–470.

Keohane, Robert O. *After Hegemony: Cooperation and Discord in the World Political Economy*. Princeton: Princeton University Press, 1984.

Kiss, Alexandre and Dinah Shelton. *International Environmental Law*. London: Graham & Trotman, 1991.

Klein, Eckart. "International Regimes." In *Encyclopedia of Public International Law*, ed. R. Bernhard, pp. 202–207. Netherlands: Elsevier Science Publishers B.V., 1986.

Krasner, Stephen D., ed. *International Regimes*. Ithaca: Cornell University Press, 1983.

Lang, Winfried. "Diplomacy and International Environmental Law-Making: Some Observations." *Yearbook of International Environmental Law* Vol. 3 (1992), pp. 108–122.

Mathews, Jessica Tuchman, ed. *Preserving The Global Environment*, NY: W.W. Norton & Co., 1991.

McDougal, Myres and Associates. *Studies In World Public Order*. New Haven: New Haven Press, 1987.

McDougal, Myres S. and Harold D. Lasswell. "The Identification and Appraisal of Diverse Systems of Public Order." *American Journal of International Law* Vol. 53, No. 1 (January 1959), pp. 1–29.

Mitchell, Ronald B. *Intentional Oil Pollution At Sea*. Cambridge, Mass: MIT Press, 1994.

Nitze, William A. *The Greenhouse Effect: Formulating AConvention*. London: Royal Institute of International Affairs, 1990.

Nordhaus, William. "Greenhouse Economics." *The Economist*, 7 July 1990, p. 113.

________. "Economic Approaches to Greenhouse Warming." In *Global Warming: Economic Policy Responses*, ed. Rudiger Dornbusch and James M. Poterba, pp. 33–36. Cambridge, Mass: MIT Press, 1991.

Pearce, David, Edward Barbier and Anil Markandya. *Blueprint for a Green Economy*. London: Earthscan, 1990.

Pearce, David, Edward Barbier, Anil Markandya, Scott Barrett, R. Turner and Tim Swanson. *Blueprint 2: Greening the World Economy*. London: Earthscan Publications Ltd., 1991.

Plant, Glen. "Institutional and Legal Responses to Global Warming." In *International Law and Global Climate Change*, ed. Robin Churchill and David Freestone, pp. 165–181. London: Graham & Trotman, 1991.

Puchala, Donald J. and Raymond F. Hopkins. "International Regimes: Lessons From Inductive Analysis." In *International Regimes*, ed. Stephen Krasner, pp. 61–91. Ithaca: Cornell University Press, 1983.

Reifsnyder, W.E. "A Tale of Ten Fallacies: The Skeptical Enquirer's View of the Carbon Dioxide Climate Controversy."*Agriculture and Forest Meteorology* Vol. 47 (1989), pp. 349–371.

Reifsnyder, Daniel A. *Remarks of Daniel A. Reifsnyder*. The '92 Seoul Symposium on UNCED and Prospects for the Environmental Regime in the 21st Century. Seoul, 2 September 1992.

Reilly, William K. *Aiming Before We Shoot: The Quiet Revolution In Environmental Policy*. Speech given at the National Press Club, Washington, DC, 26 September 1990, US EPA, 20Z-1011.

Reinstein, R.A. "Climate Negotiations." *The Washington Quarterly* Vol. 16, No. 1 (Winter 1993), pp. 79–95.

Reisman, W. Michael. "International Lawmaking: A Process of Communication." In *American Society of International Law: Proceedings of the 75th Annual Meeting*, by the American Society of International Law, Washington, DC, 1981, pp. 101–120.

________. "The View of the New Haven School of International Law." In *American Society of International Law: Proceedings of the 86th Annual Meeting*, by the American Society of International Law. Washington, DC, 1992, pp. 118–125.

Roan, Sharon. *Ozone Crisis: The 15-Year Evolution of a Sudden Global Emergency*. New York: John Wiley & Sons, Inc., 1989.

Sand, Peter H. *Lessons Learned In Global Environmental Governance*. Washington, DC: World Resources Institute, 1990.

Schachter, Oscar. "Towards A Theory of International Obligation." *Virginia Journal of International Law* Vol. 8, No. 2, 1968, pp. 300–322.

________. *International Law in Theory and Practice*. 2d ed. Dordrecht: Martinus Nijhoff, 1991.

Schechter, Michael G. *The New Haven School of International Law, Regime Theorists and Beyond*. Paper given at the annual conference of the International Studies Association. Mexico, March 1993.

Schneider, Jan. *World Public Order of the Environment: Towards An International Ecological Law and Organization*. Toronto: University of Toronto Press, 1979.

Schneider, Stephen H. *Global Warming: Are We Entering The Greenhouse Century?* Cambridge:The Lutterworth Press, 1989.

Sohn, Louis. "The Stockholm Declaration on the Human Environment." *Harvard International Law Journal* Vol. 14, No. 1 (Winter 1973), pp. 423–515.

Soroos, Martin S. "The Evolution of Global Regulation of Atmospheric Pollution." *Policy Studies Journal* Vol. 19, No. 2 (Spring 1991), pp. 115–125.

Springer, Allen L. *The International Law of Pollution*. Westport, Ct. and London: Quorum Books, 1983.

________. Commentary to Karl Zemanek, "State Responsibility and Liability." In *Environmental Protection and International Law*, ed. Winfried Lang, Hanspeter Neuhold and Karl Zemanek, pp. 198–201. London: Graham & Trotman, 1991.

Stone, Christopher. "The Global Warming Crisis, If There Is One, and the Law." *The American University Journal of International Law and Policy* Vol. 5, No. 2 (Winter 1990), pp. 497–511.

________. "Beyond Rio: 'Insuring' Against Global Warming." *American Journal of International Law* Vol. 86, No. 3 (July 1992), pp. 445–488.

Strange, Susan. "Cave! Hic Dragones: A Critique of Regime Analysis." In *International Regimes*, ed. Stephen Krasner, pp. 337–354. Ithaca: Cornell University Press, 1983.

Tinker, Catherine. "Environmental Planet Management By the UN: An Idea Whose Time Has Not Yet Come?" *New York University Journal of International Law and Politics* Vol. 22, No. 4 (Summer 1990), pp. 793–830.

van Hoof, G.J.H. *Rethinking the Sources of International Law*. Deventer: Kluwer Law and Taxation Publishers, 1983.

Victor, David. "How To Slow Global Warming," *Nature* Vol. 349, (7 February 1991), pp. 451–456.

Weiss, Edith Brown. *In Fairness To Future Generations: International Law, Common Patrimony and Intergenerational Equity*. Dobbs Ferry, NY and Tokyo: Transnational Publishers and UN University, 1989.

Williamson, Richard L., Jr. "Building the International Environmental Regime: A Status Report." *Inter-American Law Review* Vol. 21, No. 3 (Summer 1990), pp. 679–760.

Young, Oran R. *International Cooperation: Building Regimes for Natural Resources and the Environment*. Ithaca: Cornell University Press, 1989.

________. *Understanding International Regimes: Contributions from Law and the Social Sciences*. Paper given at the annual meeting of the American Society of International Law. Washington, DC, 1-3 April 1992.

________. "Remarks." In *American Society of International Law: Proceedings of the 86th Meeting*, by the American Society of International Law. Washington, DC, 1992. pp. 172–175.

________. *International Governance: Protecting the Environment in a Stateless Society*. Ithaca: Cornell University Press, 1995.

Young, Oran R. and Gail Osherenko, ed. *Polar Politics: Creating International Environmental Regimes*. Ithaca: Cornell University Press, 1993.

Zaelke, Durwood and James Cameron. "Global Warming and Climate Change: An Overview of the International Legal Process." *The American Journal of International Law and Policy* Vol. 5, No. 2 (Winter 1990), pp. 249–290.

INDEX

AUTHOR'S SKETCH

Lynne M. Jurgielewicz received her B.S. in 1985 from Fairfield University, her J.D. in 1988 from the Catholic University of America, and her Ph.D. in 1994 from the London School of Economics and Political Science. She has worked for the London office of the American law firm Faegre and Benson, and has served as a consultant for the United Nations Information Unit on Climate Change in Geneva. She has taught at Santa Clara University and Albright College, where she was also the women's tennis coach. At the present time, she is a consultant in environmental law and environmental politics. Her email address is lynnej@joe.alb.edu.